WHY ARE WOMEN MORE RELIGIOUS THAN MEN?

WHY ARE WOMEN MORE RELIGIOUS THAN MEN?

MARTA TRZEBIATOWSKA
AND STEVE BRUCE

OXFORD
UNIVERSITY PRESS

OXFORD
UNIVERSITY PRESS

Great Clarendon Street, Oxford, OX2 6DP,
United Kingdom

Oxford University Press is a department of the University of Oxford.
It furthers the University's objective of excellence in research, scholarship,
and education by publishing worldwide. Oxford is a registered trade mark of
Oxford University Press in the UK and in certain other countries

First Edition published in 2012
First published in paperback 2014

Published in the United States of America by Oxford University Press
198 Madison Avenue, New York, NY 10016, United States of America

British Library Cataloguing in Publication Data
Data available

Library of Congress Cataloging in Publication Data
Data available

ISBN 978–0–19–960810–2 (Hbk)
ISBN 978–0–19–870972–5 (Pbk)

Contents

Preface

Our publisher, who in every other respect is always wise, wanted to call this book *Gender and Religion*. We resisted because very many publications with those terms in the title are mainly concerned with the way that various religious traditions treat women and are highly partisan. This work is neither. It is a social scientific attempt to explain why women are apparently more religious than men.

We begin by presenting a range of information about women's participation in religious organizations and rituals and by making some preliminary general observations that inform the competing social science explanations that we consider in the later chapters. As one major fault line in the debates is universality—are women in all societies more religious than men?—we encompass a broad range of examples, but much of the book is concerned with contemporary modern industrial societies. There are two reasons for this arguably narrow focus: one theoretical and one methodological.

As we explain in Chapter 1, pre-industrial societies tend to be collectively religious. That is, religious beliefs and values so permeate a culture that it is somewhat misleading to see 'being religious' as an individual characteristic and hence somewhat difficult to distinguish degrees of personal religiosity. Of course some people were particularly pious and attentive to the demands of their faith, but, given the consensus that there was a supernatural realm, the all-pervasive nature of superstition, and the considerable cultural domination of basic (and some were very basic) Christian beliefs, it is difficult to identify in communities of the Middle Ages the widespread indifference to and ignorance of religion that it now commonplace. It is generally only with the onset of secularization, when a population perceptibly divides into the more or less godly, the religious and the unreligious, that it becomes possible to see if that division follows such other social divisions as age, race, ethnicity, class, or gender.

The second reason for a focus on the modern West is the availability of information. Despite the excellent work of pre- and early modern historians, we know a great deal more about the gender composition of the nineteenth-century Shakers than we do about the make-up of the early Christian Church. And the large-scale surveys of beliefs and attitudes that we now take for granted are available only from the 1950s. Furthermore, the rise of feminism in the 1970s posed new research questions. It became common to ask if women's and men's experiences of the world differed, and that generated a great deal of new data. It also generated a great deal of argument about the nature and origin of gender differences.

This study is, we believe, timely. We do answer our own question, but our conclusions are less important than the presentations of data and argument that precede them. Our primary purposes are to bring together in one convenient location a mass of descriptive material and to lay out as clearly as possible the range of explanations that are currently offered for such patterns as scholars claim to find. That is, we fully expect many readers to disagree with us and have tried to make is as easy as possible for those who do to see why they do. As Churchill put it, we see this book, not as the end of an argument or even the beginning of the end but as the end of the beginning: a collating of resources that should allow the argument henceforth to be better informed.

Acknowledgements

We have incurred a great many obligations along the way. It is a welcome sign of the cooperative spirit that can exist even among scholars who disagree that so many of our colleagues have been willing to supply us with information about the gender composition of the movements they have studied. We would like to acknowledge the assistance of Rob Balch, Paul Heelas, Nancy Ammerman, Penny Long Marler, Phil Zuckerman, Siobhan McAndrew, Clive Field, Martin Riesbrodt, James Lewis, Burke Rochford, David Bromley, and James Levi Martin.

A particular obligation is owed to two colleagues with whom we have worked on joint projects and publications, and whose statistical expertise has greatly improved our work: Tony Glendinning of the University of Aberdeen and David Voas of the University of Essex. We would also like to thank the staff of Oxford University Press and its anonymous reviewers for helping us to develop the original proposal and Hilary Walford for her painstaking copy-editing of the typescript.

Finally, we would like to thank the University of Aberdeen for providing a working environment in which we could write this book and the Leverhulme Trust for the Senior Research Fellowship that allowed Bruce to work full-time on this and related projects.

I

The Great Divide

Introduction: Four Snapshots

We will introduce our problem by describing four photographs of chapel front doors from County Durham, in the north of England. The first is of the Methodist chapel in Harwood, a remote and sparsely populated township in the upper reaches of Teesdale. Its members are lead miners, subsistence farmers, and their families. Taken in 1887, it records the reopening of the chapel after renovation and extension. The women are dressed from ankle to neck in thick black material and wear small black hats. The men are wearing thick dark tweeds and black bowler hats. Of the twenty-three adults in the picture, eighteen are men.

Our second photograph comes from a few miles down the dale and shows the congregation of Ebenezer Primitive Methodist chapel in 1907, celebrating their twenty-fifth anniversary. The eighty or so members are lined up in four ranks, with the children kneeling at the front and the men at the back standing on pews they have brought out from the chapel. Black is still the preferred Sunday colour for the older women, but the hats are now larger and ornately decorated with cloth flowers. The younger women show a greater variety of dress styles and colours under their overcoats. For most men, the hard black hat has been replaced by the broad soft tweed cloth cap. Of the fifty or so adults, half are men and half are women.

The third photograph is again of the Harwood chapel. It is now 1960. The men still wear dark suits but the women are in a variety of bright dresses, and their overcoats—a common feature of outdoor photographs in the upper dale, even in summer—are light-coloured, as are the hats. In this picture there are nineteen children, ten men, and seventeen women.

The fourth photograph is the only one in colour. It shows a group outside the Primitive Methodist chapel in the Durham village of Cox-hoe. It is the spring of 1964 and the picture has been taken to mark the closure of the chapel and the transfer of its members to the former Wesleyan Methodist chapel at the other end of the village. The photograph graphically illustrates the reason for the amalgamation. There are only fourteen people in the picture, all of them appear to be over 60, and only two are men.

The photographs are not entirely representative. We know from the membership rolls of the chapels that some women members are missing from the first Harwood picture and that a few men are missing from the final service at Coxhoe, but the snapshots do illustrate a general trend (apart from the increasing colourfulness of the clothes): the growing reliance of the Christian churches on women. Precisely when men started to disappear will depend on which social class, region, or strand of Christianity one examines and what index of involvement one uses. The following is not intended to be an exhaustive review of the data. More will be introduced in subsequent chapters. But it should be enough to justify asking 'why are women more religious than men?'.

Gender and Religiosity: Great Britain

Infant baptism was once universal, and, although less than a third of English children are now baptized, baby girls are no more likely than baby boys to be baptized.[1] Baptism is generally a family choice that is applied to all children or none. Gender first becomes relevant with confirmation, which for Protestants is a rite administered in the teenage years and hence requires some degree of cooperation from the candidate. Confirmation was once regarded as a routine mark of status passage from childhood to maturity, but, as church involvement declined over the twentieth century, we find a gender gap emerging. In the 1930s there was already a gender difference of ten percentage points in the likelihood of being confirmed in the Church of England and by the 1950s that had grown: in 1956, for every 1,000 teenagers, 41 girls but only 28 boys were confirmed.[2]

In general we can say that, the weaker the measure of religious involvement, the less the gender gap. The 2001 census asked Scots: 'What religion, religious denomination or body do you belong to?'

Just over two-thirds claimed a denominational identity or, to be strictly accurate, had it claimed for them by the member of the household who completed the form. The population as a whole was 52 per cent female. The Church of Scotland and Roman Catholic categories were both 54 per cent female. The 'Other Christian' group, which consists mostly of conservative Protestants, was 56 per cent female.[3] The categories in which women were under-represented were the 'No Religion' group and that of people who claimed to be 'Christian' without any further denominational detail. A major survey conducted the same year allows us to see a little more detail. Women were 57 per cent of the survey but 60 per cent of those who identified with the mainstream Protestant denominations, 62 per cent of Catholic identifiers, and 71 per cent of Conservative Protestants.[4] It is worth adding that this over-representation of women is not concentrated in any one age band and is thus independent of the well-known relationship between age and religion.

Statistical evidence of a gender gap in church membership is scarce for the national churches, which, until the second half of the twentieth century, regarded as members everyone in the parish who did not openly dissent. But we have clear evidence from the Nonconformist sects and denominations. 'In terms of gender, Baptist and Congregational membership has consistently displayed a female majority of two-thirds, except for the late eighteenth century. This ratio has been greatly in excess of the wider society. For most of its history the imbalance in Methodism's membership was generally less pronounced but has also reached two-thirds from the 1960s.'[5] Before the Second World War, the gender gap was less for church attendance than it was for membership (which brought with it the expectation of attending midweek classes as well as Sunday services), but thereafter male attendance declined more rapidly, so that the two measures came into line. In 2001, 69 per cent of Methodist church attenders in England and Wales were women; the average for other churches was only slightly less skewed at 65 per cent female.[6] In Scotland in the late 1960s, Church of Scotland membership was 67 per cent female, while 66 per cent of the members of the smaller Protestant sects and denominations were women.[7] In 2009, 65 per cent of communicants and 62 per cent of non-communicant adherents in the Scottish Episcopal Church were women.[8] Clive Field concludes a magisterial review of the social composition of affiliates, attenders, and members of all the major

Nonconformist bodies with the general observation that 'men gravitate towards the least demanding of the various levels of religious allegiance and commitment, with women seeking the maximum degree of involvement'.[9]

The gender gap is also apparent in social surveys. A 1947 English poll's question 'what did you do last Sunday?' had 18 per cent of women but only 12 per cent of men claiming to have attended church. That difference was not confined to an inner core of weekly attenders. Over a quarter of women but only 18 per cent of men said they attended roughly once a month.[10] Four years later a survey with over 5,000 respondents showed once a month or more frequent church attendance being claimed by 22 per cent of women but only 13 per cent of men. A 1955 survey that divided attenders into 'frequent', 'occasional', and 'non' found that the population divided roughly equally between the three categories, but, while only 19 per cent of men were frequent attenders, 28 per cent of married women (who were rather quaintly described as 'housewives') attended frequently, as did 40 per cent of single women: a reflection of the larger number of older women in that category. The gender divide could also be seen at the other end of the scale: 46 per cent of men but only 34 per cent of married women and of single women never attended.[11] In 1979, men were 49 per cent of the population but, according to clergy estimates of the gender breakdown of their congregations, only 45 per cent of church attenders. In 1990, only 41 per cent of attenders were men, and the figures for 2005 and 2007 were 38 and 35 per cent respectively.[12] A very detailed study of the Christian Church in rural areas of England found the same gender gap. Three-quarters of men, but only 58 per cent of women, never attended, and twice as many women as men attended once a month or more.[13]

That the gender gap increases with the rigour of our measure is clear from the two columns in Table 1.1, which show the proportion of women among those who belong to each denomination or denominational group and who claim to attend either rarely or regularly. In every case the gender gap is greater among the core adherents than among those whose affiliation is slight.

The gender gap in prayer appears even larger. In 1951, 58 per cent of women but only 31 per cent of men said they prayed once a day or more often. Another survey fourteen years later produced very similar figures.[14] Other marks of religious interest also show clear gender

Table 1.1. Gender and church attendance, Britain, 1983–2008

Denomination or group	Attendance	
	Rare (% female)	Regular (% female)
United Reformed	62	66
Baptist	59	67
Anglican	58	68
Methodist	58	69
Presbyterian	56	67
Roman Catholic	54	64
Other Christian	61	66
Christian—no denomination	53	60

Note: N for this item is 65,000. 'Rare' is less than monthly. 'Regular' is monthly or more often. It is unfortunate that churchgoing in Britain is so unpopular that we have too few members of charismatic and independent evangelical churches to separate them out of the 'Other Christian' group.

Source: British Social Attitudes surveys, 1983–2008. We are grateful to David Voas for providing these data.

differences. Surveys routinely show women as more likely than men to describe themselves as religious. They also show that women are more likely to assent to statements of Christian faith. 'The difference between the sexes, with women more inclined to unqualified faith in God, is one which runs through all religious attitudes.'[15] In rural England in 1990 more than half of women but less than a third of men said they believed in life after death.[16] A recurrent national survey showed that, although male and female responses to this issue fluctuated, with women being 23 points ahead of men among those born in the 1940s but only 15 points ahead for those born in the 1950s, the gap was never less than 10 points and for those born in the 1980s it was 27 percentage points.[17]

Gender and religiosity: USA

There are many ways in which the religious life of the USA differs from that of Britain—the most obvious being that currently there is more of it—but it too is marked by gender and periodically has been since the earliest settlements. In 1660, 'women comprised the majority of communicants in every New England church whose membership records have been preserved'.[18] A century later, women formed a clear majority of Congregational churches in Connecticut. In New London, for example, in 1757 and thirty years later, there were twice as many women as men on the membership rolls. Some of that disparity can be explained by the proportions in the population at large, but only a small part.[19] If we move forward another century, this time to Muncie, Indiana, we find a similar female preponderance. In the 1920s, Robert and Helen Lynd reported that church membership in *Middletown* (the pseudonym they gave their research site) was skewed 60:40 to women and added that this was not new: the ratio in 1893 had been 64:36. They found a similar ratio in church attendance.[20]

Since 1945, the Gallup polling organization has consistently found that, on every index used, American women are more religious than men and not by small margins.[21] The difference in church membership and regular attendance is 10 percentage points. The difference in the numbers saying that religion is very important to them is 20 points: 68 to 48 per cent. Men make up 58 per cent of Americans who claim 'no religion', 70 per cent of Americans who self-identify as atheist, and three-quarters of those who describe themselves as agnostic.[22] George Gallup summarizes it as follows:

A mountain of Gallup survey data attests to the idea that women are more religious than men, hold their beliefs more firmly, practice their faith more consistently, and work more vigorously for the congregation. In fact, gender-based differences in responses to religious questions are far more pronounced than those between any other demographic categories, such as age, education level, or geographic region. The tendency toward higher religiosity among women has manifested over seven decades of scientific polling, and church membership figures indicate that it probably existed for many decades prior to the advent of survey research in the mid-1930s.[23]

A similar pattern can be found in data derived from studies of congregations. A 2001 study based on over 100,000 respondents in 453 congregations found that, although women were just 51 per cent of the population, they were 61 per cent of church participants, and the gender difference was apparent in every age cohort. The gap increased with age, but even for the youngest cohort (those aged 15 to 24) women were 57 per cent of participants.

The gender difference went beyond mere presence; women got more out of their involvement. The survey asked if participants 'During worship always or usually experience...' and offered a variety of nouns to complete the sentence. Women were markedly more likely than men to claim such positive experiences as feeling 'God's presence', 'inspiration', and 'joy' (with the gender gap being almost 10 per cent for those). For 'awe or mystery' and 'spontaneity' the total scores were lower and the gender gap only 5 per cent. The only two items on which men scored higher than women explain why fewer of them attended: they were 'frustration' (5 per cent of men and 4 per cent of women) and 'boredom' (7 per cent of men and 5 per cent of women).[24]

There are considerable differences in the gender gap between various strands of Christianity in the United States. A 2008 survey of the general population with 54,000 respondents showed that the largest gap was to be found among the most theologically conservative and demanding traditions: women were 16 percentage points ahead of men among self-identifying Pentecostalists and Charismatics and 14 points ahead among Baptists. They were 12 points ahead among mainline Protestants, 10 points ahead among Mormons, and 8 points ahead among Catholics. It is only when we get to varieties of irreligion that the gender ratio is reversed. Sixty per cent of those who ticked the 'non' box, three-quarters of those who described themselves as 'agnostic', and 70 per cent of the 'atheists' were men.[25]

This sort of survey taps nominal identification. As three-quarters of respondents claim some religious affiliation but estimates of churchgoing range between 40 per cent at the top and 20 per cent at the bottom end, we know that claimed religious affiliation tells us more about family background than about personal commitment. It may be that the apparently greater female presence in conservative sects is a product of men (on average less religious than women) being more likely to identify with a large liberal denomination than with a conservative sect. Such an interpretation is supported by the fact that the smallest gender difference is in that category that consists of people whose affiliation is almost certainly no more than nominal: those described only as 'Christian Generic'.[26]

It may seem like flogging a dead horse to keep listing statistics that point to the same conclusion, but, for reasons we will explain below, it is important to show that the existence of a significant gender gap is supported by a wide range of different sources and research strategies. There has been much detailed study in the USA of patterns of drop-out from the churches, and, although there is not yet consensus about such details as the relative impact of the nature of the denomination, the religious complexion of the home of origin, and marital status, there is agreement that, 'even controlling for differences in religious socialization, women were less likely to drop out than men'.[27]

Gender and Religiosity: Other Christian Societies

It is important to establish that the gender disparity in religion is not a particularly British or US phenomenon. In New Zealand in the early 1980s, women made up 55 per cent of those who identified as Presbyterians in the national census but they were 70 per cent of the communicant membership of the Presbyterian Church.[28] In Australia in 2001, women were 61 per cent of churchgoers.[29]

A variety of very large data sets has been used to compare the gender profile of a range of religion indices for Britain, the USA, Canada, Australia, and New Zealand. With only slight variation, all five societies produced the same two findings. First, all showed a clear gender gap in religious affiliation, church attendance, and religious beliefs, with women between 5 and 10 points ahead of men. Second, the gap was generally maintained over the period of decline. So, in 1986, 87 per cent of New Zealand women and 80 per cent of men claimed a religious affiliation; in 2006, the figures were 67 per cent and 60 per cent. Australian women born before 1912 were some five points more likely than men to claim religious affiliation, as were those born between 1962 and 1972; the difference was that the graph lines for both had dropped ten points.[30]

As the Catholic Church does not have a category of member narrowly defined but regards itself as encompassing the entire population of the societies in which it is the dominant church (or at least all those who have not dissented enough to join some competing body), we generally lack data on Catholic church membership and attendance, and hence for predominately Catholic countries we are reliant on general social surveys. The large cross-national *Religion Monitor* survey in 2008 contains data on Catholics in eight countries. Taken as a group, those societies show the same gender divide we find in Anglo-American societies: 41 per cent of women but only 27 per cent of men describe themselves as 'highly religious'. In Italy the difference is 60 to 38 per cent.[31] A 1995 survey offered Italians six frequencies of confession from 'Never' to 'Several times a month'. Almost three-quarters of men and 53 per cent of women said they made their confession once or twice a year or less; only 27 per cent of men but 42 per cent of women confessed several times a year or more often.[32] Three out of four Finnish women describe themselves as religious, as compared with only half of men. Two out of three women 'find comfort and strength in religion, compared to a little more than one third of men'. Fifty-eight per cent of men say they attend religious services once a year or less; only a third of women attend as rarely.[33]

The magisterial World Values Survey (WVS) shows the same pattern. Of the thirty-eight countries in which a question about the nature of God was asked in the early 1990s, women were more likely than men to say they believed in a 'personal God' in all but one: only in the Netherlands were men ahead. For a question about the importance of God, the Netherlands was joined by Austria in its deviance. In all the other countries surveyed, women were more religious than men and often by a large margin: 23 percentage points in Spain, 18 in Italy, 21 in Northern Ireland, and 17 in Canada.[34]

As this review of evidence is in danger of shifting from the comprehensive to the tedious, we can defer to a scholar who has spent a decade analysing European data and simply note that Grace Davie says: 'It is indisputable that there are more women than men in the European ... churches.'[35]

Gender and Religiosity: Non-Christians

One of the challenges for the social scientist is to know roughly in what realm we should seek the explanation of the patterns we discover. If the differences in religious interest and activity we have described above are to be explained by features of gender that transcend particular cultures (for example, biology), we need to demonstrate that the gender divide is found in non-Christian societies. Cross-cultural comparison of any sort is always a little fraught, because considerable skill and sensitivity are required to be sure that we accurately understand the conventions and norms of cultures very different from our own:

the lost-in-translation problem. Cross-religion comparisons of the links between gender and religion are especially difficult, because gender is not just any old independent variable; it is also the subject of much religious teaching. All religions have behavioural codes, and (with too few exceptions to detain us at this point) those codes prescribe different social roles for men and women, and set different religious requirements for men and women. While the religious legitimation of gender differences is almost universal, the content of what is endorsed (and prohibited) is highly variable. In many Islamic societies, for example, women are not expected to attend prayers at the mosque. For Orthodox Jews, women are excluded from the *minyan*: the communal prayers said by a quorum of at least ten adults. Such inter-religion differences mean that some measures of religious interest—in particular those that depend on public participation—will not work well across cultural boundaries.

In the 2008 American Religious Identification survey there were only four categories in which men outnumbered women: Muslims, Eastern Religions (Hindus, Sikhs, Buddhists, Confucianists, and Daoists), New Religious Movements, and Other Religions and None. For the first three the difference was small—4–6 per cent—and for the first two it is explained by the high proportion of young male immigrants in those groups. That last point is less of a consideration in Britain, where non-Christian communities have been longer established. However, as we can see from Table 1.2, the gender profile of those Britons who claim a non-Christian religious identity is still markedly

Table 1.2. Gender and non-Christian worship, Britain, 1983–2008

Religion	Attendance	
	Rare (% female)	Regular (% female)
Hindu	49	53
Jewish	56	55
Muslim	59	32
Sikh	61	53
Buddhist	46	46

Source: ABC Television, *Television and Religion* (London: University of London Press, 1965), 28.

Table 1.3. Percentage of respondents actively practising, England and Wales, 2008–9

	Christian	Muslim	Hindu	Sikh	Buddhist	Other
Men	25	79	65	66	64	46
Women	38	82	78	66	69	51
All	32	80	70	66	66	51

Source: C. Ferguson and D. Hussey, *2008–09 Citizenship Survey: Race, Religion and Equalities Topic Report* (London: Communities and Local Government, 2010), tables 15 and 17.

different from that of the Christian identifiers. In two cases—Muslims and Buddhists—the gender balance is reversed: men are a majority of the regular attenders and for both Sikhs and Jews female preponderance is greater among the rare attenders than among the regulars.

A slightly more helpful picture can be derived from a large-scale survey that boosted the number of non-Christian respondents and asked the more general question 'Do you consider that you are actively practising your religion?'. As we can see from Table 1.3, although the overall levels of religious observance vary from a low of less than a third for nominal Christians to a high of 80 per cent for nominal Muslims, the direction of the gender difference is consistent. In no tradition are men more likely than women to describe themselves as observant. Sikh men and women are unusual in being on a par; in all the others, women score more highly than men.

Finally, we turn to non-Christian societies. There is something a little preposterous about treating most of the world in less space than we give to Britain, but, as we noted in the Preface, there are good theoretical reasons for concentrating on societies with a high degree of religious indifference. There is also the practical problem that we are relatively short of reliable data about the religious preferences and habits of men and women in China or the Middle East. However, such data as we do have seem clear. In the 1990s, the WVS asked if respondents 'get comfort and strength from religion'. In Japan, 40 per cent of women but only 30 per cent of men said they did. In Taiwan the proportions were 77 and 59 per cent. In India the figures were 82 and 74 per cent. Similar differences were found for responses to that item in Turkey (92 to 85 per cent), Azerbaijan (77 to 70 per cent), and Albania (63 to 42 per cent).[36] Other questions about religious beliefs and self-identification as 'a religious person' produced consistent and similar results. Generally, the larger the figures, the less the gender difference. This is what we would expect: the more religious the society, the more similar the views of men and women. But the key observation for our interests here is the consistency of the data. There is not one single question, asked in eight non-Christian countries, on which men score more highly than women.

Gender and Non-Materialist Beliefs

The above is enough to establish that in very many societies women are more committed to, attached to, involved with, or interested in religion than are men. Explanations of the gender gap may well involve considerations that go beyond conventional notions of the religious. To introduce two purely hypothetical possibilities, we might want to explain greater male indifference to organized religion as being a consequence of men's greater insensitivity or their greater rationality. In either case, we would look to support the case by providing evidence of male insensitivity or rationality from areas of social life other than religion. Hence the value in initially extending the range of self-images, beliefs, and practices beyond the conventionally religious.

Such an extension assumes something we have not yet presented: a definition of religion. Most people define religion in terms of its supposedly unique content by focusing on a divine or supernatural being or force. Some social scientists try to define religion by its apparent social functions. As we have argued at length elsewhere, taking something such as social cohesion, which is sometimes but not always a consequence of belief, as the defining feature of religion, is counterproductive, because it builds into the definition precisely the sort of thing we need to establish empirically. We define religion substantively as beliefs, actions, and institutions that assume the existence of a supernatural being or beings (or impersonal powers or processes) possessed of moral judgement.[37] Such a formulation seems to encompass what most people mean when they talk of religion and will serve our purposes.

As its name would imply, alternative spirituality sits at the edges of such a definition. Much of it involves the supernatural, even if it is in the attenuated form of a divine power within each of us, but it often lacks the element of moral judgement. There may be some general behavioural expectations (such as the notion that the spiritual person should be unusually nice), but there is rarely the clear injunction found in conventional religion that, unless one behaves in a particular way, the God or Gods will punish you.

A detailed study of the holistic spirituality milieu in a small north-west English town showed that '80 per cent of those active in the holistic milieu in Kendal and environs are female; 78 per cent of groups are led or facilitated by women; 80 per cent of the one-to-one practitioners are women'.[38] Major sample surveys show a similar pattern. Table 1.4 summarizes the findings from a survey that asked respondents to describe themselves as religious, spiritual, or neither and then asked about various degrees of involvement and interest in a variety of putatively spiritual activities. The first third of the table shows the gender differences in self-description. The second and third parts show levels of engagement in two types of alternative spirituality practice that attract very different sorts of people. Those New Age activities concerned primarily with well-being (yoga, meditation, physical therapies, and healing) tended to attract middle-class university-educated respondents; divination (tarot, fortune-telling, horoscopes) tended to attract working-class respondents with no post-school education. As we see from the top third of the table, women are more likely than men to describe themselves as religious or as spiritual: 16 to 14 per cent. However, there is a 23 percentage point difference between men and women when it comes to trying yoga, meditation, and the like. Among the much smaller number of people who have tried such activities but do not regard them as important, the gender gap is smaller: only 7 points. But it increases again among the even smaller number of the seriously involved. The same pattern is clear in the divination cluster of activities.

The gender gap continues beyond spirituality into the mists of superstition. A British survey showed that women were 21 percentage points more likely than men to believe in premonition and 17 points more likely than men to believe in fate.[39] Just over half of the women polled in one survey but only 28 per cent of men claimed to believe in ghosts and 18 per cent of women but only 8 per cent of men said they had seen a ghost. Almost half the women but only 18 per cent of men claimed to believe in angels and 24 per cent of women but only 9 per cent of men claimed to 'have been helped by an angel'.[40]

Table 1.4. Spirituality and alternative practices by gender, Scotland, 2001

(*a*) **Personal spirituality** (%)

	Women	Men	Total
Spiritual not religious	16	14	15
Religious	36	30	33
Neither	48	56	52
	100	100	100

Chi-square(2) = 11.33, p < 0.01

(*b*) **Use of complementary and alternative medicine, yoga** (%)

	Women	Men	Total
Important	30	14	23
Used but not important	31	24	27
Never used	39	62	50
	100	100	100

Chi-square(2) = 83.40, p < 0.001

(*c*) **Use of horoscopes, tarot** (%)

	Women	Men	Total
Important	13	4	9
Used but not important	56	30	45
Never used	31	66	46
	100	100	100

Chi-square(2) = 205.78, p < 0.001

Source: Scottish Social Attitudes 2001. We would like to thank Tony Glendinning for his assistance in analysing data.

There is, of course, a great deal of flexibility involved in 'believing in' something. We are on surer ground when people go to the trouble of paying for some service. Over a third of women but only 11 per cent of men had 'ever sought advice from a fortune-teller, palmist or Tarot card reader or medium'.[41] Another poll asked 'Have you ever consulted a psychic or medium?' and offered three positive responses: 'Yes but only for fun', 'Yes once or twice and not just for fun', and 'Yes, more than twice and not just for fun'. Women were much more likely than men to have dabbled 'for fun': 17 per cent to 6 per cent. But they were even more likely to have taken it seriously: pooling the two 'not just for fun' responses gives us 19 per cent of women but only 4 per cent of men.[42] And it is not just in the consumption of forms of divination that women lead men. A 1951 survey asked if respondents could tell fortunes: three times as many women as men claimed this skill.[43]

It would be unwise to suppose that all of the content of magazines directly reflects the preferences of readers, but it is noticeable that magazines intended for women are much more likely then men's magazines (which in this context is not a euphemism for pornography) to feature horoscopes. In 1991, *Esquire* magazine ran what it billed as 'the first intelligent horoscope for men' but quickly abandoned it when the staff found that readers were not taking it seriously.[44]

Clarifying the Issue

What needs explaining can be put very simply. In thoroughly religious societies everyone is religious. To put it like that is misleading, because it disguises a crucial difference between pre-modern and modern societies. In the small-scale societies studied by anthropologists or in England in the Middle Ages, the entire culture was so pervaded by religious beliefs, values, and assumptions that it makes little sense to talk about individual religiosity. Although some people were more devout and pious than others, religiosity was a property more of the society's culture than of any individual's personality or preferences. Historians differ about the extent of adherence to the formal teachings of the medieval Christian churches, but no one doubts that the big themes of the Christian faith were embedded in the popular culture, that rites of passage and agricultural seasons were celebrated in church, that Christian signs and symbols were casually and routinely deployed in everyday life, and that people believed themselves to inhabit a world pervaded by the supernatural. Actually, 'knew themselves to inhabit' such a world better conveys the taken-for-grantedness of a religious world view in traditional societies. Social characteristics such as age, class, and gender might be associated with different forms of devotion and expressions of belief. The rich left enough in their wills to hire priests to say Mass for their souls, while the poor left enough for an altar candle. The gentry wore amulets that they had purchased at the shrines they visited on pilgrimage; their farm servants wore holy medallions purchased from a travelling pedlar. But a basically Christian world view, a belief in magic, and a general culture of superstition were so thoroughly pervasive that we cannot identify major social divisions in belief in the supernatural.

If we imagine a thoroughly secular society (and there are parts of northern Europe, Canada, Australia, and New Zealand that are close to that condition), we will again find no strong links between social characteristics and religiosity. We do not imagine secularization as the complete elimination of religious sentiments and ideas. On the contrary, the decline of a dominant religious world view opens the way for increasing innovation and increasing diversification of religious and spiritual resources. However, as none of these has the numerical support to become influential, their take-up is largely idiosyncratic. That is, for what are in effect unpopular choices, the reasons why people choose to hold particular beliefs will be explained by features of their biography, personality, and life circumstances that are particular to them and are hardly susceptible to sociological explanation.

What concerns us is the period between the two extremes of religion as pervasive world view and religion as idiosyncratic personal choice. Why, over the course of the twentieth century, did Methodism in Teesdale change from attracting men and women equally to being overwhelmingly female? We can put the same question in a larger frame. Norris and Inglehart divide all the societies that are surveyed by the WVS into agrarian, industrial, and post-industrial. In agrarian societies men and women are equally likely to participate in religious worship, but the participation rate in industrial societies is 26 per cent for women and 22 per cent for men, while in post-industrial societies (those with economies based primarily on providing services rather than manufacturing goods), the participation rate is 26 per cent for women and only 18 per cent for men.[45]

Just in case the gender disparity in religion is not in itself sufficiently interesting, we can note that the preponderance of women has an almost ironic relationship to the apparent appeal of the major religious traditions in modern liberal democracies. The modern defenders of orthodox Christianity, Judaism, Islam, Hinduism, and Buddhism claim that the sexism found in those faiths is the fault of the various cultures in which they grew rather than the faiths themselves. They may also assert that women are treated as 'separate but equal'. None of that changes the fact that all the major world religions have, for most of their histories, been intensely patriarchal and have treated women as second-class citizens. That women are apparently more religious than men may not be as counter-intuitive as turkeys voting for Christmas or Thanksgiving, but it certainly seems similar to manual workers voting for conservative political parties. There is something to be explained.

Methodological Issues

As most readers will not share our interest in the details of research methodology, we have not dwelt on the methods involved in the studies whose conclusions we report, nor have we done more than touch on the many technical issues involved in conducting and analysing such research. However, there are a few general observations of a methodological nature that should be made once to save future repetition.

The Validity of Measures of Religious Interest

A common experience for those of us who lecture on changes in patterns of religious involvement, especially when delineating decline, is to be challenged by someone who asserts that we cannot know if people are 'really' religious. Secularization can be made to disappear if we suppose that those who took communion at Easter in the Middle Ages were merely bending to social pressure and that those who now take no part in any religious activities might none the less be as religious as churchgoing ancestors. As well as implying an insensitive distinction between what people do voluntarily and what they are in some sense pressed to do by others, that seems an unnecessarily bleak response to the difficulties of social research. Because religion has often been extremely important to many people and because religious institutions have often been among the most adept social bodies at collecting and preserving information, we probably know rather more about the religion of our forebears than we do about most other aspects of their lives. Peter Laslett's *The World We Have Lost* is able to tell us precisely which of the 276 residents of Goodnestone-next-Wingham in Kent took Easter communion in 1676, because the report of the parish curate to his bishop has been preserved.[46] We know how important religion was to the people of Exeter in the sixteenth century because a large collection of their wills has been preserved, and those wills show that leaving money to the church and to pay people 'to pray to our Lord God to have mercy on my soul and all Christian souls' was commonplace.[47]

Although we would hesitate to claim to know what any of our contemporaries 'really' believe, we have a mass of data from religious institutions (which have a powerful interest in monitoring their performance) and from secular sources such as social surveys that tells us what people say they believe and what they say they did. We also have data (such as church records and government censuses of church membership and attendance) that allow us to test what people say about their actions. Far from the study of religion being uniquely hampered by its ineffability, the sociologist of religion is probably better supplied with data than students of most other areas of social life.

The problems we face in interpreting that data do not seem different in kind from those faced in any field of the social sciences and we feel no less confident than our colleagues in other fields that difficulties can be overcome with skill and expertise. For example, experience tells us that a higher rate of claimed church attendance will be produced by a survey question that asks directly 'Did you attend church in the last seven days?' than by one that asks 'Which of the following did you do last weekend?' and has 'Attend church' as one of a long list of options. To give another example, it is often claimed that congregational membership figures will be artificially deflated for denominations that impose a levy on congregations based on their size. It is equally often claimed that clergy will inflate statistics of membership or attendance in order to boost their own self-esteem. But such concerns should be stimuli to better research, not reasons for giving up. Pollsters and those who use their data are not (as the critics of quantitative research often imply) particularly credulous. They are generally better aware of the weaknesses and strengths of their work than are their critics and they are generally cautious in the claims they make. The validity of congregation statistics is not naively taken-for-granted by scholars who compile them: we routinely test them against other sources. It is possible, for example, to compare the membership figures for specific British Methodist chapels in the nineteenth and twentieth centuries against the roll books and attendance records. Sometimes clergy reports of attendance can be compared with actual counts of attendance produced by outsiders. Reassuringly, such checking generally shows consistency and accuracy.

One often-overlooked facet of empirical research should satisfy general scepticism about the reliability of the data: quantity usually improves quality, because idiosyncratic variations will come out in the wash of large numbers. It would be foolish to conclude anything about the popularity of Methodism, Protestantism, Christianity, or religion in England from the membership of the Wheatley Hill, County Durham, Primitive Methodist chapel, which fell from 25 in 1881 to just 4 in 1891: that was a result of the local colliery closure removing almost the entire village population. But it would be equally foolish to conclude nothing from the membership data for all the chapels in England over a century.

Our experience of trying to estimate degrees of religious interest and involvement suggests that a greater problem than the supposed unknowability of the phenomenon is the shifting relationship between different measures of different facets. In order to make comparisons over time and space and—the crucial issue for this book—to make comparisons between the sexes, we need some common units of currency. For Christians, church attendance is a good measure. For Catholics, canon law made Mass attendance an obligation for all the faithful, and the Catechism describes deliberate failure to attend as a 'grave sin'. It was hardly less of a burden for Protestants. Every Protestant church, sect, and denomination strenuously encourages its adherents to gather together to worship and to provide mutual edification and education.

Generally speaking, the three aspects of religious interest that we can measure relatively easily—self-identification or stated affiliation, assent to particular beliefs, and attendance at worship—do go together. We can demonstrate this in two ways. We can graph change in the three measures for a very large number of people over time: the three trend lines do not quite move as one, but their trajectories are very similar.[48] Or we can take a large survey sample, create three sets (one for each measure), and see how much they overlap. At the level both of the group and of the individual, such indices tend to fit together in the obvious ways. It is rare to find a large number of survey respondents who describe themselves as religious, say they are Christian, claim to believe in a personal creator God, say that religion is important to them, but do not attend church regularly. Equally the number of people who say they have no religion but then attend church once a month or more often (we presume many of these are companionable spouses of believers) is very small: less than 2 per cent of the 19,000 people who disclaimed a religion in the pooled British Social Attitudes survey.

The above holds true for a certain time and place. As the arguments over female religiosity tend to rest on gender patterns that transcend a particular time or place, we need to be aware not only that religious traditions differ but also that any one religion may well change so that the significance and value of some measure also changes. For example, although the Mass has always been a central part of Catholic worship, Protestant churches differ considerably in the importance they assign to the Eucharist (or Communion) and to the frequency with which is it is celebrated. And within particular Protestant churches that has changed. In the nineteenth century many Church of England incumbents celebrated communion rarely. By the 1960s family communion was common. Thus we see a pattern of communicant numbers rising while total attendances were going down. We can make the same point at a higher level of abstraction. In the nineteenth century, when membership of sects such as the Primitive Methodists and the Baptists was a highly prized privilege and intending members had to serve a period 'on trial', it was common for church attendance to be higher than membership. As membership and attendance declined over the twentieth century, the relationship between them switched. In the 1860s attendance in some Durham chapels was two or three times the membership. By the 1960s it was two-thirds and by the end of the century only half the members attended regularly. But this is neither difficult to understand nor an obstacle to empirical research. It simply means that, when we consider gender differences in this or that measure of religious interest, we need to be careful about precisely what any measure describes and cautious about the inferences we draw from it.

As we note at the start of Chapter 8, measuring religious interest and involvement becomes more challenging once we move beyond Christianity. What is required of a 'good Muslim', for example, differs in many interesting ways from what would qualify someone as a 'good Christian'. More challenging for our purposes, Islam, Hinduism, and Judaism make different demands of men and women. Hence the greater attention given in Chapter 8 to qualitative studies. None the less, some survey questions work well cross-culturally.

All of the above may seem like a very long way round the houses, but, given the frequency with which a social scientific approach to religion is criticized, the points are worth making. They can be summarized in two simple propositions. First, the increasingly diverse sources of evidence we have the better. Second, it is unwise to make too much of weak patterns that appear only occasionally.

Choice, Feedback, and Amplification

That our materials are self-aware people rather than chemicals has a variety of important consequences for social science explanation. One is that small initial differences that we explain in one way can become amplified into major differences by other considerations. We can illustrate the point from years of observing how our students sign up for option courses. Sign-up sheets for courses such as the sociology of sport, sociology of law, sociology of religion, and the like were mounted on the department notice board and remained for a week so that students could alter their choices once they had sorted out their other timetable commitments. Year after year we found the same pattern of changes. At first a few women would sign up for the sociology of sport and a few men would sign up for the course 'Femininity and Masculinity'. However, as soon as the lists for these courses started to show a clear gender difference, the deviant early enrollers would return and change their enrolments, so that, by the time the courses first met, the sport option was almost entirely male and the gender course was almost entirely female. Almost all of the few remaining deviant students would then ask to change courses. Students very quickly took the fact that the vast majority in the class were of the other gender as signifying that this course was not suitable for them.

This is not at all unusual. What we have learnt from decades of studies of the diffusion of innovation, of interpersonal influence, and of religious conversion is that a sense of similarity between promoters and potential converts is important in persuading people that something new is worth trying.[49] People in the evangelism business appreciate that, if you want to appeal to young people, you use a young evangelist. When the Moonies first arrived in the USA from Korea, they recruited only very very slowly: the Korean missionaries had trouble attracting serious interest from white Americans. Only once they were able to deploy young white middle-class Americans did they start to recruit young white middle-class Americans.[50] Even when the innovation in question is technical (a new seed variety, for example) and might best be promoted by an expert (in this case an agronomist), the farmers being targeted proved most open to being persuaded by other like-situated farmers rather than by the experts. The simple point is that in many situations of choice people are more likely to trust those who are in crucial respects like them than people who are different. What the good evangelist does is present himself as being very much like his audience except that, since conversion, his life is so much better. The similarity point is important, because he has to convey the impression that this product will 'work for you'. The guru, the founder of the movement, can be different. Indeed, if she or he is claiming some charismatic authority, it helps to be exotic, but the local sales rep for the new life, the new persona, the new idea, must be someone in whom the targets can see themselves.

Most of us are extremely skilled at reading signs. When a middle-aged middle-class man walks into a large bar with shiny chrome fittings and loud techno music, full of young people with a lot of hair product on, he immediately knows that this is not his place and these are not his people. A few of us are adventurous and are frequently drawn to the unusual and the exotic. Many of us are occasionally drawn to the danger inherent in transgressing social and cultural divisions: Lady Chatterley can stand as an example. But most of the time, most of us draw on implicit notions of what we are like and of what we like in making choices and we use social similarity as a time-saving device for simplifying those decisions.

Which brings us to our main point. Gender is one of the most obvious social divisions and social markers of division. To pre-empt a likely criticism, we should add that, at this stage, we are not committing ourselves to any particular explanation of why that is the case. We simply note that most people assume that the selves, circumstances, and hence interests of men and women are often different and that much of what appeals to one will not satisfy the other. Once a gender preference pattern is established, it becomes self-reinforcing. This can come through the free choice of potential participants, for the reasons outlined above. Men simply look at the existing participants and think 'These people are not like me so this is probably not my thing'. Organizers then respond by accepting that their audience is female and portraying the activity accordingly—the posters for aerobics in our local gym exclusively feature women in tights, leotards, leg warmers, and sweat bands—and structuring it accordingly: the aerobics classes are during the day when the crèche is available.

We stress this point about the role of feedback in patterns of choice because it may relieve us of the obligation to look for a big explanation. That there is a large gender gap in religious interest does not necessarily mean that the initial cause of that gap must be equally powerful or impressive. Because the casual rules-of-thumb we use in decision-making often give great weight to similarity, what now appears as a major difference (the gender composition of New Age activities, for example) may require only a small difference at the original cause stage that is subsequently amplified by the self-reinforcing nature of the 'like likes like' short cut.

Conclusion

This study is timely in three senses. First, it is only possible in a world where there is a significant degree of secularization. Only if a goodly number of people are patently not religious can we explore the social causes of differences in personal religiosity. It is timely in a second sense that the social sciences now pay systematic attention to gender differences. Leaders of the Christian churches have been worrying about the 'feminization' of their organizations for more than a century: sociologists of religion are now catching up, and we have a considerable body of data that distinguishes the religious preferences of men and women. Thirdly, we now also have a large number of putative explanations for those differences. The purpose of this book is to bring together the now considerable body of research on gender and religion to consider whether it is indeed the case that women are more religious than men and, if so, why. The data presented in this chapter certainly seem a *prima facie* case.

2

New Religions

Introduction

We begin with a pointed barb overheard in a Dublin bar. Two men were talking about the possibility of the Catholic Church ordaining women. One thought it would never happen. The other thought the Church would eventually ordain women priests and added, with feeling, 'and it'll claim it has always had them'. Religions generally claim to be unchanging. Some, such as Hinduism and Buddhism, claim to have identified invariant principles of how the world, natural and supernatural, works. Judaism, Christianity, and Islam have historical points at which the divine revealed itself, but those points are many centuries in the past and what was then revealed was timeless in its application. As too-obviously editing God's revelation might cause people to question the message's authorship, religions tend to be conservative, and change is almost invariably presented not as novelty but as the rediscovery of the original essence. The avowedly new, though not unknown—Scientology is an example—is much rarer than the revival and the restoration.

The previous chapter described the gender divide in adherence to the dominant religious traditions of a variety of societies and to widely accepted expressions of the supernatural. All those illustrations could be read as implicitly supporting the notion that women are more religious than men because they are more conservative, docile, or conformist. As a 1947 report on religious attitudes in London put it: 'Women are regularly more inclined to accept, or welcome, the fait accompli than men, and less inclined to criticise the *status quo*.'[1] As the willingness (or otherwise) of women to be involved in deviant and delinquent activities has some bearing on explanations of the gender gap in religiosity, we will now supplement the data of the first chapter with some account of the gender composition of radical or innovative religion. In this chapter we consider the role played by women in a variety of eighteenth- and nineteenth-century movements and in the post-1960s new religious movements.

Millenarian Visions

To imagine that God created the world invites the corresponding possibility that God will bring it to an end. Adherents to some strands of Shia Islam expect the imminent return of the Hidden Imam.[2] To many followers of the Lubavitch sect of Orthodox Judaism, Menachem Mendel Schneerson, who died in 1994, is the Messiah whose return will herald a glorious age.[3] The early Christians clearly expected Christ to return soon to end this world and usher in the next, and, although the major Christian churches reconciled themselves to an indefinite future on this earth, the stability of Christianity has periodically been shaken by millenarian movements committed to an imminent major upheaval. Many were associated with the specific expectation of Christ's return instituting a thousand years' reign of righteousness; hence the label 'millennialist'.

Ann Lee (1736–1784)

The members of the United Society of Believers in Christ's Second Appearing are, to furniture experts at least, better known as the Shakers. That name was an abbreviation of an amalgam of insults: the 'Shaking Quakers' were so called because many early recruits were Quakers (which name itself referred to the habit of trembling during prayer) and because they shook in two ways. They still became agitated during emotional prayer meetings but they also devised a style of social dancing that was somewhere between jogging on the spot and close-order drill.

The Shakers were originally English. In 1747 Jane Wardley, a Quaker from Bolton-le-Moors near Manchester, felt that she was being instructed by the Lord to announce that Christ's return was imminent. Ann Lee, a Manchester mill-worker, joined the Shakers by 1758 and brought to the leadership of the small community an intense dislike for sex, which first displayed itself in an unwillingness to marry and was then reinforced by eight pregnancies, four of which resulted in the children dying in infancy. Combining her own experiences with a rather literal interpretation of the story of Adam and Eve's expulsion from the Garden of Eden, she concluded that 'the world's wrongs— war, disease, slavery, famine, poverty, the inequality of the sexes, human "depravity"—were all the result of "concupiscence"'.[4] In her vision of the future kingdom of God, as in the Shaker fellowship, there was 'neither marrying nor giving in marriage'.

By 1774, Ann Lee and a small band of her followers had emigrated to America and settled near Albany in the State of New York. After a long period of obscurity and a short period of notoriety in which they were persecuted for treason to the cause of American independence, they attracted a considerable following from the fringes of the evangelical Protestant revival known as the 'Great Awakening'. However, their insistence on celibacy and sexual segregation meant that they could not build on their initial recruitment, as most movements do, by breeding new members. They created about 500 communes and attracted a large number of converts (many of them orphans given into the movement's care), but there was also considerable turnover, and the peak of around 6,000 members in 1840 was followed by a rapid ageing of the member- ship and an equally rapid decline of the movement, which is now known primarily not for its millenarian faith but for its simple furniture styles. As Shaker communities segregated the sexes, it made sense for the women's 'line' to be led by a woman, but women also occupied the most senior position in the movement. Ann Lee was succeeded by Joseph Meacham, but after his death in 1796 Elderess Lucy Wright became the head of 'what was now an established order'.[5]

None of the principal historians of the Shaker movement directly address the relative number of men and women, but, in his listing of leading Shaker personalities, Andrews names twenty-nine women and thirty-seven men. Details of particular communities suggest that men and women joined in roughly equal numbers, which is only to be expected, given that conversion generally ran through families. Often the woman converted first and brought the rest of her family into the fold. That single women did join on their own initiative is clear from the reports of mob violence that was directed against Shaker settle- ments in the 1810s: 'in each case the object of the invaders was the procurement of some child or young sister in the society.'[6]

Elspeth Buchan (1738–1791)

The great eighteenth-century Scots poet Robert Burns wrote of a notorious local woman: 'she pretends to give [her followers] the Holy Ghost by breathing on them, which she does with postures and practices that are scandalously indecent' and 'they lodge and lye all together, and hold likewise a community of women, as it is another of their tenets that they can commit no moral sin'.[7] Burns, no stranger to moral sin himself, was thoroughly familiar with this millennialist sect: a young female member was one of his many lovers.

Elspeth Buchan was a servant from Banffshire in the north-east of Scotland. A religious enthusiast from teenage years, she was a keen member of informal religious fellowships. Her increasingly deviant beliefs caused friction, and in 1781 she moved to Glasgow, where she attracted a small audience for her teaching. It was in the Ayrshire town of Irvine that she had her greatest impact. She went to hear the preaching of Hugh White, minister of the Relief Presbytery church at Irvine, and became convinced that he had a part in her divinely ordained scheme. Like Joanna Southcott discussed below, Buchan believed that she was the woman described in chapter 12 of the Book of Revelation and she persuaded White that he was the man-child described in the same biblical text. The end of the world was nigh. Those who cast aside social conventions such as marriage and private property to join her would not die but would be lifted up, alive and intact, to heaven. Buchan and White sufficiently offended the townsfolk that in 1784 the Burgh magistrates expelled them. Taking only what they could carry, the forty-six Buchanites were harried out of the town. They were eventually given shelter by a farmer at New Cample, near Thornhill in Dumfriesshire. In return for unpaid labour, he allowed them to build a plain barn in which the men and women slept crowded together, with no regard to previous marital status. This 'free love' attracted much odium, as did the blasphemies published in 1785 by White and Buchan as *The Divine Dictionary; Or, A Treatise Indicated by Holy Inspiration, Containing the Faith and Practice of that People (by This World) Called Buchanites*. When Buchan's first prediction of their bodily translation heaven-ward failed, she concluded that they were held back by a 'want of faith' and instituted a forty-day period of fasting. Thus prepared, in July 1786, they built wooden platforms on nearby Templand Hill, discarded their possessions, cut off all their hair except for a small tuft by which the angels would catch them up, and gathered on the hill for their ascent. At the end of the day of disappointment, 'the company of half-famished looking creatures' retraced their steps to the barn.

Buchan again explained that their ascent was still promised but was still delayed by their lack of faith. With the date of the end of the world now unknown, the community leased farm land in Galloway. Buchan died in March 1791, and Hugh White led the twenty or so members who could afford the passage to America, where they dispersed. The last surviving Buchanite, Andrew Innes, who had followed Buchan since her Glasgow days, died in Thornhill in 1848.

The gender composition of the Buchanites cannot be precisely known, because contemporary commentators did not think it important enough to note. Most of Buchan's followers joined as families. The better-off brought their female servants, but this was offset by the single recruits being mostly men. There is an interesting aside in Innes's comment on sleeping arrangements in the barn, which prefigures our comments below on women's recruitment to communal new religions in the 1970s:

there [was] no distinction of persons among us—those who had wives being as if they had none. But if our Friend Mother [Buchan] and Mrs Gibson [the wife of the wealthiest member] be excepted, the women were greatly behind the men in their compliance, for there was scarcely one, either old or young, who did not retain a partial hankering after either husband or sweetheart; but, as there was no law to be put in force, and no punishment to be apprehended, it was all matter of choice with us.[8]

Joanna Southcott (1750–1814)

In 1792, Joanna Southcott (or Southcote), a middle-aged upholsteress and domestic servant from the south-west of England, became convinced that she possessed supernatural gifts of prophecy. What distinguished her from all the forgotten village visionaries was that she was a prolific writer. Despite being uneducated, she wrote her prophecies and interpretations of scripture passages, and mixed in fragments of biography and commentary on daily life. She funded the production of her first pamphlet from her savings. Later patronage and sales income allowed her to produce sixty-five pamphlets and a similar volume of unpublished work in the twenty-two years between her first revelation and her death in 1814. When her claims to prophecy were rejected by her fellow Methodists and by the local Anglican clergy to whom she then turned, she was taken up by followers of Richard Brothers. He was a millenarian prophet whose works were sufficiently politically radical for him to be examined by the Privy Council on suspicion of treason. Lacking evidence of political intent, his persecutors had him confined as a lunatic.[9]

With backing from a few wealthy patrons, Southcott's writings were widely distributed.[10] Equally popular were her seals: so called because, after the fashion described in the Book of Revelations, these charms 'sealed' or assured the salvation of the possessor. They were small pieces of paper with the formula 'The Sealed of the Lord—the Elect Precious—Man's Redemption to Inherit the Tree of Life—To be Made Heirs of God and Joint Heirs with Jesus Christ' written inside a circle. More than 10,000 were sold for between half a guinea and a guinea. Sales apparently dried up after one member of the Elect, a healer called Mary Bateman, was hanged at York Assizes for murdering at least one of her clients. A gruesome footnote testifies to the enduring power of superstition: although Bateman was held to be a charlatan, strips of her skin were sold as magic charms.[11]

Like Buchan, Southcott was not just the messenger: she was also a central player in the drama of the endtimes. She believed herself to be the woman described in the following passage from the Book of Revelations (12: 1–6):

And there appeared a great wonder in heaven; a woman clothed with the sun, and the moon under her feet, and upon her head a crown of twelve stars. And she being with child cried, travailing in birth, and pained to be delivered...And she brought forth a man child, who was to rule all nations with a rod of iron: and her child was caught up unto God, and to his throne.

At the age of 64 she announced that she was pregnant with the new Messiah. Hardly surprisingly, the baby failed to appear on the due date, and Southcott died shortly after.[12] The movement, which at its peak had some 100,000 adherents, did not die with her but declined gently over the course of the nineteenth century. One source of notoriety was a box of prophecies that was to be opened only in a time of national crisis and in the presence of all the then-twenty-four bishops of the Church of England. During both the Crimean War and the First World War, the bishops declined to play their part in this revelation. Eventually in 1927 the Bishop of Grantham was persuaded to be present at the box's opening, but it was found to contain only some unimportant papers and a few oddments, among them a lottery ticket and a pistol. The followers of Southcott later claimed that the box that had been opened was not the real one.

Southcott's legacy was extended in the 1920s by the Panacea Society, a movement led by Mabel Barltrop, the widow of an Anglican curate. After being hospitalized in a mental institution for a number of years for melancholia, Barltrop gradually attracted a following of women interested in Southcott's writings, which she freely expanded with her own revelations. She declared herself to be 'Shiloh' or the Messiah and took the name Octavia. The female basis of the movement was not an accident. Barltrop believed that, as the problems of the world had been created by a woman—Eve—so they would be solved by women. She also decided that a small part of the nondescript English town of Bedford where she had settled was both the site of the original Garden of Eden and the place where Christ would return. Others bought houses adjacent or close by, until a small community of 'single, middle-aged women, confirmed spinsters and widows' was formed.[13] The community was remarkable in the world of utopian movements for its middle-class gentility: paradise as a well-run ordered hotel. The wealthier members bought houses and lived on the interest from inherited capital. Poorer members worked as servants for the wealthy. They attracted little attention and caused no scandal. The historian Jane Smith captures perfectly the essence of the Bedford community when she says: 'If Jesus taught ethics through his parables, then Octavia taught them through the sensibilities of Edwardian middle-class etiquette.'[14] Octavia was an obsessive micro-manager who issued the most detailed instructions for living the life of an Edwardian middle-class lady: 'Never take butter with your own knife. Do not call a dinner napkin a "serviette". Eat asparagus with your fingers.'[15]

According to the *Panacea*, the purpose of the Society was to gather together those who would never die and prepare them for immortality by 'Overcoming': an active process of leaving the self behind through monitoring and criticizing one's own faults and the faults of other members. Like Southcott, Octavia 'sealed' her followers in the twin sense of affirming their definite inclusion on the list of the 144,000 people who, according to the Book of Revelation, would never die and of providing them with a seal that would ward off various evils. Later these seals became the basis of a worldwide healing ministry. Cardboard (later linen) slips on which Octavia had breathed were held to impart curative powers, which transferred to water in which they were soaked. In the first year of advertising the curative seals, the Society had 3,389 requests, which doubled in the second year. Interest in healing far outstripped interest in the millennialist teachings. Between 1923 and 1934, more than 70,000 people applied for healing, but there were only 1,285 sealed members and only 60 or so of them joined the Bedford community.

Those who applied for healing seals were requested to report regularly on their efficacy, and, as part of their Overcoming, non-resident members wrote regularly about their emotional and spiritual problems. Together those letters form an extraordinary archive, which very strongly suggests two things. First, far more women sought healing for their husbands than vice versa. Second, many women had problems with sex. Octavia's initial response to requests for guidance was to endorse the traditional position of the grim wing of Christianity—that sex within marriage for the purpose of procreation was permitted—but she added that Overcoming would remove the sexual urge. Married couples were encouraged to become chaste because only when the Chosen had renounced sexual relations would 'the necessary adjustment of relations between the sexes... bring about the Second Coming of Christ'.[16]

Although the Society received a severe shock when the putatively immortal Octavia died in 1934, neither recruitment nor requests for healing seals faltered until the Second World War. But, as with the Shakers, the rejection of sex removed the primary source of new members, and the appeal of the lifestyle of elderly Edwardian ladies stretched little beyond its own time. The Society declined after 1945 until it became so small that the Charity Commission required it to sell off a proportion of its by-then-considerable assets to retain charitable status. The core properties in Bedford were retained. Some became a museum. Others were refurbished to receive Octavia and Jesus when they chose to return.

Apparently Southcott had prophesied that 2004 would see the Day of Judgement, and the Panacea Society argued that, if the contents of her box had not been studied beforehand, the world would have had to face judgement unprepared. The year 2004 turned out to be rather unmemorable.

Ellen White (1827–1915)

Ellen White was a prolific Christian author and one of the founders of the Seventh-Day Adventist (SDA) Church: so called because it celebrated the Sabbath on Saturday rather than Sunday and because it expected the Second Coming (or Advent) of Christ. Her family were Methodists from Maine who were involved in William Miller's millenarian movement. Miller, a Baptist preacher, had persuaded himself, by reading the prophecies of the Book of Daniel, that Jesus Christ would return to the earth during the year 1844. The prediction was narrowed down by another preacher, Samuel S. Snow, to 22 October. On that date thousands of followers, some of whom had followed the Buchanite method of divesting themselves of their possessions, waited expectantly, but, as we know, nothing happened. It was soon after the Great Disappointment that Ellen White had the first of her many visions.

At this time I visited one of our Advent sisters, and in the morning we bowed around the family altar. It was not an exciting occasion, and there were but five of us present, all females. While praying the power of God came upon me as I never had felt it before, and I was wrapt up in a vision of God's glory, and seemed to be rising higher and higher from the earth and was shown something of the travels of the Advent people to the Holy City.[17]

Over the following years White received a large number of visions, which helped create a viable reinterpretation of the 1842 disappointment: they had been right about the date but wrong about the nature of the event. The 'sanctuary' that would then be cleansed was not the earth but heaven. So Christ was preparing a place for his people and the Adventist movement could continue to proselytize in the expectation that the long-awaited lifting-up was not too far off. White's many visions combined religious instruction, advice for individuals, and predictions. Her frequent contributions to the *Review and Herald* and other church publications helped give shape to what in 1863 became the Seventh-Day Adventist Church. As this is a theme to which we will return a number of times, it is worth noting that, as well as being a religious teacher, White was a keen promoter of dietary regimes and health programmes.

Mary Baker Eddy (1821–1910)

Mary Baker was born in Bow, New Hampshire, in 1821 to a Congregationalist family. She was a pious and sickly child who, from an early age, heard voices. Her persistent ill-health seems to have been a psychosomatic reaction to her father's Calvinist view that our fate (heaven or hell) was 'predestined' before birth. During one of their arguments she developed a serious fever, which finally caused him to moderate his beliefs.

> My mother...bade me lean on God's love, which would give me rest if I went to Him in prayer, as I was wont to do, seeking His guidance. I prayed; and a soft glow of ineffable joy came over me. The fever was gone and I rose and dressed myself in a normal condition of health. Mother saw this and was glad. The physician marvelled; and the 'horrible decree' of Predestination—as John Calvin rightly called his own tenet—forever lost its power over me.[18]

Her first husband died in the first year of their marriage, leaving her with a son. Her second, whom she eventually divorced, was a thoroughly bad lot. He reneged on a commitment to adopt her son, who had been placed in the care of neighbours, he was unfaithful to her, and he was a poor provider. Mary was frequently bed-ridden with depression and with ailments that may well have been psychosomatic. Her ill-health led to her to experiment with a wide variety of quack therapies, the most effective of which was the 'mesmerism' or hypnosis practised by Phineas Quimby from Maine.

After a severe fall caused a major spinal injury in February 1866, Eddy found comfort in one of the New Testament stories of Christ healing the sick: 'And, behold, they brought to him a man sick of the palsy, lying on a bed: and Jesus seeing their faith said unto the sick of the palsy; Son be of good cheer; thy sins be forgiven thee...Arise take up thy bed, and go unto thine house. And he arose, and departed to his house.'[19] After her unexpected recovery, she began to formulate what became Christian Science. She rejected drugs and the conventional therapies of her day on the grounds that Christ did not use them. 'The tender word and Christian encouragement of an invalid, pitiful patience with his fears and the removal of them, are better than hecatombs of gushing theories, stereotyped borrowed speeches, and the doling of arguments.'[20] If her condemnation of medicine seems extreme and foolhardy, it is worth remembering how little evidence-based medicine there was in the 1860s.

In 1875, two years before she acquired the 'Eddy' name from her third husband, Mary Baker published her discovery in the book *Science and Health*. She spent the rest of her life promoting her principles, training healers, and establishing the Church of Christ, Scientist. Fifty years later there were almost 2,000 congregations with around 141,000 members, of whom three-quarters were women.[21]

Madame Blavatsky (1831–1891) and Annie Besant (1847–1933)

Theosophy was founded by one woman and maintained by another. The Theosophical Society was founded in New York in 1875 by Helena Blavatsky, a Russian émigré spirit medium with a talent for self-promotion, and Henry Steel Olcott, an army officer, journalist, and lawyer. It was originally inspired by Spiritualism (of which more in the next chapter): its first stated purpose was the investigation, study, and explanation of mediumistic phenomena. After a few years Blavatsky and Olcott moved to India, and then to Sri Lanka, where they took the Five Precepts and became Buddhists, before returning to India in 1882. The Society's purpose was now to form the core of a universal brotherhood without distinction of race, creed, sex, caste, or colour; to encourage the study of comparative religion, philosophy, and science; and to investigate the unexplained laws of nature and the powers latent in man. Blavatsky claimed mediumistic powers that allowed the Mahatmas, a class of especially wise guides, to provide her with spiritual guidance that would help the race evolve. There was a minor scandal in 1885 when two co-workers accused her of faking her more impressive displays of mediumistic power and a sympathetic investigator of psychic phenomena agreed. But such was her popularity in India, where she was seen as an important promoter of Indian religious culture, that she managed to ride out the criticism. In August 1890, with a neat hint at her own self-image, Blavatsky formed an 'Inner Circle' of twelve disciples: six men and six women. She died the following year.

The theological core of Theosophy is difficult to identify. Blavatsky received copious instruction from the Mahatmas, some of it in the form of letters that were 'materialized' by her mediumistic skills. The first serious account of her teachings, *Isis Unveiled*, is impenetrable and inconsistent, and she was widely accused of plagiarizing ideas she had not understood. Like many people of the period interested in esoteric knowledge, Blavatsky had a distinctive view on evolution and race.[22] She thought that the Aryans (a clutch of peoples that had little in common other than that she liked them) originally came from Atlantis. In contrast, Semitic peoples had become 'degenerate in spirituality and perfected in materiality'. To justify retaining the philosophical elements of Hinduism and Buddhism while dropping the associated Gods, shrines, sacrifices, taboos, and rituals, she argued that, during the

Vedic period, people had become sufficiently enlightened to do without them, but the trickery of idol worship was brought back by such inferior 'survivals' as the Chinese and Africans. None the less the future looked bright. The racial 'failures of nature' would become extinct and the 'higher race' would ascend.

Annie Besant's background was not in occultism but in social reform. She was a Londoner who became a prominent speaker and writer for the National Secular Society and close friend of Charles Bradlaugh. In 1877 they were prosecuted for publishing a book by birth-control campaigner Charles Knowlton. The scandal made them famous, and Bradlaugh was elected MP for Northampton in 1880. He refused to take the religious oath of allegiance to the Crown, and his parliamentary seat was declared vacant. He was re-elected four times by the people of Northampton and ejected three times before the dispute was settled with the 1888 Oaths Act, which allowed members of both the House of Commons and the Lords to affirm their loyalty in a secular manner. Besant was a member of the Fabian Society and the Social Democratic Federation and an active promoter of trade unionism. She was elected to the London School Board for Tower Hamlets, topping the poll, even though few women were qualified to vote at that time. In 1890 she met Blavatsky and gradually shifted her interests from secular political agitation to Theosophy. She became President of the Theosophical Society in 1890 and began to steer it away from Buddhism and towards Hinduism. She also helped to tutor Theosophy's Messiah.

Krishnamurti was born into a Telugu Brahmin family. His father worked for the Theosophical Society as a clerk and it was while living close to the Theosophical Society headquarters at Adyar in Madras that he was noticed by Charles Leadbeater, a former Anglican clergyman who became a leading Theosophist. Leadbeater was convinced that the boy had such spiritual gifts that he could be the 'World Teacher' the movement was expecting. Leadbeater and Besant schooled him in Theosophy teachings, but as a young man he rejected his allocated role and gradually abandoned Theosophy. None the less he spent the rest of his life as a popular speaker and writer in what would now be recognized as a 'New Age' vein: popular psychology mixed with vague Eastern wisdom.

Two years after Blavatsky had died, a World Parliament of Religions was held in Chicago, and Hindu, Buddhist, and Jain leaders were given an unprecedentedly respectful hearing. Blavatsky's chaotic gluing-together of every esoteric and eastern theme that came near her became the template for New Age philosophy, but she was premature. Theosophy's borrowing of Eastern religious themes was not that successful. In 1926 there were 223 groups in the USA with a combined membership of around 7,000. The primacy of women in leadership was reflected in the membership: 65 per cent of the members of the American Theosophical Society were women.[23] Its London membership was also overwhelmingly female. As Robert Pearsall notes: 'emancipated girls with college educations went into it, cocking a snook in the face of their square elders.'[24]

We can draw a number of general observations from this brief review of female-led religious innovations. In an ideal world we would know precisely how many people in any period joined such religious innovations, we would know their gender composition, and we would be able to calculate precisely what proportion of men and women were attracted to such enthusiasms. Lacking such data, we have to rely on our impression formed from a great deal of historical reading, and we guess that women were at least as likely as men, and probably slightly more so, to be attracted to millennialist movements. We hesitate to commit ourselves as thoroughly as Rodney Stark does when he says: 'So far as is known, throughout recorded history religious movements have recruited women far more successfully than men, except for those that excluded women from membership.'[25] But we certainly find enough evidence of women being involved in religious innovation to call into question the claim that women are more religious than men because they are more conservative and conformist.

Second, we note the social utility of divine inspiration as a justification for defying social norms. The rules of men may confine women to second-class status but, if God has chosen, then his will trumps human convention.

Third, we note the close relationship between Godliness and health. Persistent frailty and sickness often formed the backcloth to revelation. Its role in the careers of White, Lee, Baltrop, and Eddy has already been mentioned. Blavatsky dated her first Theosophical inspirations to a period of ill-health. And the new faith was often curative. It was centrally so in the case of Christian Science, but the Seventh-Day Adventists, Theosophists, Panaceans, and Shakers all promoted dietary and exercise regimes as part of the new life.

Finally, we draw attention to the sexual puritanism of most female-led religious innovations. For two good reasons, new religions are often accused of sexual licentiousness and perversion. Such pioneers often raise the topic themselves in that they are critical of some or all aspects of the institution of marriage. And accusations of sexual perversion always have a certain plausibility simply because they are difficult to disprove.[26] However, with the exception of the Buchanites—and their impropriety seems to have been more theoretical than actual—and Theosophy, the movements discussed here all promoted sexual continence and abstinence. With the exception of the Panacea Society, we know little or nothing of the attitudes to sex of the ordinary members, but, as these movements were relatively successful we can suppose that the views of the leaders were to some extent representative. In most cases religious enthusiasm was associated with (we cannot say 'caused by') a desire to avoid sexual intercourse and its consequences in frequent pregnancy. In addition to directly prohibiting or restricting sexual intercourse, most movements promoted diets intended to reduce sexual desire. The historian of the Panacea Society notes one example of a member who was troubled by her husband's wish to give up sexual relations, but generally the pursuit of piety was closely associated with notions of bodily purity that allowed women to curb male sexual demands.[27]

New Religious Movements of the 1960s

If the range of religions on offer is a symptom of religious interest, then the second half of the twentieth century appears to rebut any suggestion that the West has become increasingly secular: the counterculture of the 1960s produced an astonishing array of new religious movements (NRMs).[28] The International Society for Krishna Consciousness (or ISKCON or Hare Krishna), Transcendental Meditation (or TM), the Divine Light Mission, and the Healthy-Happy-Holy movement of Yogi Bhajan (a variant of Sikhism) were imports from the East. Others were what Paul Heelas has called 'self-religions': Erhard Seminar Training (or *est*, always spelt with lower-case letters), Insight, Exegesis, and Scientology were quasi-religious psychotherapies. They took the ideas of Sigmund Freud, Carl Jung, Wilhelm Reich, and others, inflated their therapeutic claims, and broadened their reach so that cures for the sick became tools for general improvement.

The apparently counter-intuitive connection with secularization is simply explained. Cheaper travel and better communications made the entire world's religious repertoire practically available to the citizens of the West, but they became *socially* available only when the power of Christianity to stigmatize alternatives as dangerously deviant waned. Our grandparents knew about Hinduism and Buddhism, but they saw them through the hostile judgements of a strongly Christian culture. Secularization created space for people to take seriously alternative religious traditions, and innovation flourished.

What prevents this being a rebuttal of secularization is that the numbers attracted to NRMs were considerably smaller than those lost to the mainstream churches. Their promoters and their detractors shared a common interest in inflating the importance of a phenomenon that, for all its exotic fascination, attracted memberships that rarely reached the thousands. Millions became aware of Transcendental Meditation because of the Beatles' visit to the ashram of Maharishi Mahesh Yogi and George Harrison's 'My Sweet Lord'. Thousands learnt the basic TM meditation technique. Only small hundreds stayed with the movement for more than a few months.

There is much that can be said about the new religions of the 1960s, but a helpful distinction that summarizes much that is important about them is Roy Wallis's contrast between world-rejecting and world-affirming movements.[29] World-rejecting movements are salvation oriented. They take people out of the mundane world and into full-time religious work, the purpose of which is to purify the members and prepare them and the world at large for salvation. Such movements are generally ascetic and puritanical: the things of the flesh are bad; the things of the spirit are good. In contrast, world-affirming movements are generally not salvation oriented. Their focus is this life rather than the next, and they have one or more of three related aims: empowerment, reconciliation, and restoration. They empower adherents to be more successful in the material world, usually by teaching them how to access some hidden psychic energy. They also reconcile people to their current circumstances; the success that is delivered may be change, not in the status quo, but in one's attitude to it. They may also offer to restore the authentic self and the potential for truly human relationships that those who have devoted themselves whole-heartedly to the pursuit of career success have lost in their Faustian compact.

With the exception of Theosophy, all the religious innovations discussed above were variants of Christianity, and hence recruitment to them could be seen as an extension of people's prior religious socialization. Early adopters of Seventh-Day Adventism or Christian Science may have been thought odd, and in places the Shakers got the same rough treatment meted out to the early Mormons, but they were arguably still part of the Christian tradition. Many of the 1960s NRMs were genuinely novel for Westerners, and hence the decision to join cannot be explained as simply a continuation—with added pep—of whatever explains conventional religiosity.

Lorne Dawson concludes a review of NRMs by saying that, while some groups might attract more of 'one sex than another, there is no strong evidence that women are any more susceptible to joining NRMs than men'.[30] It is interesting that he feels the assertion that needs to be rebutted is that women are particularly credulous, and we will return to that, but our immediate response is that we know more than he implies about gender and NRMs. Table 2.1 presents the gender breakdown of a variety of NRMs in various times and place and three columns of information about characteristics that may explain their appeal. The letters 'C and 'NC' under the heading 'Living' indicate whether the group was communal or non-communal. The 'WR' or 'WA' under 'Slant' indicates world-rejecting or world-affirming. The 'E' and 'W' under 'Origins' indicates whether the group's core beliefs were primarily Eastern (as in Hindu or Buddhist; none was inspired by Islam) or Western (the spiritualized psychotherapies). Obviously such dichotomies simplify, but they do economically convey important information about the group or movement in question.

The examples are ranked by the proportion of adherents who are female, so that the NRMs that appealed most to women are in the top half of the table. A quick glance at the last three columns shows that most of the examples fall into two very different blocks, which attract men and women in quite different proportions. By and large those movements that were Eastern in origin, expected full-time residential commitment, and were world-rejecting in ethos had a male majority. Those that were Western in origin did not require communal living, and those that were world-affirming were either balanced or had a female majority.[31]

A study of thirty-five Eastern-inspired communes reported that on average women made up 40 per cent of the residents (with a standard

Table 2.1. Gender profile of new religious movements

Name	% female	Date	Place	Living	Slant	Origin
Brahma Kumaris	80	2011	UK	NC	WR	E
Soka Gakkai	70	2007	USA	NC	WA	E
Soka Gakkai	68	1997	USA	NC	WA	E
Soka Gakkai	66	2003	Aus.	NC	WA	E
Endtime Family/ Children of God	60	1997	WW	NC	WR	W
est	60	1970s	USA	NC	WA	W
Soka Gakkai	57	1990	UK	NC	WA	E
Brahma Kumaris	55	1992	Aus.	NC	WR	E
TM Technique	51	2010	UK	NC	WA	E
Heaven's Gate	50	1990s	USA	NC	WR	W
Exegesis	50	1980	UK	NC	WA	W
Rajneeshpuram	50	1980s	USA	C	WA	E
Insight	50	1979	UK	NC	WA	W
Various Eastern communes	40	1980s	USA	C	WR	E
San Francisco Zen Center	40	1970s	USA	C	WR	E
Bo and Peep	40	1970s	USA	C	WR	W
Brahma Kumaris	40	1970s	Aus.	NC	WR	E
Zen Buddhism	39	2007	USA	NC	WR	E
ISKCON	33	*c.*1978	Aus.	C	WR	E
ISKCON	33	1970s	USA	C	WR	E
Children of God	33	1970s	WW	C	WR	W
Unification Church	33	1980	UK	C	WR	W
ISKCON	30	1966–77	WW	C	WR	E
TM Residential	25	1970s	USA	C	WR	E

Note: WW = worldwide; C = communal; NC = non-communal; WA = world-affirming; WR = world-rejecting; E = Eastern; W = Western.

Sources: The data for the table come from the following:

Bo and Peep: Rob Balch, personal communication.

Brahma Kumaris Australia: J. D. Howell and P. L. Nelson, 'Demographic Change and Secularization in an Asian New Religious Movement', *Research in the Social Scientific Study of Religion*, 11 (2000), 225–39.

Brahma Kumaris UK: Astrid Bendomir, personal communication.

Endtime Family/Children of God: Association of Religion Data Archives <http://www.thearda.com/Archive/Files/Descriptions/ENDTIME.asp> (accessed 7 Nov. 2010) and S. Palmer, *Moon Sisters, Krishna Mothers, Rajneesh Lovers: Women's Roles in New Religions* (Syracuse, NY: Syracuse University Press, 1994), 239.

est: S. Tipton, *Getting Saved from the Sixties* (Berkeley and Los Angeles: University of California Press, 1992), 103, 182.

Exegesis: Paul Heelas, personal communication.

Insight: Roy Wallis, original research notes.

ISKCON WW: E. Burke Rocheford, personal communication.

ISKCON 1970s: Palmer, *Moon Sisters.*

ISKCON Australia: L. O'Brien. 'A Case Study of the "Hare Krishna" Movement', in A. Black and P. Glasner (eds), *Practice and Belief* (Sydney: George Allen and Unwin, 1983), 134–52.

Moonies: E. Barker, *The Making of a Moonie: Brainwashing or Choice?* (Oxford: Basil Blackwell, 1984), 206–7.

TM technique UK: TM headquarters and two TM practitioners, personal communication.

SGI Australia: D. A. Metraux, 'Globalising Japanese Religion: Soka Gakkai in Australia', *Virginia Review of Asian Studies*, 2003 <http://www.virginiareviewofasianstudies.com/files/archives/2003/Australia_metraux.pdf> (accessed 1 July 2011).

SGI UK 1990: B. R. Wilson and K. Dobbelaere, *A Time to Chant: The Soka Gakkai Buddhists in Britain* (Oxford: Oxford University Press, 1998), 39.

SGI USA 2003: as for Endtime Family/Children of God.

SGI USA 2007: *The Pluralism Project at Harvard University* <http://pluralism.org/view/71659> (accessed 3 Mar. 2011).

TM: <http://en.wikipedia.org/wiki/Transcendental_Meditation_movement> (accessed 8 Nov. 2010).

Zen Center, San Francisco: Tipton, *Getting Saved*, 103.

Zen Buddhism USA 2007: Pew Forum, *US Religious Landscape Survey.*

Various: C. A. Larkin, 'Gender Roles in the Experimental Community', *Sex Roles*, 21 (1989), 629–52.

Various Eastern communes: S. Fuller and J. L. Martin, 'Women's Status in Eastern NRMs', *Review of Religious Research*, 44 (2003), 354–69.

deviation of 20 per cent).[32] We have no information on the thousands of people who learnt to meditate with the Maharishi Mahesh Yogi's Transcendental Meditation (or TM) movement in the 1970s, but, according to one source, the ratio of men to women in TM's residential programmes in the USA was 3 to 1.[33] In the San Francisco Zen Buddhist Center in the early 1970s there were three men for every two women.[34] Forty years later, the gender gap among those who described themselves as Zen Buddhists in a major national survey was greater: 61/39 per cent male to female. The male representation in the International Society for Krishna Consciousness (aka ISKCON or Hare Krishna) was slightly higher again. When he died in 1977, the founder Prabhupada had initiated some 5,000 disciples, of whom 3,500 were men.[35] Elizabeth Puttick argues that university-educated women were put off by the patriarchal nature of many such movements.[36] In particular, a series of sex scandals associated with the San Francisco Zen Center, with ISKCON, and with the leading Tibetan Buddhist Chogyam Trungpa were read as evidence of the generally exploitative attitude towards women.

Although they were accused of licentiousness, the members of the Unification Church (aka the Moonies) were actually puritanical. And, although its founder was Korean, its teachings had more in common with Christian millenarianism than with Hinduism and Buddhism. None the less it was firmly world-rejecting, and it was patriarchal in the sense that great play was made of the family as a model for social harmony and of Moon's status as the Divine Father. Those two things might explain why, in its early years, the sex ratio in Britain and the United States was two to one in favour of men.

Although its philosophy was so eclectic as to defy classification, the flying saucer cult led by Bo and Peep (as Marshall Applewhite and Bonnie Nettles then called themselves) in Oregon in the early 1970s also attracted more men than women. They liked to have their followers solicit donations in male–female pairs, but, as Rob Balch recalls 'there were some male–male pairs but no female–female pairs'.[37] However, twenty years later, with Nettles dead and Applewhite the leader of what was now known as Heaven's Gate, the gender balance was closer. When the close transit of the Hale–Bop comet triggered a communal suicide, there were twenty-one men and eighteen women among those who abandoned their bodies so they could be lifted up to 'the next level'. Although the group was so small that we should not make too much of any change in composition, it may well be that the peripatetic lifestyle of the early years discouraged women, and hence more women joined once its leaders had settled in San Francisco and involvement became more compatible with normal life. That the requirement for communal living and full-time involvement may be as big a consideration as the theoretical world orientation of the NRM is further suggested by two deviant cases. A detailed study of two non-residential Thervadan Buddhist centres (one in Cambridge, Massachusetts, and one in Philadelphia) showed that, in contrast to the SF Zen Center, women were over-represented: in both places women made up two-thirds of the attenders.[38]

On the basis of Wallis's analysis we might expect that movements such as *est* and Scientology would have appealed primarily to men. If the pitch is that working hard to get on in the public world of work causes people to sublimate or stifle the authentic self, then we would expect that men, as a large majority of those who in the 1970s occupied positions of power in corporations and companies, would be the beneficiaries of *est*, Exegesis, Insight, and such therapies. This does not seem to have been the case. Writing of the late 1970s, Steven Tipton says: 'Roughly 60 per cent of all *est* clients are women, who generally report themselves more influenced by the training than men do.'[39]

Arianna Stassinopoulous became famous in the USA as the wife of Michael Huffington, a right-wing Republican congressman from California, and as a right-wing commentator and political candidate in her own right and then later as the founder of the *Huffington Post* (one of the pioneering online news outlets). Before that she was well known in London as a broadcaster and writer in London and as the lover of celebrated journalist Bernard Levin. She introduced first Levin and then London society to Insight, an *est*-like form of training that promised to free people from

the melodrama that goes on in our heads most of the time; the fear, anxiety, guilt and recrimination; the burden of the past which dominates our present responses...from crippling images...self-limiting images which makes us feel that we are not terribly worthwhile...from the sense of oneself as victim.[40]

The audiences for Insight training were evenly male and female, as were the graduates of the Exegesis seminar training, a UK-based organization similar in style and ethos to *est*.[41]

One plausible way of reshaping the Wallis explanation shows the innate difficulty of proving causal connections. Wallis sees the restorative element of the world-affirming movement as appealing particularly to successful middle-aged men who have won the world but lost their souls: Bernard Levin was by his own account such a person. But what distinguishes humans from lower animals is that we can anticipate future states. A young woman such as Stassinopoulous did not have to wait until the problem arose before seeking a solution; she could imagine it and take pre-emptive action. We can thus broaden the Wallis picture of the world-affirming NRM's clientele to include educated ambitious young women who wished for worldly success but also sought protection against the loss of sensitivity and humane relations with their fellows. The problem with so expanding *est*'s appeal is that we now have less of an explanation.

It is perhaps easier to see why women were less likely than men to be drawn to world-rejecting movements. The notion that the patriarchal culture of Hindu and Buddhist-based NRMs was a chill factor for young women seems plausible for later periods in the history of such movements—once their nature had become the subject of popular discussion. But it may not work as well as an explanation of gender patterns where they were evident from the start. Barker considers this for the Moonies:

Another possible explanation which occurred to me was that the Unification Church is decidedly unsympathetic towards modern ideas of female emancipation...but I had to abandon this as a plausible explanation when I went through the thousand-odd application forms for a two-day workshop and found that only a third of these (and of the application forms for the twenty-one-day course) were from women, and potential recruits would have been unlikely to know much about the movement's attitude towards women at that stage.[42]

However, what would have been apparent from the very first encounter was that this was a conservative world-rejecting religious movement, and it may be that the gender gap is explained by the same consideration that explains the absence of two other demographics: racial and ethnic minorities and the working class.

Many world-rejecting movements are 'religions of the oppressed': their appeal is to those who have little or nothing in this life, and it is based on inverting the social hierarchy.[43] To the poor they promise that the meek shall inherit the earth. For those who cannot or do not wish to rebel against their low status, a puritanical religion, such as the fundamentalism of the agrarian south of the USA in the 1930s, has considerable socio-psychological value. It promises that the current status hierarchy will be reversed in the next life. It denounces the rich, guarantees salvation to the poor, and assures them that they are really better than their masters. It thus turns privation into a mark of merit. The target audience of such movements as the Moonies was not the conventionally poor: they were much more likely to be found in conservative evangelical and Pentecostal churches. The world-rejecting new religions of the 1960s appealed primarily to those who, courtesy of their parents, enjoyed a comfortable niche in the world and whose futures looked bright. For the few months that was the typical membership of most recruits, well-off white kids criticized their own social class. Why young white men should find this temporary rebellion more attractive than did young black and Asian men and young white women might be explained simply by the difference in the expectations of success held by those different demographic groups. Professional career opportunities were only just opening up for women and racial minorities and could not be sufficiently taken-for-granted for them to be scorned, even temporarily. This perhaps puts it a little harshly, but rich white boys could afford to play at being monks. Those who had found their way to wealth, status, and power blocked by their gender, class, or race were less likely to be attracted by a critique of the material success they sought.

Women had a second problem with world-rejecting NRMs. Members were expected to serve the movement full-time and either to abandon or to defer plans for conventional careers and for marriage and children. For those women still attached to the traditional roles of women as wives and mothers, joining an ashram required a considerable sacrifice. And it was no less a sacrifice for progressive young women who wanted to take advantage of the new opportunities in higher education and rewarding professions.

Finally, after discussing gender differences *between* NRMs, we can consider the gender composition of the spectrum as a whole. As we noted for the nineteenth century millennialist movements, it would be nice if we could calculate the gender composition of the 1960s NRMs as a whole, but the very high turnover and the short lifespan of many movements makes such membership and adherence figures as we do have extremely unreliable, and adding them together simply compounds the uncertainty. The best we can do is note that women generally outnumbered men in world-affirming movements and lagged behind in world-rejecting ones. The former type of movement was much more popular than the latter. So, although we cannot put a figure on the overall gender gap, we can reasonably conclude that women predominated in the 1960s NRMs.

Conclusion

We thus disagree with Dawson's conclusion that 'there is no strong evidence that women are any more susceptible to joining NRMs than men'. Dawson was responding to the sort of explanation of female religious enthusiasm advanced by Whitney Cross in his discussion of religious revivals in the first half of the nineteenth century in western New York state.[44] Cross noted the preponderance of women and explained it as being because they were 'less educated, more superstitious, and more zealous than the men'.[45] We have no difficulty with the third of those descriptions. The first two seem, like Dawson's use of susceptibility, to rest on a distinction between routine church adherence and dangerous enthusiasm. We would argue that, if we recognize that women tend to predominate in all forms of religion—institutionalized and innovative—there is no need to make pejorative judgements of those women who were recruited to the new religious movements of either the nineteenth or the late twentieth century or to defend such women against the accusation of being suckers. We can simply observe that in most settings women tend to be more religious than men and then add appropriate qualifications about the appeal of particular kinds of religious innovation.

3

Spirits and Bodies

Introduction

If this introductory review of women's religious interests was being arranged chronologically, Spiritualism would have been introduced in the previous chapter between the Shakers and the Seventh-Day Adventists. We have singled it out because its appeal introduces some new elements that are worth highlighting.

It is a mark of both the secularity and the cynicism of modern culture that Spiritualism now seems eccentric and its audiences seem credulous. It is worth stressing that, though it had many contemporary critics, Spiritualism was for a short time popular and prestigious. Victoria Woodhull had an extraordinary career that took her from selling sex and hokum medicines to selling shares as the first female New York stockbroker and to addressing a Congressional committee on votes for women. She also acted as a spirit medium for many of the leading social reformers of the 1860s. Her advocacy of 'free love' and her criticisms of the oppressive nature of the institution of marriage earned her far more enemies than did her claims to commune with the dead. When the American spiritualist D. D. Home moved to London in 1855, he attracted the patronage of such London society figures as Lady Waldegrave (a leading Liberal party hostess), Lady Downshire, the Duchess of Somerset, Lady Londonderry, Lady Fanny Jocelyn (one of Queen Victoria's ladies-in-waiting), and Lady Salisbury. The Queen herself engaged in a spot of table-turning.[1]

Initially Spiritualism was more a mixture of science and parlour game than a religion. It did make claims about the supernatural. Indeed, its original primary purpose was the dramatic demonstration, through contact with them, that the spirits of the deceased lived on in some non-material world that was separated from us only by a thin veil. But it lacked the other characteristics of religion: there was no particular ethical code nor any sense of divine judgement. In the twentieth century, as the entertainment and showmanship elements receded, it came to resemble other Protestant sects and denominations. This chapter will present a brief history of Spiritualism and introduce possible explanations for its particular appeal to women. It will also introduce some highly suggestive data on women's attitudes to the disposal of the dead and to the human body in general.

Spiritualism

Modern Spiritualism is generally credited to the Fox sisters of Hydesville, New York: Leah, Margaret, and Kate. When Kate was 12 and Margaret 15, the family moved to a reputedly haunted house where they reportedly heard strange rapping noises. One night in 31 March 1848, Kate challenged the invisible noise-maker, presumed to be a 'spirit', to repeat the snaps of her fingers, which it did. She asked it to rap out the ages of the girls, which it also did. The neighbours were called to witness what gradually became a complex series of communications based on raps, which could be yes or no answers to questions or could indicate a letter of the alphabet.[2] The girls addressed the spirit as 'Mr Splitfoot', a nickname for the Devil. Later the sounds were attributed to the spirit of a peddler named Charles B. Rosma, who had supposedly been murdered five years earlier and buried in the cellar. No such missing person was ever identified.[3]

Kate and Margaret were sent away to Rochester during the excitement, and it was found that the rappings went with them. Their hosts, a leading Quaker couple and long-standing friends of the Foxes, Isaac and Amy Post, became convinced of the genuineness of the phenomena, and they helped to spread the word among their radical Quaker friends, who came to form the core of the Spiritualist movement. The Fox girls became famous, and their public séances in New York in 1850 attracted such notable people as James Fennimore Cooper, author of *The Last of the Mohicans*, and William Lloyd Garrison, a leader of the anti-slavery movement.

The Foxes also attracted imitators, and, during the following few years, hundreds of people would claim the ability to communicate with spirits. For many that skill was exercised in one-to-one consultations that combined putting the client in touch with some deceased loved one and treating some psychological or physical ailments. Mary, the wife of Horace Greeley, the owner of the *New York Tribune* and one of the founders of the Republican party, was so stricken with grief at the loss of her young son that she insisted that her husband find Kate Fox and employ her to be a regular bridge to her lost child. A large potential clientele of bereaved mothers such as Mary Greeley was ensured by the high infant mortality rate, but it was inflated in the 1860s by the American Civil War, in which at least 600,000 people died:

The movement... was at its zenith at the end of the Civil War. The unbearable death of a generation of young men—the hope of America—encouraged the belief that these souls had simply 'passed over'. They were reachable in a land just beyond the living where they could be called upon to comfort and support the bereft they left behind.[4]

For the British, the First World War provided a similar stimulus.

The deaths occurring in almost every family in the land brought a sudden and concentrated interest in life after death. People not only asked the question 'If a man die shall he live again?' but they eagerly sought to know if communication was possible with the dear ones they had lost.[5]

Those words were written by Sir Arthur Conan Doyle, the author and creator of Sherlock Holmes. His wife had died in 1906, and his son Kingsley died in 1918 from pneumonia contracted while convalescing after being wounded at the Battle of the Somme. He also lost his brother, his two brothers-in-law, and two nephews shortly after the war. In Spiritualism he found a cure for his depression. Conan Doyle's interest in Spiritualism might seem at odds with the attitudes he gave to his most famous creation. In the detective stories, the hard-headed and ruthlessly scientific Holmes invariably shows that apparently supernatural phenomena have natural causes. Conan Doyle's attachment to Spiritualism may seem like a change of heart but that misses the point that the communication with the dead that he and others believed possible was thought to be thoroughly natural.

The best of the mediums who provided a personal service were sufficiently good readers of people that they could learn more about their clients than the clients knew they were giving away and re-present that knowledge to the client as proof of supernatural sources. They could also use that sensitivity therapeutically to treat the psychosomatic ailments that were common among a class of women who had few legitimate outlets for their ambitions and abilities, who were oppressed by the burden of unrestricted childbirth, and who were frustrated by a drastically inegalitarian culture that denied them all but the most basic civil rights. Many mediums were like Woodhull in offering healing, dietary advice, and counselling in their consultations.

Spiritualism also provided a new form of domestic entertainment. The wealthy hired professional mediums; others engaged family and friends in amateurish efforts with Ouija boards and rappings. But communicating with the dead also became highly popular and lucrative public entertainment. Showmanship became an increasingly important part as professional mediums toured provincial towns competing for paying audiences with ever more florid displays of sounds and signs.

Not surprisingly, this spirit-filled branch of vaudeville attracted considerable sceptical attention. There were investigations, and some mediums were prosecuted in the courts for fraud. The most successful de-bunkers of Spiritualism were professional conjurers, who were able to demonstrate how glasses could be moved around the letters on a Ouija board and how apparitions could be produced with the aid of sticks, strips of cloth, and sleight of hand. In retrospect it seems strange that audiences were so easily persuaded that the conditions required for making contact with spirit guides were precisely those that fraudsters would have chosen to protect their sleights of hand: very dim light, seclusion in a cabinet, and a sympathetic audience. This last condition provided a useful explanation of failure in the presence of investigators: the spirits were scared off by hostility.

The most famous act of the Davenport Brothers was the box illusion. The two brothers were tied in sitting positions inside a large cupboard that contained musical instruments. Once the door was closed, the instruments would sound. When the door was opened, the brothers were found still tied in their original positions; therefore the drums must have been struck, and the trumpet blown, by spirits. After a decade touring the USA, the Davenports visited England to catch the Spiritualism boom there. A watchmaker and amateur magician John Maskelyne exposed the act by building his own spirit cabinet and repeating the trick, without spirited assistance.[6] During the 1920s, professional magician Harry Houdini undertook a well-publicized campaign to expose fraudulent mediums. He concludes the introduction to his account of those investigations with the judgement: 'Up to the present time everything that I have investigated has been the result of deluded brains.'[7]

As well as de-bunkers, the Spiritualists also attracted serious academic interest. The Society for Psychical Research was founded in London in 1882 to investigate scientifically mediumship and related psychical phenomenon. William James, one of the founders of modern psychology, investigated a number of mediums and published generally positive conclusions. Typical of the lengths to which the abilities of mediums were tested was the experiment conducted by Sir William Crookes on Florence Cook, who was apparently able to materialize a spirit called Katie while remaining in a trance. Conveniently, Cook could contact the spirits only when protected from audience negativity; she would operate only in a large cupboard or separate room. To ensure that she did not move, Cook was connected to a galvanometer by pieces of blotting paper soaked in ammonium nitrate, sovereign coins, and copper wire: the meter would register an abrupt change in current if she left her place. Despite Cook's galvanometer readings remaining reasonably stable, Katie

looked out from under the curtain, three minutes later she showed her hands and in ten minutes she was out and about among the audience, putting her hands on Crookes's head. Katie asked for paper and began to write. The audience heard Miss Cook moaning like a woman in a nightmare. During the writing the galvanometer did not vary.[8]

Florence Cook passed that test, but many other mediums, particularly those who materialized spirits, were exposed as frauds.

Forty years after the first rappings, Margaret Fox confessed that they had been a hoax.

When we went to bed at night we used to tie an apple to a string and move the string up and down, causing the apple to bump on the floor, or we would drop the apple on the floor, making a strange noise every time it would rebound. Mother listened to this for a time. She would not understand it and did not suspect us as being capable of a trick because we were so young.

In October 1888, Margaret, accompanied by Kate, gave a large New York audience a demonstration of her ability to produce the rapping sounds at will with her toe joints.

That I have been chiefly instrumental in perpetrating the fraud of Spiritualism upon a too-confiding public, most of you doubtless know. The greatest sorrow in my life has been that this is true, and though it has come late in my day, I am now prepared to tell the truth, the whole truth, and nothing but the truth, so help me God!...I am here tonight as one of the founders of Spiritualism to denounce it as an absolute falsehood from beginning to end, as the flimsiest of superstitions, the most wicked blasphemy known to the world.

She also gave an extended confession to a newspaper in which explained the technique:

[Leah] took Katie and me to Rochester. There it was that we discovered a new way to make the raps. My sister Katie was the first to observe that by swishing her fingers she could produce certain noises with her knuckles and joints, and that the same effect could be made with the toes. Finding that we could make raps with our feet—first with one foot and then with both—we practiced until we could do this easily when the room was dark.[9]

She attributed the rest of her apparent communication with the spirit world to the susceptibility of the audience:

Some very wealthy people came to see me some years ago...and I did some rappings for them. I made the spirit rap on the chair and one of the ladies cried out: 'I feel the spirit tapping me on the shoulder.' Of course that was pure imagination.[10]

According to press reports, Kate joined her sister in repenting of their past: 'I regard Spiritualism as one of the greatest curses that the world has ever known.'[11]

It is not often that the founders of a new religious movement denounce their creation, and it is perhaps to be expected that many refused to believe the sisters. There were two techniques for rejecting the bad news. The first was to explain why the sisters should now be lying, and that was easily done. Kate and Margaret were alcoholics and desperate for money, and the newspaper that sponsored their public recantation paid handsomely for the coup. Kate had fallen out with Leah, because the older sister did not think Kate capable of raising her children, and Kate and Margaret clearly wished to harm Leah and other leading Spiritualists. Margaret had a second motive. In 1852 she had married a Catholic, converted, and given up mediumship, which she resumed only after her husband had died in 1857. Thirty years later and ill, she was contemplating a return to the Catholic Church. According to those who believed the Fox sisters really were channels for spirit communications, it was the combination of Catholic pressure, spite, and poverty that persuaded Kate and Margaret to lie.

The second way to neutralize the confession, which also worked for the exposure of fraud, was to develop the implications of the fact that the medium was undoubtedly involved in the process. Although mediums generally presented themselves as passive (and sometimes very reluctant) channels, they still did something, so it was possible for the sympathetic to suppose that mediums might be unaware of precisely what part of the communication was theirs and what part the spirit's. That Margaret thought she was making it up did not rule out the possibility that there really was something else involved. That a medium cheated sometimes did not mean that she cheated always. When Woodhull passed on to Commodore Vanderbilt spirit guidance as to when to buy and sell gold in the run-up to the collapse of the gold market in 1869, her source was very firmly this-worldly: a friend who was party to the plans of the schemers who were manipulating the market. But her own responses to her voices and visions clearly show that she was often entirely sincere, especially when summoning up her spirit guides to help her face otherwise daunting challenges such as addressing a Congressional committee or a large suffrage audience.[12]

Institutionalization

Over the twentieth century Spiritualism developed in three directions. Individual practitioners continued to contact spirits on behalf of clients and some also performed in public, though there was no return to the vaudeville of the previous century. Second, there was a growth in the use of contact with the spirit world to provide ethical, political, social, and moral guidance. What Helene Blavatsky had pioneered with her wisdom from the Mahatmas evolved into New Age 'channelling'. Third, there was a line that added formal organization, training and accreditation, ritual and ideology to become the Spiritualist churches.

Training in Spiritualism was consolidated in the 1920s with the foundation of the Arthur Findlay College at Stansted Hall in England and the Morris Pratt Institute in Wisconsin, USA. Membership of Spiritualist churches in the USA is difficult to estimate, because many did not affiliate to either the National Spiritualist Association of Churches, founded in 1893, or the National Spiritual Alliance (a breakaway that differed from the first body by believing in reincarnation). In net terms, the high point for those organizations was 1946, when they had a combined membership of around 17,500. As a proportion of the available population, their peak was in the 1920s, and by the end of the twentieth century, when population had more than doubled, membership was less than 5,000.[13] The UK's main body—The Spiritualists' National Union—was founded in 1890, when there were probably 25,000 Spiritualists in the UK. The movement grew during the First World War and peaked in 1920 with around 100,000 members. It remained popular through the 1930s, but, perhaps surprisingly, gained no boost from the carnage of the Second World War. There were around 32,000 members in 2003 and 17,000 in 2007. These figures almost certainly flatter Spiritualism, probably because they include people who also have a stronger affiliation to a more mainstream denomination. The England and Wales version of the 2001 census asked for religion in only general 'faith' terms, but the Scottish version asked for specific affiliation, and from that we know that only 868 Scots identified as Spiritualists. Assuming a similar proportion in England, Wales, and Northern Ireland would give us around 10,000 Spiritualists for the UK as a whole.[14] Interest, of course, is greater. Far more people consult a Spiritualist once or twice than attend a Spiritualist church regularly, and multi-channel cable and satellite TV has allowed a number of Spiritualists to become well-known performers and entertainers.

British Spiritualist churches usually display the Seven Principles, made suitably sombre by being painted in gold gothic script on a black background: The Fatherhood of God; the Brotherhood of Man; Communion of Spirits and the Ministry of Angels; the Continuous Existence of the Human Soul; Personal Responsibility; Compensation and Retribution Hereafter for All the Good and Evil Deeds Done on Earth; and Eternal Progress Open to Every Soul.[15] There is nothing there that would make it specifically Christian, but also nothing that could not, with a little fudging, be acceptable to Christians. This is an important consideration, because many of those who attend Spiritualist churches also attend mainstream Christian churches. 'The form of the service, though not its content, has been largely taken over from familiar Nonconformist models.'[16] The lay leader begins with a short prayer and introduces the visiting medium. There is then a hymn, prayer, and short address from the medium. Another hymn is followed by the service centrepiece: the medium's display of clairvoyance. The lay leader then reads out notices and introduces the final prayer and hymn. The hymns used in British churches are generally taken from the Church of England's *Hymns Ancient and Modern* or the Methodist hymn book. As Bernice Martin explains, those that were theologically vague have been left intact. Others have been doctored. For example, replacing the first two words of 'Jesus Lives! Thy terrors now can, O death, no more appal us' by 'Loved ones live!' creates a perfect Spiritualist hymn.[17]

Surviving and Caring

One interesting feature of the public perception of Spiritualism is that its sense of the gender profile of mediums was inaccurate, at least in the early days. The profession was seen as primarily female, though a US survey in 1859 counted 121 women and 110 men.[18] The gender balance undoubtedly shifted when the vaudeville style, largely a male preserve, died out. But the public misperception of the early days may well have been a consequence of the sorts of characteristics attributed to mediumship. To be a good medium one had to be unusually sensitive, and sensitivity was what women supposedly had in spades. Sensitivity was associated with physical fragility. Some of the best-known US mediums were extremely hard-working and must have been robust to engage in the long tours that were necessary to find new audiences for a standard performance. Nonetheless, mediums frequently presented themselves as frail invalids. Long periods of poor health were a routine part of the biographical background to the discovery of mediumship powers. Bodily weakness was presented as one cause of the trance-like state into which most mediums fell before they made effective contact with the other side. Helen Duncan, the last British woman to be tried as a witch, was an obese semi-invalid with 'pulmonary, renal, cardio-vascular, glandular, urinary and intestinal malfunctions'. Even when she was mobile, 'her lurching blood-sugar levels made fainting a fact of life'.[19] Along with fragility came passivity: mediums presented themselves as the impassive and sometimes reluctant recipients of communications from the other side. This was particularly important for those trance speakers who took questions on difficult scientific or cultural subjects from the audience and whose ability to produce cogent answers was taken as proof of a spirit world. The more the medium could appear dull or ill-educated, the more the messages acted as proof. In further conformity to contemporary gender roles, the putative spirit guide was often a high-status male. Not just because they were exotic but also because they represented cultures that were known for venerating ancestors, American Indian chiefs were popular, as were Chinese Mandarins.

There seems to be widespread agreement that women were particularly attracted to mediumship by the rare opportunities it offered. The anthropologist I. M. Lewis distinguished between spirit possession in organized cults and peripheral possession.[20] In central possession cults, ecstasy is a routine part of the dominant religion, the spirits are moral, and possession is confined to people of high status: normally men. Peripheral possession is importantly different. The spirits are external and amoral. The possessed are generally low status, often women. In contrast to approaches that saw spirit possession as akin to mental illness, Lewis's explanation treats peripheral possession as a rational response to social impotence. The historian Barbara Goldsmith makes the same connection when she says of Woodhull and her contemporaries: 'At a time when women had no power to achieve equal rights, they relied on the "other powers" provided by Spiritualism to sustain their efforts. Through the mouths of trance speakers came words of wisdom from long-dead seers and from the spirits came the courage to go forward.'[21]

Whatever the gender of the medium, the largest part of the audience was likely to be female. Of the members of the 602 congregations of the American National Spiritualist Association and the National Spiritual Alliance of the USA in 1926, 62 per cent were women.[22] No studies of UK Spiritualists provide detailed gender breakdowns, but all are agreed that women are over-represented in membership and attendance.

An obvious explanation of this pattern is the demographic one: men die earlier. As the clientele for the work of the medium is composed primarily of people who wish to hear reassuring messages from a deceased loved one, it is not surprising that the composition of the audience reflects the patterns of death. One of the very few UK studies of Spiritualist churches that provides statistics found that in the 1970s the proportion of widows in the membership was three times that in the population at large.[23] Even if belief in the efficacy of mediumship was equally distributed between men and women, differences in life expectancy would lead us to expect more female than male clients or members of the Spiritualist churches.

But there may be something more subtle going on here that bears on our general question of the gender gap in religiosity. In 1951, with the aid of the *People* newspaper, Geoffrey Gorer arranged a survey that attracted over 5,000 respondents. One series of questions asked about life after death. As Gorer says: 'As in all matters of religious belief there is a very marked contrast between men and women: 39 per cent of men and 56 per cent of women believe in an after-life; 28 per cent of the men and 14 per cent of the women do not.'[24] A 1990s British survey found a similarly large difference: two-thirds of women but only one-third of men said they believed in life after death.[25]

In the 1951 survey, those who said they believed in an afterlife were asked: 'What do you think it will be like?' The answers were so varied that Gorer had trouble compressing them into a limited number of types, but he eventually managed to identify ten typical responses, which he summarizes as follows:

- scriptural heaven, hell, and purgatory (direct references to the Bible and to judgement);
- scriptural heaven (references to God, Jesus, the Holy Family, but no reference to judgement or punishment);
- not like scriptural heaven (explicit disbelief in angels, harps, etc.);
- beauty, rest, peace, etc.;
- absence of pain, worry, evil, inequality, etc. (no reference to God);
- rejoining loved ones;
- watching over loved ones;
- like this life;
- reincarnation;
- life on another planet.

Gorer conducted a similar survey in 1963. For most of his typical views of the afterlife, there is no major difference between men and women. Over the two surveys, the one stand-out difference was in 'rejoining loved ones', which describes the expectations of 14 per cent of women but only 2 per cent of men in 1963, and 11 per cent of women and only 6 per cent of men in 1951.[26] An example of this response is the following from a married woman in Norfolk:

I was always taught as a child to believe in God even though the road through which we travel might not be smooth. This I do and hope when I draw my last fleeting breath I shall be re-united with my mother, sister and baby daughter, in the land where there is no pain.[27]

It is surely significant that she mentions no male relatives. One can always make too much of these things, but it does seem that, in thinking about life after death, more women than men are reflecting on personal relationships: a difference that may be explained by the closer biological bond between mothers and children and by the social roles and expectations that reinforce that natural connection. It is tedious repeatedly to add obvious cautions, but propositions about the place of biology in shaping social gender roles so frequently provoke partisan misunderstandings that we should stress that we are not suggesting that *only* mothers care a great deal for their children or that *all* mothers care a great deal for their children. Our point is the narrower one that the experience of being pregnant, giving birth, and nurturing a child through its early years (the first two elements of which are exclusive to women) is likely to create stronger ties than fathers will have with their children. And that difference may go some way to explaining why, if belief in an afterlife is not universal, women are more likely than men to hold it.

Attitudes to the Body

Although the connections are not at all obvious, there does seem to be a link between hope for some sort of life after death and attitudes towards the body before and after death. We have already mentioned gender differences in attitudes to health and well-being, especially as evidenced in various forms of self-help. A number of the nineteenth-century female-led religious innovations also promoted innovative healing and dietary regimes. Christian Science, of course, was as much concerned with physical and psychological well-being as with spiritual development. Ellen White and the Seventh-Day Adventist Church she founded was also much concerned with diet and health: John Harvey Kellogg, who gave the world cornflakes and colonic irrigation, came to prominence as the chief medical officer of the SDA's Battle Creek sanatorium. Adventists adopted a vegetarian diet, abstained from alcohol and tobacco, and performed a severe exercise programme. Many of the early Spiritualists shared Kellogg's interests. Like many of those at the intersection of Spiritualism and social reform, Mary Greeley dieted to control the passions and imposed an ascetic regime on her husband Horace. What integrated both the physical and the spiritual was the ideal of purity.

The links we are making here are deliberately tentative, but it is worth mentioning one of the other well-documented gender differences in behaviour: the selection of methods of suicide. Since Emile Durkheim's classic study of 1897 *Suicide*, it has been noted that men tend to choose violent methods (such as guns and hanging) while women favour poisoning and gassing. US data from 2004 show that the most common method for men involved firearms (57 per cent of suicides) with hanging, suffocation, or strangling claiming 23 per cent of cases; for women the most popular was poisoning (38 per cent) followed by firearms at 32 per cent.[28] Firearms are much less readily available in the UK. In England and Wales the most popular means of suicide for men were hanging and suffocation (33 per cent of cases) and poisoning (20 per cent). The ranking was reversed for women: poisoning accounted for 50 per cent of cases while hanging and suffocation accounted for 18 per cent.[29] Aside from some interesting national variations, Europe-wide data from 2008 showed a similar gender difference. Men were much more likely to hang or suffocate themselves than women (54 per cent of male suicides but only 36 per cent of female cases). The second most popular method for women (25 per cent) was poisoning, which was used in only 8 per cent of male suicides.[30]

These differences can be explained in various ways. Clearly availability is relevant. Men are more likely than women to have guns. Women are more likely to be in kitchens with gas ovens. A further consideration is certainty: it has been suggested that men favour more violent means of killing themselves because they are more sure they wish to die. The possibility that intrigues us concerns bodily appearance. Put simply, the most popular male methods disfigure or distort the body: the most popular female methods leave it intact. That some women kill themselves by jumping from high places shows that we are not dealing with absolute differences, but the gender preferences are sufficiently different to support the hardly contentious suggestion that women are more concerned than men about their appearance.

We raise this because it fits with otherwise strange gender differences in attitudes to post-mortem disposal of corpses. An English survey of attitudes to the body after death produced some surprising findings, which are summarized in Table 3.1. Respondents were asked to list any fears and anxieties they might have about being buried or being cremated. The vast majority of respondents had no particular anxieties about either method of disposal, but, among the remainder,

Table 3.1. Anxieties over burial and cremation, England, 1993

	Female (no.)	Male (no)	Ratio (F:M)
BURIAL			
Being buried alive, claustrophobia	123	42	3:1
Eaten by worms	72	17	4:1
Body rotting	24	8	3:1
CREMATION			
Fear of fire, being burnt	65	28	2:1
Being burnt alive	29	7	4:1
Getting right ashes back	6	0	—

Source: D. Davies and A. Shaw, *Reusing Old Graves: A Report on Popular British Attitudes* (Crayford: Shaw and Sons, 1995), 26–7.

there is a very clear gender pattern. Women are markedly more con-cerned than men about being buried or cremated alive and they are also far more concerned than men about the decay of their bodies.

A 1960 study of what Americans feared about death produced very similar findings. Although all respondents placed 'I am afraid of what might happen to my body after death' behind such concerns as 'I could not look after my dependants', women were much more likely than men to be concerned about their bodies. The researchers believe: 'This may be related to the fact that women value themselves more in terms of their physical attractiveness than do men.'[31]

We are not for a moment suggesting that women's greater interest in religion is solely or even mainly inspired by vanity. Our point is the small one that, as concern for bodily purity is one of the persistent minor themes of religious enthusiasm, a gendered difference in the extent to which men and women's sense of self-worth and being is derived from their appearance may explain some of the differential appeal of those religious enthusiasms.

Conclusion

Although Spiritualism is marginal to the contemporary religious cul-ture of modern societies, it is of interest to us because of its leadership and its audience. It is one of the very few religious movements, using the term a little loosely, led by women, and, in the gender composition of its membership or client base, it is one of the most skewed movements we will examine. The historians of late-nineteenth-century Spiritualism make the point that mediumship offered career opportunities for women who were otherwise short of social power. In that sense Spiritualism, like the women's suffrage movement with which it overlapped, can be seen as a way station on the road to greater gender equality. But most mediums were not like Cora Richmond or Victoria Woodhull: figures of great presence delivering messages of potency to the rich and famous. They were ordinary women who counselled and consoled those who wished to make contact with deceased loved ones. Women were more likely than men to become mediums because the role required sensitivity and a caring attitude to others. For many women becoming a medium was simply an extension of the emotional work they already did in their families and friendships.

As with all our examples, Spiritualism is both an illustration of women's religious interests and a source of possible explanations for that interest. The obvious major theme, which we will take up again in Chapter 6, is continuity of gender roles and expectations: women were more attracted to the movement than men because it spoke more to their interests in a language with which they were more familiar. The movement also allows us to note the minor theme of the importance of the body. In their attitudes to both the living body and the body post-mortem, women and men seem to differ, not greatly but sufficiently for us to wonder if women's attraction to other religious and spiritual movements may in part be explained by concerns for bodily purity and completeness. Both major and minor themes will be pursued in the next chapter, where we consider New Age or holistic spirituality.

4

Spirituality

Introduction

The most popular of the 1960s new religious movements (NRMs) survived to become part of the fabric of the holistic spirituality milieu. Strictly speaking none of the NRMs was popular. They attracted attention because they were exotic or threatening, not because they were large. Membership of the Unification Church (aka the Moonies) in the USA was well below 5,000 in 2009.[1] In Canada in the 1990s there were precisely 139 adult Moonies.[2] There were never more than 1,000 Moonies in Britain at any one time. In the 2001 census only 1,781 people in England and Wales listed their religion as Scientology; in Scotland it was 58, which in any reckoning is trivial but is still twice the number of Hare Krishnas.[3] Of those new religions, those that offered to help people succeed in this world and demanded little of their adherents did proportionately better than those that required members to abandon the world. As the world-affirming NRMs came to terms with the shallow and transient commitment they could attract, they persisted into the era of what is variously called New Age, alternative, contemporary, or holistic spirituality.

A nice illustration of that adaptation was inadvertently provided by Transcendental Meditation (or TM). To collect the data in Table 2.1 we wrote to the officials of a wide range of movements. The standard part of the rubric we sent out referred to our interest in the gender profile of 'different religions'. TM's UK headquarters provided the information but added rather sniffily: 'Transcendental Meditation is not a religion. It is a scientifically validated technique which does not involve holding any faith or belief, just as in the same way it doesn't conflict with any belief that a person may already have.' As almost identical phrasing was used by two regional TM offices we had also contacted, we can suppose that this is official spin. TM certainly was a religion when the Beatles visited the Maharishi in India and George Harrison became a Hindu. That it now presents itself as one dish in a cafeteria of alternatives is typical of the transformation that many world-affirming new religions have undergone since the 1980s. They have scaled down their claims and allowed customers to treat their therapy or revelation as one of a wide variety, which the user may combine in whatever manner suits.

Core features of the New Age movement make it hard to pin down. Even the word 'movement' exaggerates its cohesion. It is best thought of as a culture and a milieu. As a culture, it is a series of loosely inter-related themes: self-realization, ecological awareness, developing internal spiritual powers, personal autonomy, individualism, and a consumerist orientation to the vast range of quasi-religious, quasi-medical, and quasi-scientific beliefs, rituals, therapies, and practices on offer. As a milieu, it is a network of organizations, publishing houses, magazines, workshops, seminars and conference, informal groups, websites, coffee houses, and shops bound together only by the overlapping interests of those who participate in it.

Spirituality (as distinct from religion) generally has three features. Its ideological core is a belief in some sort of supernatural force or entity that differs from that of conventional religion in having no loca-tion outside the self, except in some vague notion of an all-pervasive cosmic consciousness. A phrase common in the New Age centre at Findhorn, Scotland—'coming into your power'—nicely captures the sense that enlightenment involves becoming aware of what you already have, rather than subordinating oneself to some external force. Its second component involves perception: becoming spiritual changes how one sees and feels about the world. Its third component is ethical: becoming aware of our spiritual nature should make us better people. These three features fit perfectly well with what Paul Heelas and Linda Wood-head mean by spirituality—'subjective-life forms of the sacred, which emphasize inner sources of significance and authority and the cultiva-tion or sacralization of unique subjective-lives'—and which they con-trast with more conventionally religious conceptions, 'which emphasise a transcendent source of significance and authority to which individ-uals must conform at the expense of the cultivation of their unique subjective-lives'.[4]

New Science and Positive Psychology

We plan to overlook one element of the New Age. Although we suspect that examining the nature and support base for what is sometimes called 'New Science' would strengthen our argument, it is such a large topic that it requires a book of its own. We simply note that there is a milieu constructed around interest in the extraterrestrial origins and powers of pyramids, astral projection, alchemy, Atlantis, extrasensory perception, precognition, telekinesis, UFOs and extraterrestrial aliens, and crop circles. Although such interests are sometimes tinged with spirituality, they are an extension of, or challenge to, science rather than to religion. And, like the science fiction with which it shares much subject matter, New Science seems to be more popular with men than with women. A casual counting of heads in crop circle group photographs suggested ten men for every woman. An equally casual count of people discussing crop circles on the Order of Critical Believers website found eight men and one woman.[5] A more professional and much larger survey of Americans suggested that 29 per cent of men but only 23 per cent of women believed in UFOs.[6] The obvious guess—that this sort of thing, like filing music collections in alphabetical orders and computer games, appeals more to nerdish men than to women—is also likely to be correct.[7] Esoteric physics, like real science, appeals more to men than to women, especially if it can be combined with a good conspiracy theory that explains why governments have hidden from us the truth.[8]

We are also leaving aside the related realm of 'positive psychology'. This is the belief that our attitudes are powerful enough to change more than just our selves and our relations with other people, and that, by visualizing the achievement of our goals, we can ensure their achievement. Positive psychology does overlap with alternative spirituality, but most of it is secular (if misguided) in its models of how its goals are achieved, and it generally lacks an ethical dimension.

The Spiritual Gender Gap

The gender gap in the world of holistic spirituality is considerably greater than that found in the congregational world of mainstream religion. A detailed study of the holistic spirituality milieu in Kendal, a small town in the north-west of England, found that 80 per cent of those who were actively involved were women.[9] A similar gap was found in the 2001 Scottish Social Attitudes survey, data from which are presented in Table 1.4. The survey distinguished degrees of involvement by asking if respondents had ever tried, and then if they had ever paid for, and then if they found important, a variety of New Age activities, which were divided into three fields: complementary medicine, yoga and meditation, and divination. At the entry level of having tried any of the activities at least once, the difference was 30 percentage points: 85 per cent of women but only 55 per cent of men had dabbled. As we move up through the layers to more serious involvement, the totals go down and the gender gap becomes proportionately larger. So 24 per cent of women but only 10 per cent of men had tried something more than once or twice, had paid for it, and thought it important in living their lives. Because it becomes important later on, it is worth noting that the most popular activities were forms of complementary medicine. When we try to identify a clearly 'spiritual' New Age sample by isolating those respondents who describe themselves as spiritual and have any serious engagement with either yoga and meditation or divination, we find only 7 per cent of women but that is still more than twice the 3 per cent of men.

The annual Festival for Mind–Body–Spirit, which in the 1990s ran for 10 days and attracted over 50,000 visitors, is one of Britain's main contemporary spirituality events. A survey in 1990 showed that two-thirds of visitors were women.[10]

This gender gulf is not particularly British. Using data from three sweeps of the World Values Survey (1981, 1990, and 2000) for fourteen European countries, Dick Houtman and Stef Aupers find that 'spirituality is more typically embraced by post-traditional women than by post-traditional men'.[11] Joep de Hart makes the same observation for the Netherlands.[12]

Finally, before we turn to possible explanations of the gender gap we want to stress the point of scale. A US survey of 33,671 respondents found only 9 people—0.026 per cent of the sample—claiming affiliation with a pagan or Wiccan group.[13] The authors of the Kendal study found that less than 2 per cent of the population were engaged in holistic spirituality activities, arguably defined far too broadly.[14] Fortunately we do not need to argue about whether the Kendal yoga classes, Reiki healing sessions, or aromatherapy massages should be regarded as spiritual, because the respondents were asked if they were motivated by spiritual concerns. Just over half said they were not: that is, less than I per cent of the population were involved in the holistic spirituality milieu for avowedly spiritual reasons. So the gender gap we are addressing in this chapter is in degrees of unpopularity and that needs to be borne in mind when evaluating alternative explanations.

Explanation: Deprivation Compensation

It is common to explain choices (such as joining a new religious movement) in terms of compensating for some deprivation. Of course any action can accurately but trivially be explained by deprivation. In joining the Moonies, Fred is showing that he lacks Moonie membership. But we normally mean something more contentful. More often what the new activity provides is taken to be compensation for some more general lack, which is common to a whole class of people and is social-structural in origin. For example, Roy Wallis explains the appeal of world-affirming new religions such as *est* by reasoning back from their promise to help people get in touch with their authentic selves and to build properly human relationships with others to the general proposition that many people who have become materially successfully are deprived of satisfying expressive relationships. In order to become successful they have had to sublimate and control their feelings. They have had to be instrumental and rational in pursuit of their material goals and along the way they have lost their souls. Soul is what they are deprived of, and, if the opportunities arise at the right time and in the right way, they may be attracted to movements that promise to restore what they have lost or to provide some appropriate compensation.

Inspired by the reworking of the classic notions of alienation and anomie by Peter Berger, Brigitte Berger, and Hansfried Kellner in *The Homeless Mind*, Heelas and Woodhead explain the attraction of contemporary spirituality by a grander more all-encompassing version of the Wallis logic.[15] The modern world is dominated by a rational instrumentalism that is embodied in bureaucracies where people are constrained to interact on the basis of narrow social roles. It is an efficient but soulless place that prompts people to seek a solution to their alienation from their fellows and from their own human nature by joining the spiritual revolution.

An extra element is added to that depiction of the general human condition to explain why women are particularly attracted to holistic spirituality. As Talcott Parsons assumed in his discussion of the social functions of the nuclear family, men can compensate for the alienation of the modern life-world in private, personal experiences. The home provides an antidote to the impersonality and rationality of the public sphere.[16] However, women are doubly alienated. As they already occupy the private world and find it as unrewarding as men find the public world, they have to escape to somewhere else.

Post-traditional women... have to struggle against the constrictions not only of a work role but, more importantly, of the traditional women's roles—as dutiful wife and mother—which are likely to have even less scope for subjective expression and fulfilment... Lacking the occupational identity which tends to support a sense of personal identity, worth and entitlement, women who become dissatisfied with the roles of wife, mother and nurturer may embark upon 'deep' quests of self-exploration.[17]

This notion of double deprivation—alienated at work as a person and alienated at home as a woman—has a certain neatness, but it has flaws as an explanation of women's attraction to spirituality.

The first flaw is also found in explaining the general appeal of holistic spirituality as a response to modernity's lack of soul: the scale is wrong. The appeal of spirituality lies in it being a cure for the alienated nature of modern life. Heelas takes a dystopian or dyspeptic view of modernity from the most pessimistic interpretation of Max Weber's view of the prevalence of instrumental rationality. We apparently feel trapped by the 'iron cage' of rationality. The cause here is universal: we are all the victims of modernity. Yet very few of us show any interest in New Age spirituality or anything like it. The same fault defeats the application of the general explanation to the particular position of women. The deprivations of the typical woman are offered as a cause of the choices made by very few women; a universal is used to explain something very rare. We could imagine a variety of subordinate causes, but, in order to bring the initial cause—the condition of every-woman—down to the right scale, the subordinate explanations would have to explain far more of the variance than is explained by the supposed main cause.

A second difficulty is that much of the holistic milieu does not address the sorts of problems that are being presented as the cause of its appeal to women. In the Roy Wallis deprivation–compensation explanation for the attraction of world-affirming new religions, there is a clear connection between what was missing from the joiner's life and what *est* or Exegesis or the like has to offer: which is not a surprise, because Wallis has worked backwards from what the movement offers to what the joiner must have needed and then lightly tested his claim by showing that joiners are of the right class and age background for the explanation to be plausible. The same exercise fails for Kendal New Agers, because few of the holistic milieu activities identified involved spiritual questing, self-exploration, or solidaristic self-affirming group activity. Motives are difficult to untangle because the questionnaire offered a range of possibilities that frequently overlap.[18] None the less, the most popular reason for involvement was 'health and fitness', and, in so far as we can divide the reasons into mundane health and fitness concerns, on the one side, and 'looking for spiritual growth', 'personal growth', 'life crises', and 'emotional support or human contact', on the other, the mundane reasons are twice as popular as those that might be redolent of spiritual cures for double alienation.[19] In short, most participants were engaged in forms of physical therapy, physical exercise, quasi-medical therapy, and relaxation, which of themselves suggest little sign of dissatisfaction with the psychic side of life.[20]

As the double-deprivation thesis concerns social roles and expectations rather than biology, it should be the case that some women—in particular those with the least satisfying places in the public world—are more alienated than others. Social class is a rather blunt characteristic for identifying such people, but it seems reasonable to expect that the double deprivation that prompts spiritual seeking should bear most heavily on those with the least pleasant working lives. It should be the hospital cleaners and school dinner ladies, not the teachers and psychologists, who fill the meditation class. Given the lack of robust data, we need to be cautious about this, but we have no doubt that the class linkage actually runs the other way.[21] The unskilled manual workers who possess the objective characteristics one might expect to be associated with alienation in the public sphere are markedly absent from the world of holistic spirituality.

It is difficult to measure and compare alienation or patriarchal oppression in the domestic sphere. In identifying those who 'may embark upon "deep" quests of self-exploration', Woodhead talks of 'women who become dissatisfied with the roles of wife, mother and nurturer' but gives us little idea of what circumstances lead women to be more or less satisfied in these three roles.[22] However, two of those roles have objective elements and are thus testable: wives have to have husbands and mothers have to have children. So the most doubly alienated and hence most involved in the holistic milieu should be married women with children. The Kendal data do not support either conclusion: the holistic milieu participants were less likely than average to be married and had fewer than average children.

There is one other feature of the Kendal New Agers that does not fit with the general deprivation-compensation explanation: the narrow age profile. If the explanation of interest in holistic spirituality is a feature of modernity, that interest should be enduring. Modernity has not gone away. That is, the change would be a 'period effect' seen in the choices of all adults after its cause first became effective. But the Kendal New Agers are recruited from a very narrow age band. The modal age band was 50–54, 83 per cent were aged 40 or over, and there were only three people under the age of 30 among the respondents. We do know something about the children of the older New Agers. Two-thirds of respondents said that their children, by then mostly themselves adults, did not share their interests. If the explanation of New Age spirituality lies in a general feature of the social structure of modern societies, that interest should now be prevalent in every age cohort of women that has reached adulthood, married, and discovered that it is doubly deprived. As interest is much stronger in the age cohort that grew up in the hippie era than in subsequent cohorts, we can surmise that the cause lies in a transient feature of culture rather than in a permanent feature of social structure. Or, to put it plainly, interest in holistic spirituality is a fashion.

We offer a final thought on the logic of deprivation compensation: there is one time-honoured way of solving the problem that those people who are most deprived are least likely to be doing whatever is putatively explained by their deprivation: add false consciousness to the mix. Marxists pioneered this method of resolving the tension between the supposedly objective alienation of the working class and the obstinate refusal of the working classes to act as if they were alienated: because they were suffering from false consciousness, members of the proletariat could not correctly discern their condition. Only the educated middle-class vanguard of Marxist intellectuals was sufficiently clear of sight to appreciate what the world was really like. There is something of a similar explanation in the distinction between traditional and post-traditional women. The former do not realize they are double-alienated; only the latter can see just how bad life is for women. We might well reject such a defence on the grounds of bad taste: it smacks too much of the educated speaking *de haut en bas* to poor people. But we can reject it on evidential grounds. Overall the scale is wrong: a widespread feature of modernity is being presented as the cause of a very rare activity. And, taken in detailed particulars, the popularity of activities within the holistic spirituality milieu and the social characteristics of those most involved in them do not fit the requirements of the explanation.

Explanation: Familiarity and Extension

Our detailed examination of survey data suggests an alternative approach will be more fruitful. There are good reasons to think that the greatest difference in relationship to holistic spirituality between men and women who share similar educational, class, and occupational backgrounds lies not in starting predispositions (which is where the double-deprivation thesis places it) but at the later stage of deciding whether to continue with some New Age practice after tentative engagement or exploration. When asked to choose between describing themselves as 'religious', 'spiritual', or 'neither', 14 per cent of the male respondents and 16 per cent of female respondents chose 'spiritual': an insignificant difference. When we looked closely at the relative effects of occupation on involvement in holistic spirituality, we found that social class was more important than gender. Men and women who worked in social, education, and health professions were more likely than other professionals and people in skilled and unskilled manual occupations to be sympathetic towards holistic spirituality and to have tried yoga, meditation, and the like. There is an additional, separate contribution from gender. When we compare gender differences at each stage of a 'career' from thinking of oneself as spiritual, to initial experimentation, through to regularly engaging in well-being practices and finding them important, we find that more men than women drop out. Male social, education, and health professionals may be willing to try alternative practices associated with personal self-development and well-being, but they do not continue with them to the extent that women do.

Survey data do not tell us why initial male sympathy does not translate into regular engagement at the same rate as that of women but we can hazard a guess: much of the holistic spirituality milieu is designed by women for women. Woodhead rules out that possibility at the start of her deprivation explanation when she says that 'holistic spiritualities are not inherently gendered'.[23] The word 'inherently' is a red herring. What matters about the gendering of alternative spirituality is not its logical necessity (after all, very few things are 'inherently' one thing or another) but its scale. It seems obvious to us that the content of holistic spirituality milieu is heavily oriented to women.

It is important that we repeat one of the methodological cautions presented in Chapter 1. In trying to decide whether some new activity is likely to be rewarding, people often fall back on a repertoire of common-sense typifications in which they have been socialized and which they have refined through frequent use. One such device is the 'people who are like me' principle, which supposes that, as tastes and preferences tend to follow lines of social class, age, gender, race, and ethnicity, complex choices can be short-circuited by the quick test of asking 'Are these my sort of people?'. The young man who goes into a Methodist chapel and finds himself in the company only of elderly women will conclude quickly that this is not his sort of thing. And the providers may further amplify the distinctive ethos by accepting the limited reach of their activity and making it as attractive as possible to the audience they have rather than working against the tide. We stress this point about the recursive, feedback nature of patterns of choice because it relieves us of the obligation to look for a big explanation of the gender gap. It may be that the attraction of women and the repulsion of men is initially only slight and that the current gender gulf we see in New Age participation is a result of subsequent reinforcement.

One simple explanation of the gender gap is that much New Age activity is promoted by women who aim to recruit other women to pursue what are explicitly presented as women's interests. The practitioners of Dianic witchcraft (as in goddess, not the British princess), for example, 'emphasize women's oppression and point to the European Witch burnings as a "women's holocaust"... and they denounce injustices done to women in the name of patriarchy'.[24]

The Women of Wisdom Foundation is a National Women's Organization based in Seattle, providing diverse and innovative programs that offer women

opportunities for personal growth and transformation. WOW promotes wom-
en's spirituality, creativity and wholeness, and empowers women's voices and
their contributions to the world, honoring the Divine Feminine in all. Wom-
en's events include a range of mind body and spirit topics for a full healing
experience.[25]

Or consider the 'Mists of Avalon pilgrimage to England' organized by
Sacred Journeys for Women, which is 'open to all women who would
like to spend a week in the beautiful English countryside' but closed
to similarly pastorally inclined men.[26]

   There is a more subtle type of closure. The following is the advert
of Patricia Dancing Elk-Walls:

Working primarily through feminine energies and combining ancient knowledge with contemporary therapies is how I work to assist you in identifying
and clearing those areas of your life that keep you 'stuck', holding you in patterns of fear, anger, insecurity, illness, addiction, poor relationships and all those
other bothersome roadblocks on the way to healing and enlightenment.[27]

She does not reject men as clients, but few are likely to get past the
'feminine energies' in the first line.

   Or consider this advertisement for a St Brigdhe (or St Bridie) Goddess conference in Glastonbury:

We will be honouring all Her aspects, especially those connected to Her four
fires, the fire of inspiration and poetry, the fire of love, the fire of healing and
the alchemical transforming fire of smithcraft. We will walk Her sacred swan
landscape here in Glastonbury, join in local Bridie ceremonies, make pilgrimage to Bride's Mound, and visit the holy wells where She is honoured here
today. We will journey to meet Her and bathe ourselves in Her healing energies, letting go of the darkness of winter and opening ourselves to Her renew-
ing fire.

The flyer concludes: 'We will make Bridie Dolls and Bridie Eyes. Bring
ribbons, beads and materials to decorate yours. We will also make a
healing girdle to wear when we offer healing in Her name' and 'There
will be a special ceremony for those who wish to dedicate themselves
as a Priestess of Brigdhe. Please bring white ceremonial clothing, veils
and headdresses.'[28] Of forty-six people identified as organizers or contributors, only three are men.

   That a large part of the world of alternative spirituality constructs
itself around gender is no surprise. After all, one of the common
elements of contemporary spirituality is a deliberate rejection of

patriarchy, especially in the form of the idea that the divine creator is male. Another common strand is the ecofeminist idea that industrial capitalist production is male and that cooperative craft production is female. That does not, of course, preclude men, but there is a clear challenge to men running through that sphere and hence little surprise that most men are not attracted to it.

Slightly less 'inherently gendered' are ideas and activities that are closely related to something in the secular world that already has a clear gender preference pattern. The inclusion of doll-sewing in the Goddess conference mentioned above is an example: few men sew dolls. But there is a considerable range of activities that have a less obvious gender bias in their secular forms: group singing and dancing are more popular with women than with men and that alone would explain why women are more likely than men to be attracted to spiritual growth practices that involve singing and dancing. Much the same point can be made about that range of therapies often called 'bodywork'. Men might be attracted to a locker-room style of massage administered by strong men who smell of liniment; they are less likely than women to be attracted to forms of massage and healing therapy that are presented as extensions of the perfumery, beauty parlour, and health spa. It has been suggested that this depiction is a male insult to women:

Precisely because this sphere is women-dominated, it is also inhospitable to the many forms of male identity based upon negation of the female. The way in which both academic and popular discourses often dismiss such spirituality as 'pseudoscientific', 'pampering', 'trivial', 'diverting', 'irrational', 'psychobabble'—often without any experience of this milieu—is a sign of this unease.[29]

We would not use the terms 'irrational' and 'psychobabble'; they are too judgemental. We would happily describe the theory of Reiki healing as 'pseudo-scientific' because it uses vaguely scientific language to describe an anatomical model quite at odds with that developed by medical–scientific research, and we have no doubt which is superior. We would also stand by our descriptions of the numbers involved in the holistic milieu (when, for example, comparing them to mainstream religious movements such as Methodism), as 'trivial'. And the term 'pampering' was not introduced to the debate by hostile men. The introduction to the 'Pampering 4 Life' website, written by a woman, says:

Thank you for following me and learning more on how you can live your 'Best Life' each and everyday just by doing exciting things to awaken and pamper what is most important in your life. Pampering4life is a lifestyle of pampering all aspects of one's life. It is the ultimate indulgence of pampering your mind, body, and freedom. Please make sure to take time for yourself at least 10 minutes a day. Relax and feel your desire to live the life God has given you after all 'Pampering4life' is a celebration of you...[30]

Or consider this from 'Soul Pampering'

[The programme] involves art and healing techniques that in other words creates beauty in wounded places! Pampering and taking time away is an amazing tool for awakening creative energy so we have combined ceremonies with expressive art therapy workshops to facilitate growth and healing. Through writing, poetry, vision board, music, meditation and improvisational play among other tools we can awaken individual creativity and we can gain profound emotional and spiritual healing. Our retreat combines these experiences to awaken the creative life force within all of us.[31]

Our final observation relates more to the providers than the consumers (although this is only a small distinction, as many providers of one therapy or revelation are consumers of others). In many senses the role of therapist, healer, or counsellor is a continuation of the carer role that many women will have performed in their private and their working lives. Sole to Soul—a holistic chiropody/podiatry and therapy centre near Lancaster in the north-west of England—offers counselling along with medical herbalism, naturopathy, homeopathy, acupuncture, 'and more'.[32] Even where counselling is not listed, many New Age practitioners, such as the spirit mediums discussed in Chapter 3, are often as important to their clients for the sympathetic hearing they offer them as for the specific service they offer.

A simple way to summarize our point is to consider the range of activities on offer in Glastonbury, England's premier New Age site. Billing itself as the 'unique free guide to holistic Glastonbury', the *Oracle* is a monthly free sheet that advertises regular events (such as the weekly meetings of the Buddhist group) and special events (such as the annual Mystic and Earth Spirit Fayre and the Avalon Faery Ball). It also contains many advertisements from individual practitioners. Of ninety-two event or service adverts in the October 2010 issue, 71 per cent were promoted and led by women. Almost a quarter had no identified leader or were promoted by men and women together, usually a husband and wife team. Only 5 per cent of the events or services were provided or led by men and two of those—an alchemy class and an astrology workshop—

were led by the same chap. Some adverts were accompanied by an illustration. Where the illustration featured a person of identifiable gender—mostly photographs of practitioners—women led men in a ratio of 3 to 1. A teenage boy who accompanied us on one of our visits to Glastonbury flicked through the *Oracle* and unprompted concluded: 'It's all for girls.'

Health and Efficiency

So far we have mainly been discussing those activities in the holistic spirituality milieu that are overtly concerned with the spiritual. But, as we have already noted, Goddess worship, angels, divination, and voyages of deep spiritual exploration are a very small part of the milieu. The most popular activities tend to be those concerned with physical and psychological health and well-being. The men (and they often are men) who teach yoga and meditation are patently inspired by spiritual concerns, but the majority of their customers are like the yoga novice who, when asked how she got interested in Hinduism, replied: 'What's that got to do with yoga?' Having followed yoga with a Pilates course, she now runs a Curves women-only exercise centre.

Research tends to make one blinkered. The initial research problem may so shape perceptions that we miss what would be obvious to anyone starting from a different point of view. Because the research projects described above were concerned with estimating and then explaining involvement in contemporary or alternative spirituality, and with exploring the relationship between traditional religion and spirituality, all the attention has been on the spiritual. An alternative way of looking at the research results is to note that there is a fascinating world of customer-driven self-help medical and physical therapy that is dominated by women. The key question then becomes, not why are women more spiritual than men, but why are women apparently much more interested than men in a certain type of health and exercise. Though this may seem like a distraction from the question we posed in this book's title, it seems too much of a coincidence that concerns with diet, with healing, and with exercise regimes keep re-emerging. We saw them in the interests of the various nineteenth-century millennialist movements described in Chapter 2 and we saw them again in Chapter 3's discussion of attitudes to the disposal of bodies.

A very wide range of US studies conclude that gender is one of the most important sociocultural factors that influence 'health-related behaviour... Women engage in far more health-promoting behaviours than men and have more healthy lifestyle patterns.'[33] Women are more likely than men to make beneficial changes in their exercise habits and are less likely to be overweight. There are major differences in how men and women use medical facilities. Although the gender differences tend to disappear the more serious the illness, adult men make far fewer visits to doctors than do women (once those associated with reproduction are removed from the equation). The primary reason for this seems to lie in the very ways that gender stereotypes are constructed. Men see the denial of pain and weakness as part of being robust and strong: 'men are demonstrating dominant norms of masculinity when they refuse to take sick leave from work.'[34] There are plenty of British sources that point to the same patterns. British men are not only more likely than British women to make unhealthy choices, but, when they are ill, they are slower to do anything about it.[35] This suggests that the gender differences visible in two elements of the holistic spirituality milieu—health-promoting group activities such as yoga and individual healing consultations—may well be a continuation of 'secular' patterns. One can imagine an 'Extreme Team' yoga, with competitions, scores, player performance statistics, and physical violence, that would appeal to men, but as currently practised it seems the negation of everything associated with masculinity, as do most holistic therapies. If the explanation of men's reluctance to seek conventional health-care treatment—that it demonstrates weakness—is at all plausible, most alternative therapies will be even less attractive, because the general ethos that underpins 'healing' is the notion that we are responsible for our own ill-health because we have not been positive enough.

Conclusion

Any explanation of the appeal of holistic spirituality has to start from the observation that it is unpopular. Most women, like most men, are even less interested in contemporary spirituality than they are in conventional mainstream religion. We need to explain a large gender difference in a very small world.

We cannot explain why, in an increasingly secular society, some people remain interested in the religious and the spiritual. When the percentage of the population involved in religious and spiritual activities is large, we can expect that there will be some social underpinning to the patterns: one particular region, or class, or ethnic group will be more religious or spiritual than another. Once the proportions get down to 3 or 4 per cent of the population, the explanations are likely to involve idiosyncratic features of an individual's biography: family upbringing, chance encounters with personally impressive religious or spiritual people, accidents of career that close one door and open another, strains of personal relationships that lead someone to look for cosmic explanations for his or her fate, and the like.

What we can say is that prior interests and experiences predispose a few women to find elements of the New Age plausible and worth exploring. We should divide those elements into two very different strands. One is concerned with health and well-being; the other with spiritual enlightenment. That fewer men than women are interested in the holistic spirituality milieu's health and well-being activities seems simply explained by the way that conventional notions of masculinity shape men's attitudes to health in general.

The same principle of continuity explains why women are more interested than men in those elements of the milieu that display a caring and nurturing ethos and that offer to improve people's skills in these areas. Without needing to commit ourselves to any particular explanation of the observation, we can note simply that in most societies women are more likely than men to be involved in paid and unpaid caring and nurturing work.

Finally we can note that the very small part of the milieu that is avowedly concerned with the spiritual—Dianic witchcraft, for example—is also very obviously intended to recruit women rather than men. That is, the gendering is done in the construction of the activities and hence does not require a prior explanation at the level of deprivation causing gender differences in receptivity. To that we can add an obvious point about the relative lack of alternative outlets and opportunities. Although many of the Christian churches now ordain women and are deliberately trying to make their theology and rituals more gender-blind, it remains the case that the world of conventional religion does not offer women the freedom to innovate that they can find in the free market and entrepreneurial world of contemporary spirituality.

5

Conservative Religion

Introduction

It is not news that feminists generally do not like the three religions that revere Abraham. After all, the three Hebrew Patriarchs—Abraham, his son Isaac, and grandson Jacob—give their title to 'patriarchy': the concept that most succinctly summarizes what feminists oppose. Patriarchy is rule by men, ideologically bolstered by the claim that men and women are innately different and men innately superior. And Judaism, Christianity, and Islam have been, and mostly still are, profoundly patriarchal, both in their own organizations and in their legitimation of patriarchal social structures and cultures.

For most early Western feminists the primary target was Christianity. Some could imagine an inclusive version of Christianity that treated men and women as equals. Others believed it beyond reform.[1] Overall, Christianity was considered oppressive and restrictive for women, and those who stayed in the churches were cast as victims of false consciousness. However, that the churches continued to be more strongly supported by women than by men made this simple dismissal rather unsatisfactory. That was especially so in the USA, where the rise of feminism coincided with a shift in numbers and influence within Protestantism, as the liberal and mainstream churches were overtaken by growing evangelical, fundamentalist, and Pentecostal churches. Much of that conservative growth was due to demographics rather than relative appeal to outsiders: members of conservative denominations such as the Southern Baptists tended to have larger families than Unitarians and Episcopalians. But, even if juvenile membership of avowedly patriarchal churches could be explained by young women not knowing any better, that so many remained part of a religious culture that was providing most of the support for the anti-feminist politics of the new Christian right required a more thoughtful answer than the assertion of false consciousness.

In the 1980s and 1990s the emphasis shifted from a blanket negative view of organized religion to the more sympathetic interest in women's interpretations of their membership of socially conservative religious groups. Studies in this vein had at their heart the classic idea that oppression and resistance always coexist and are mutually dependent.[2] Such publications focused on American women in Orthodox Judaism, evangelical Christianity, and conservative Catholicism. The strict gender script in these religions makes a good starting point for analysing the interaction between oppression and liberation. It is much easier to study gender norms and people's view of them in churches where those norms are clearly delineated than in more liberal and flexible mainstream churches. As the USA is a democratic, industrialized nation with relatively high levels of religiosity, it is a unique site for studying the coexistence of secular liberalism and conservative religion.

One of the challenges of teaching sociology to undergraduates is that we are often asking people to grasp and evaluate sociological explanations of phenomena of which they have little understanding. So we teach the sociology of crime and deviance, the sociology of the family, or the sociology of work and industry to people who have little or no acquaintance with crime and deviance, work and industry, or any family other than their own. In our case, the difficulty is that even those readers who are religious will generally be familiar only with their own confession, church, denomination, cult, or sect. One solution would be for students to read the many rich and detailed ethnographies of religion that our colleagues produce. In this chapter we provide unusually full summaries of some first-rate qualitative studies, which we hope will serve both as an inducement to read the originals and as sufficient background to make sense of our analytical conclusions.

Evangelicals in North America

What the studies of women in conservative religions show is that patriarchy in religious settings can be shut out, pushed aside, and comfortably ignored, precisely because of the seemingly restrictive gender segregation on which the groups are based. An example is Brenda

Brasher's study of two evangelical Christian congregations, which explores how women can acquire power and influence by creating a female enclave in an essentially male-dominated organization. Brasher's participants valued the strictly gendered set-up of the congregation because it allowed them to run a wide range of women-only programmes, including a women's ministry, Bible studies, aerobics classes, a sexual abuse victims group, and a counselling agency, to name but a few.[3] Through numerous female-only activities, contained under the 'sacred canopy' of the congregation, the women created and strengthened bonds with other members of the group and, more importantly, reinforced their belief in radical differences between men and women. They embraced gender difference and condoned the idea of marital submission, yet at the same time they supported equal pay for both genders, and acknowledged the importance of legal protection of women from sexual harassment and domestic abuse. The key aspect of the female-led subgroup of the congregation was that, very much like Catholic convents, they were self-governed and relatively independent of the main congregation. The group provided its members with a ready-made and highly efficient life-support network that was guided by a spiritual agenda. Judith, one of Brasher's participants, sums it up as follows: 'My sole purpose in going to a woman's ministry was that there wouldn't be men there. I felt very safe personally because there would be other women. It had nothing to do with their age, experiences, or anything else, other than that they were women.'[4]

The sense of God's loving presence is mediated through the all-female group where participants derive comfort and security from being around others like themselves. Women's Aglow Fellowship, a Pentecostal prayer organization, is an even better example because of its international and transdenominational status. Aglow was formed in 1967, in Seattle, by Christian women who wanted to transcend denominational boundaries. Over 4,600 Aglow female-led groups exist worldwide. In the comprehensive and brilliantly written *God's Daughters: Evangelical Women and the Power of Submission*, R. Marie Griffith cogently explains the appeal of the organization to women.[5] Most importantly, there is little scope or need for theological dispute in Aglow, as the members are united by the loose Christian label and by their gender. In monthly worship meetings, after the official closing prayer, many women stay on in order to discuss their personal problems. Although life could be hard and the world is a hostile place, 'with the strength given to them by their Aglow sisters and the assurance that Jesus accompanies them in their troubles, the women move forward in an effort to face the world with confidence and tranquility'.[6] Like Brasher's evangelical women, members of Aglow bond by reinforcing the idea that men are from Mars and women are from Venus. In practice, the Aglow women behave much like any other group of women on a Saturday night: joking about typical male behaviour, making generalizations about men's 'nature', and emphasizing the inability of men to understand women.[7] Griffith interprets such behaviour as a humorous way of letting off steam and diffusing tension and frustration caused by gender-related problems in their lives.

These examples demonstrate the appeal of female-only religious groups as safe havens for women who seek friendship, belonging, help, and support with everyday problems and a sense of community with others like them. Britain is too secular and the Catholic tradition of much of Europe has little history of religious small groups. Hence British and European women would have to find secular alternatives for such female solidarity, and to an extent they find them in book clubs, fitness classes, walking groups, clothes swapping parties, and mothers-and-toddlers coffee mornings, and also in a wide range of networking and mentoring clubs for businesswomen and women in male-dominated professions. The list of explicitly secular charities and support groups for women from all walks of life available on the Web is endless. American women can find their support groups in churches and para-church organizations, because church membership is normal. The women described above are predisposed to religiosity in the sense that they all come from some sort of a religious background, even if they experienced a hiatus in religious involvement before converting to evangelical Christianity. For example, only one participant in Brasher's study was brought up as an 'atheist–Buddhist', while all the others were nominally Christians.[8]

If the sort of attraction we have just described is actually largely secular, with 'church' providing the venue and the opportunity, there is another part of the attraction that is distinctly religious. The potential for healing in such groups is of crucial importance. As Griffith points out: 'Aglow stories are filled with pain.'[9] Many women who come to Aglow meetings have experienced emotional and physical abuse and struggled with emotional problems. Griffith tells us that several of her participants suffered from serious health problems prior to conversion.

For example, Vivian was healed from multiple sclerosis after she cried out to God for help in desperation and Jesus appeared to her. Soon after, at an Aglow meeting, she was baptized in the Holy Spirit and her symptoms disappeared completely. Another woman, Sandra, recovered from incurable cystic fibrosis after she had discovered faith healing at the age of 17. A more extreme case involved a woman in a wheelchair who suddenly began praying during her suicide attempt. She survived and later came to believe that her subsequent recovery from spinal injuries was a direct result of her prayers. More trivial cases, such as a woman's desire to reduce her breast size, are also taken care of by God, according to the Aglow women.[10] Emotional healing occurs along a similar pattern: a woman in despair cries out to God and receives inner strength, joy, and peace that allow her to confront her problems in a positive and constructive manner. The theme of miraculous healings is, of course, typical of the evangelical tradition, and particularly of its charismatic version. In their conversion narratives Brasher's evangelical women quote personal crisis and emptiness as the defining features of their pre-conversion lives. In both studies, the women seek solutions to unhappiness, marital disappointment, and frustration. The fact that they opt for conservative religion can be explained partly by their background and partly by the fact that evangelicals have adopted what they saw as helpful aspects of secular therapy and reconceptualized them in Christian terms. The language of recovery and healing was particularly attractive to women, and it was actively marketed to them. The main point is this: evangelical women believe that secular therapy can achieve only so much, but the 'real healer is Jesus'.[11] In Brasher's study, the women refer to their involvement in the congregations not as religion but as a relationship. According to Brasher it allows them to protect what they do from criticism of religion as pre-modern and to validate their faith as a personal experience.

However, the clash between the socially conservative teachings of their religion and their secular convictions regarding gender inequalities cannot always be ignored or avoided.[12] Some considerable creative work is often required to reconcile feminist beliefs and religious norms. Most of the Protestant, Catholic, and Jewish middle-class women studied by Elizabeth Ozorak recognize the existence of gender inequalities within their religious traditions but employ cognitive strategies to reduce their frustration and discomfort.[13] They reinterpret the tradition favourably, substitute their own (non-sexist) words and images for conventional religious ones, and, most importantly, stress the value of connectedness and community experienced with other religious women. In other words, benefits outweigh costs in the interpretative framework they create for themselves. Thus, for example, some believe that 'a group of women is more likely to generate solid emotional support than a group that includes men'.[14] Others stress the lack of competitiveness among women (instead there is cooperation and inclusiveness). They elevate female spirituality to the status of the 'real thing', whereas they see masculinity in itself as an obstacle in following Jesus. Consequently, men are dismissed not only on social but also on spiritual grounds as somewhat inferior and less capable than women. The women also emphasize serving others as a crucial element of religious practice and present their faith as based on emotions and intuition rather than rationality and understanding.

Of course, not all American women in conservative religions are there *despite* their faith's conservative attitude to women. Some consciously seek stricter guidelines and rules on how to live their lives. Deborah Kaufman's account of women returning to Orthodox Judaism demonstrates that they do so to rebel against the secular, and in their eyes overly masculine, society.[15] These voluntary returnees find the omnipresent individualism and freedom of choice in secular society constraining, rather than liberating. Liberal culture produces short-lasting or failed relationships with men unable to commit. Orthodox Judaism fixes the problem. It holds femininity and women in high regard. Women's special status gave the participants in Kaufman's study a sense of dignity and control over their bodies. In a secular society where 'infidelity has become a norm', it is much more challenging to remain in a marriage or a long-term relationship.[16] Conservative religion creates a world in which it is not only possible but desirable.[17]

Prior to conversion, the women in Kaufman's study had the luxury of experiencing a secular way of living and being brought up in a liberal environment. They were baby-boomers who grew up just as second-wave feminism was becoming an influential social movement and religion was radically changing. They returned to Orthodoxy out of choice and equipped with a feminist toolkit to reinterpret the apparently conservative religious norms as liberating. Unlike women born into strict religious traditions, they continue to exercise free choice.

Another aspect of conservative religion that the converts appreciated was the mutuality of expectations between men and women.

Submission is required of both spouses. The gender-specific rules of conduct work both ways, and in some instances women have more power to make certain demands on the husbands than they would in the secular world.[18] Where rules are ambiguous, or non-existent, no points of reference can be drawn on, and demands cannot be made easily. When expectations are clearly defined, individuals who fail to fulfil them can be challenged legitimately. They can be reminded of their accountability to the higher power, not just to other people.

Pentecostalists in Latin America

In the examples just discussed, the puzzle for scholars is the willingness of modern women to accept the patriarchal beliefs of conservative religion. The assumption of gender equality is so pervasive that it is almost taken-for-granted (even in conservative circles women often work full-time in high-status jobs), and women who find something they want in conservative religious traditions have creatively to re-evaluate and readjust their interpretations of both what their religion requires and what their female pride can accept.

The situation is different in such other parts of the world as Latin America and South Africa. Here the tension is not between a general climate of modern secular liberalism and conservative religion but between differing forms of supernaturalist religion. The rise and success of Pentecostal churches in the southern hemisphere has attracted a lot of academic attention, and gender has become one of the dominant themes in these accounts.[19] We will look closely at two case studies: one is an exploration of female converts to evangelical Christianity in Latin America; the other examines women in Pentecostal charismatic churches in South Africa.

Latin America is so called because, since the Portuguese and Spanish conquests in the fifteenth and sixteenth centuries, it has been Hispanic in language and Roman Catholic in religion. Despite strenuous attempts by Protestant missionaries, Catholic domination was not seriously challenged until the 1960s. Coincident with the decline of the hacienda system of agriculture and the movement to the cities, evangelical and Pentecostal Protestant churches began to make serious inroads. In the last quarter of the twentieth century the evangelical, charismatic, or Pentecostal population—we will not concern ourselves with the differences—grew from less than 5 per cent to more than 25 per cent of the population.[20]

Elizabeth Brusco's *Reformation of Machismo* explores the domestic lives of converts to evangelical Christianity in Colombia.[21] Colombian women benefit from converting to evangelicalism because the religious framework enhances their feminine status and promotes female interests in an otherwise macho culture. Religion is often associated with the polarization of male and female roles and spheres—one of its main flaws in feminist eyes, especially when the religious culture portrays women as both weak and the primary source of sin. Although evangelical Protestantism is conservative and formally patriarchal, in contrast to Latin Catholicism it is progressive. Colombian evangelicalism pushes men and women toward collaboration and joint effort in maintaining the family life and the household. It provides tools for women to reform *machista* and, more importantly, it provides tangible rewards for the male convert.

Machismo, Brusco argues, is primarily defined as a public role, which is why male domination of the household is more of a myth than reality: Colombian men have no script for the roles of husband and father. This makes the household the woman's domain. The man's absence makes it possible for women to assert a high degree of control, but at the same time the woman carries the burden of providing for the family as well as acting in tune with the ideology of *marianismo*: the obligation to emulate the Virgin Mary's sexual purity, moral strength, selflessness, and spiritual superiority.[22] Devotion to motherhood and family lies at the core of this version of femininity. The male and female values are diametrically different: men's lives revolve around individualistic aspirations in the public sphere while women practise maternal altruism at home by devoting all symbolic and material resources to the good of the family.[23] Women are largely responsible for running the household but they rely on men for financial support. If men's priorities are out of synch with those of their wives, then the latter are in a difficult position. Machismo allows men to avoid supporting their families, and women are forced to perform a double (or even triple) shift in order to fill the gap. On average, women are paid much less than men in Colombia, which makes it hard for them to survive without their husbands' income. Moreover, divorce and the break-up of a home are problematic in more than just the emotional sense. Obviously, divorce carries social stigma in any strongly Catholic culture, but financial hardship for the woman is a more immediate consequence of dissolving a marriage. When women convert to charismatic Christianity, they increase their capital as morally superior parties in the marriage and they are better positioned to save men from the perils of machismo, such as the culture of violence and drunkenness. The logistics of traditional courtship in Colombia mean that women have more power over men prior to the couple getting married. Once married, the man conducts his life mainly in the public sphere, and his wife's moral influence becomes restricted to the home. The symbolic separation of the two spheres causes real problems for married couples, because men and women apparently have no common ground. It is only when the husband is forced to withdraw from the public sphere that the wife has a chance to influence his attitude to the household and the marriage.

According to Brusco, many men convert to Pentecostalism as a result of being healed at evangelical services to which their wives have taken them. This is significant as a logical outcome of the encounter between machismo and the weakness of physical illness. When a man becomes ill, he withdraws into the home and hence into the sphere of female influence. Moreover, he becomes physically dependent on his wife. As Brusco notes, his converted wife 'is armed with the logic of the church to argue that his illness is the result of his *vicios* (vices), and that only by giving them up will he be well again'.[24] More generally, the ideology of machismo can be demanding on Colombian men, and conversion liberates them from the culturally imposed role. The male convert no longer feels the need to validate his masculinity through drunkenness and physical violence. Evangelical Christianity equips women and men with similar desires and aspirations, which means that the household ceases to be an exclusively feminine domain and instead it is shared by both spouses. Brusco illustrates the difference between Catholic and Pentecostal households by comparing the patterns of consumption. In Catholic households, the first significant purchase would be a radio; Pentecostals would invest in a dining table.[25] This example underlines the importance of the private family realm to the lives of evangelical Christians.

The great footballer and alcoholic George Best is reputed to have said of his lost fortunes: 'I spent a lot of money on booze, birds and fast cars. The rest I just squandered.' Machismo with its hard-drinking and womanizing is wasteful. The Pentecostal emphasis on asceticism leads to greater financial security, and, quite often, to upward mobility of the whole family. This economic advantage of conversion is of particular importance to women. Not only does it decrease their worries about maintaining the household but it also gives them the possibility of educating their children and giving them a better start in life than they themselves had. Most importantly, Brusco stresses the curious interaction between Pentecostalism and Colombian femininity. Evangelical churches appeal to women because of their emphasis on the importance of the family and the domestic realm. But female converts also influence the shape Pentecostalism takes in Colombia. For example, home services are more effective than church-based ones in attracting new members. These are private, intimate, and safe affairs, which is what makes them more appealing to Colombian women, who are uncomfortable in large, open-air rallies. Women's organizations are formed within Pentecostal churches, and women frequently preach in a style that Brusco describes as 'compellingly female' and filled with metaphors of spiritual cleanliness and sustenance. Brusco does acknowledge the possibility of a more sceptical reading: churches could be accused of deliberately including themes such as courtship, marriage, family roles, and so on in their sermons in order to draw women in. However, she suggests that, as women have been present and active in the Colombian Pentecostal churches from their inception, the religion itself has been shaped by feminine concerns and values. Therefore:

The tangible changes and improvement in the standard of living of women and children in dependent households is only a symptom or an indicator of something much more remarkable that is happening. With conversion, machismo is replaced by evangelical belief as the main determinant of husband–wife relations. The machismo role and the male role defined by evangelicalism are almost diametrical opposites. Aggression, violence, pride, self-indulgence, and an individualistic orientation in the public sphere are replaced by peace seeking, humility, self-restraint, and a collective orientation and identity with the church and the home.[26]

In this situation the key to altering the unequal gender relations in Colombia lies not in individual freedom for women but rather in the empowerment of both men and women via an alignment of their values through evangelical religion. In this sense, Pentecostal Christianity manages to achieve the transformation of social roles for both genders, which is admittedly something secular Western feminism has struggled with to some degree.

Pentecostalists in Southern Africa

The story is very different in South Africa, which we will examine through Maria Frahm-Arp's ethnography of young, professional black women in two Pentecostal churches in Johannesburg and Soweto.[27] Frahm-Arp demonstrates that these churches aid the transition to a new social and economic reality but their focus is less on the private and more on the public realm of transformations. For aspiring black women who strive to take advantage of the educational and economic possibilities that opened up after the fall of the apartheid, these churches are sites of comfort, encouragement, and practical support. Overall, black women benefited little from the post-apartheid economic and political change.[28] Traditional family and kinship networks that used to act as channels for finding work became redundant in post-apartheid South Africa. Ambitious entrepreneurs who wanted to climb the career ladder fast had to look for alternative social networks. Charismatic Pentecostal churches provided an ideal environment for introduction to other like-minded people (both in the religious and the professional sense) and equipped converts with suitable cultural capital, which enabled them to function successfully in the corporate world. Protestant charismatic pastors preach that women and men have a God-given purpose in the world and should not waste their potential to achieve it. In this sense, the gospel is traditionally masculine in content and it is delivered in a masculine language. For example, the pastors advocate spiritual warfare against evil as a personal mission, Christian dominance of the world, leading and influencing people at work, and gaining victory over people and over the forces of evil. It is easy to see that the professional and the spiritual go hand in hand in the discourse promoted in these churches.

The demands that Pentecostal charismatic churches place on women are potentially as contradictory as the ones in the secular world. Female members are told to be successful professionals but also good mothers whose main task is to raise the future generations of South African citizens.[29] As a result, they suffer from the same split consciousness as Western women who attempt to juggle careers and families. The difference for Pentecostal women is that their pastors advocate that they prioritize their children and husbands. However, they are expected to find husbands in the first place. Most women in the study were unmarried at the age when family and friends wished to see them embark on the life of motherhood and home-building. Their singleness was partly the outcome of their upbringing. In most cases, fathers were largely absent and as a result the women claim they feel unable to trust men. However, they are also victims of their professional success, because men are intimidated by their high social and economic status. These women seem to be caught between the demands of the professional and the personal. On the one hand, by working hard and succeeding they are pleasing God; this legitimates their single status to some extent. On the other hand, marriage and motherhood are idealized and presented as desirable by their church communities, which makes singleness socially problematic. Many women felt that the standards for personal relationships were too high in the light of objective possibilities and circumstances. They went to church to meet eligible Christian men who hold similar values with regard to fidelity, purity, and work ethic, but the fact that women outnumber men made the mission of finding a husband much more difficult.

Churches provide a training ground for professional women in this-worldly sense but they also give them more abstract tools—such as God's approval—to manage their personal issues. In their professional lives the women employ rational thinking to solve problems, but, when faced with personal difficulties, they turn to God for guidance. Teachings on sexual restraint during courtship for both sexes remove the burden of reforming male sexuality from women and allow them to maintain control over their own sexuality and body: a difficult task in the sexually liberated and promiscuous culture of post-apartheid South Africa. Male church members are instructed to take responsibility as heads of household and family. This in turn enables women to demand respect, support, and fidelity from their husbands. Just as in the Colombian case, submission is a two-way process. Female converts see Pentecostal Christian marriage as a healthy alternative to its secular equivalent. Because of strict rules of conduct for both parties, such marriages are considered as potentially safe from the problems of infidelity and divorce, widespread in mainstream secular society.[30] Men, for their part, are attracted to the model of nuclear family because it gives them a clearly set out role. Pentecostal women treat marriage in relatively utilitarian terms, in contrast to the romantic model of love promoted in the secular Western culture. The notion of calling extends to women's private and intimate lives, which turns marriage into a higher,

God-ordained, purpose. Thus, even women who previously rejected marriage changed their minds after conversion, and the nuclear family model promoted in their church became their main goal.[31] The nuclear family as a symbol of urban middle-class South Africans works well in conjunction with the message of professional success. With upward social mobility, professional black women could buy houses that are both socially and physically suitable for the nuclear family. Under apartheid the family suffered from disintegration, but Pentecostal churches not only taught these women about forming families but also gave them the family they never had.[32] The message preached in the churches is simple: adherence to a strict moral code in personal life ensures a stable family and economic success for Pentecostal Christians.

It is plain to see that Pentecostal Christianity guides women through the maze of old and new cultural expectations in the twenty-first-century South Africa. They are second- or third-generation urban-dwellers who have little familiarity with traditional African ideologies, philosophies, religion, and practices. Pentecostal churches create an environment in which the women feel less pressure to conform to the African tradition, and pastors give them a religious message compatible with modern life. Conversion to Pentecostal Christianity also assuages the sense of guilt many may feel about distancing themselves from the communal family. They still support their relatives financially but are released from many cultural practices, such as week-long mourning customs, for example, by virtue of their association with Pentecostalism, where professional work and its demands are highly valued. Rational and efficacious religion fits well with the new rational and goal-oriented economic system. While, under apartheid, material wealth was associated with the white oppressor, in the new social reality it is a sign of black liberation, additionally, spiritually legitimated by the Pentecostal churches. In fact, the practical support and spiritual legitimation were the most important aspects of the churches' appeal to black professional women. As Frahm-Arp notes herself: 'The vast majority of women I interviewed said what they valued and appreciated the most in their churches was the teaching they received on how to work most effectively in business and how to succeed.'[33]

Unsurprisingly, juggling the demands of professional, private, and spiritual realms meant that many of Frahm-Arp's participants experienced emotional stress, anxiety, and a sense of failure. Their reliance on God's guidance also meant that, when they did not find a job that naturally fitted the high qualifications they had worked so hard to obtain, they questioned God's plan for them as well as their own potential to fulfil it. The churches handled such problems by providing a counselling service that promoted such typically Christian solutions for personal problems as prayer, self-belief, purity, and struggle against the devil. None the less, some women leave the churches when they become disillusioned with the mismatch between the teachings and the reality of their own lives. Frahm-Arp conducted follow-up interviews with several women three years after her original research. Of the forty-three professional women, 27 per cent had left the churches, mainly citing God's broken promises as the reason for their disillusionment. They became angry when the perfect life promoted in their church did not materialize for them. Curiously, they left their churches at the same time as they began to feel unappreciated in their jobs.[34] Once the women had exhausted the practical resources that enhanced their cultural capital for advancing their position in the workplace, the more spiritually based coping strategies offered by the churches did not suffice in the face of institutional sexism, racism, and the complexities of a society in transition. They experienced their problems at work as spiritual, because failing as professional women meant failing as Christians.

This case study could be seen as a gendered example of religion working in cultural transition. When a society experiences relatively fast economic, social, and cultural shifts, religions that offer a clear behavioural code become popular, because they operate as a lifeboat for those potentially lost in the sea of change. They save individuals and equip them with tools to cope with the emerging social reality. It is clear from both the Colombian and the South African example that Pentecostalism, as a highly adaptive religion, works particularly well for women, because it combines the public and the private in its message. In the Colombian case, the private and the feminine are glorified, partly because of the historical circumstances in which evangelical Christianity arose, and partly because of the self-fulfilling prophecy of women being attracted to what they perceive as feminine, or female friendly, in a particular cultural context. In South Africa, the gospel itself may well have been masculinized, but, as black women entered the public sphere via the professional and largely masculine world of business, they found the teachings useful from a practical but also from a spiritual point of view. They participated in workshops, lectures, small group activities, and networking, but they also prayed, received divine guidance, and derived emotional strength from their faith. All of these seemingly private acts were reinforced by collective worship and rituals in their churches.

The women in South Africa used Pentecostal churches to reconcile the dilemma of career versus motherhood, because both were promoted as equally important by the pastor and the congregation, which legitimized their lives in both a social and a spiritual sense. Although in theory family mattered more than professional success, in practice the two were inextricably intertwined. In South Africa, the importance of race as a stratifying element changes the dynamic and makes a rational and business-oriented style more suitable and helpful for people, particularly women, whose social positioning is in flux. Race defines social relations to such a great extent that male domination, or male absence from the household, are not the main oppressive forces. In Colombia, on the other hand, it is the feminization of evangelical Christianity, with the emphasis on the reformation of machismo, that works as the strongest magnet for women.

Conclusion

One does not have to be a feminist to recognize that religions generally treat women badly. Leaving aside the part that religious ideologies play in justifying gender discrimination in the secular world, we can simply point to the clergy. The majority of religions do not permit women to hold office, and those that do confine them to the lowest orders. In most varieties of Buddhism, the lowest male monk outranks the most senior female monk. Most strands of Islam and Judaism bar women from office. Only in our lifetimes have mainstream Protestant churches ordained women, and one of the largest, the Church of England, has permitted them into the various grades of the clergy with the enthusiasm of a child being fed Brussels sprouts. Of course, religious institutions deny that excluding women from office is discrimination, but one has only to replace gender by race in such justifications to get their measure.

It is that background which makes the topic of this book all the more intriguing. If men were more religious than women, we would not be seeking an explanation in the mysteries of socialization or the unintended consequences of gender roles. We would simply point to self-interest and rational calculation. We would say that men are more religious than women, because in a variety of ways religious institutions and ideologies privilege them.

In this chapter we have looked at women's involvement in types of religion that, superficially at least, promote a particularly patriarchal view of the world. We draw three somewhat obvious conclusions. The first is that some women like patriarchy. The second is that women can ignore or subvert what they do not like. The third is that close acquaintance with the material may reveal benefits that are not obvious from a distance.

We would like to add a dull but necessary theoretical note to correct a potentially misleading impression. We have explained why Colombian women are attracted to Pentecostalism by identifying its benefits or, as sociologists often prefer, functions. Although it is a convenient shorthand, functional explanation has two paradoxical dangers that we will briefly address. First, it can unduly imply that people have a cynical or utilitarian attitude to their faith. When we note that Pentecostalism is attractive because it offers opportunities to tame the culture of machismo and thus improve women's family lives, we come close to suggesting that these secondary benefits (or latent functions) are the main appeal and that the core religious beliefs of Pentecostalism are adopted as a mere convenience. It is important to appreciate that the conversions are genuine. The various beneficial social consequences might be openly perceived, as when the preacher points out the financial advantages of sobriety. They might be implicitly sensed, as when the potential convert notices that Pentecostalists are better dressed, have tidier houses and cleaner children, and seem more self-confident. But the convert accepts Pentecostalism, not because she wanted those things (though she does), but because she sees those things as evidence that Pentecostalism is right. That is, the beneficial side products are taken as circumstantial evidence that the new beliefs should be seriously entertained. The new behavioural patterns are adopted, initially with a degree of 'role distance', and only as the novice feels the new life to be working is the belief-system that legitimates it fully accepted. The latent social functions or the good social consequences are not desired separately from the religion but add to its plausibility.

The important point to remember is that when we use notions such as needs and functions to explain the popularity of religion we are, for convenience, skipping a vital line in the equation: the plausibility of religion. In the final analysis, personal religiosity rests on belief, on faith. In trying to uncover the rational base for religious conversion, we are not suggesting that people cynically pretend to hold unconvincing supernaturalist beliefs in order to gain some this-worldly benefit. We are saying that this-worldly benefits are part of what makes a belief-system plausible.

6

Biology, Roles, and Attitudes

Introduction

Scholars wrangle over the meaning of 'religious', but arguably the hard part of the question 'Why are women more religious than men?' is the word 'women'. We do not mean that is difficult to distinguish women from men; that is another argument. We mean that it is not obvious what it is about women that would explain heightened religiosity: is it the things they do or the sort of people they are?

As a method of describing and explaining the social world, sociology has always emphasized environmental factors and interactions as the main determinants of human behaviour. The neglect of biology is in part professional necessity: biological and genetic influences had to be downplayed for the discipline to develop its distinctive perspective.[1] But there are better reasons. The first can be put as an empirical observation or as an ethical posture. The empirical point is that the anthropological and historical record shows a degree of variation in human behaviour that is hard to reconcile with the idea that our biology much constrains us or much explains our actions. We may talk casually of a maternal instinct or a will to survive, but we find cultures in which women do not behave in a terribly maternal manner, and suicide is common. The same point can inform an ethical position. If we accept that gender or racial differences are a biological given, then all manner of discrimination can be justified as being the 'natural' order of things. However, if we demonstrate that gender categories are not fixed but malleable, there is a greater degree of flexibility and potential for change in gender relations.

A further reason for downplaying biology is that attempts to use innate characteristics to explain real world behaviour have to date not been impressive. Cesare Lombroso's nineteenth century the *Criminal Man* claimed that criminals were born criminal and could be identified by such physical marks as sloping foreheads, oddly shaped ears, and unusually long arms: the *Criminal Mind* is now an intellectual curio on the same shelf as the phrenologist's skull.[2] Research linking IQ and race has fared little better. The mapping of the human genome seemed to offer the prospect of finding the criminal or the gay gene, but as yet we are no closer narrowly to linking social behaviour and human physiology.

Until the eighteenth century philosophers and scientists assumed that the male sex was the only one, and that women's internal genitalia were simply the inverse of men's genitalia: the womb and vagina were penis and scrotum turned inside out.[3] By the late nineteenth century, however, differences between men and women were established as a scientific fact, not least as a result of the development of Darwin's theory of the origins of the species and the findings of evolutionary biology. The differences between the sexes came to be perceived as natural and thus necessarily immutable. Feminine and masculine identities were the product of differing biological and hormonal constitutions. The sociological response was to distinguish between the biology of sex and the sociology of gender. Whatever the former contributed to women and men's personalities, behaviour, and attitudes was clearly shaped by cultural expectations. More recently, gender scholars such as Judith Butler have gone a step further and proposed that sex itself is subject to environmental influences and is more fluid and indeterminate than it would appear at first glance.[4] However, the female potential to give birth remains the fundamental biological difference between men and women that continues to structure their respective places in social life. In this sense, biology matters as the major determinant of many women's lives. We do not mean to say that biology is destiny, but it cannot be denied that it puts women in a social position that places particular expectations on them from the start.

Fortunately much of the nature-versus-nurture argument need not concern us, because we start one step up. There are exceptions (for example, in the discussion of risk in Chapter 7), but generally we need not explain why gender roles are composed as they are or how notions of masculine and feminine acquired their specific content. We are trying to understand why those roles and personalities might make religion more or less plausible or attractive.

In this chapter we consider the various activities and roles of women that might have some connection with religion: giving birth, child-rearing, and caring for the sick and dying. We also consider whether there is explanatory value in moving from the gender categories to some more abstract notion of femininity and masculinity. In particular we consider the aesthetic appeal of certain forms of religion to some gay men.

Giving Birth

Being born is patently an important rite of passage, and all religions offer a variety of rituals and celebrations to accompany the event. Most strands of Christianity have regarded baptism as a sacrament: a ritual act that changes the status of the person by bringing him or her into the body of the church. Many have regarded baptism as so central to the post-mortem fate of the person that midwives were taught a simple formula to recite over any newborn child so sickly that it seemed unlikely to live long enough for a priest to perform the official ritual. A further mark of the ritual's importance was that it trumped deeply rooted Reformation divisions in the Scottish Hebridean islands. Some small islands had a resident Catholic priest or a Presbyterian minister but not both. In the eighteenth and nineteenth centuries, many families would ask the 'wrong' clergyman to perform the ritual if the right one could not readily attend.

Although the ceremony of the churching of women had largely died out in the Western Christian church by the end of the nineteenth century, it continues in some Eastern churches. Reflecting the Old Testament convention that a woman was impure for a period after giving birth, Christian churches offered a special service to give thanks for the women's survival and to welcome her back into conventional society after a period of confinement to the home. The churching service could take place in the home, but more usually it took place in church, with the woman wearing particular clothes and seated in a special position. According to the 1549 Book of Common Prayer, the woman was to be 'nigh unto the quire door'. In the revised version, she was to be 'nigh unto the place where the Table (or altar) standeth'.[5] The woman being churched was expected to make some offering, such as the chrisom placed on the child at its christening.

It is not surprising that religious societies should surround child-birth with religious rituals. Our task is to explain why in societies that are becoming increasingly secular women remain more religious than men, and the religious significance of childbirth seems to offer a good explanation. Women who are personally pious will enthusiastically embrace the religious affirmations offered, but even those who are not particularly religious will find themselves drawn into a positive relationship with the church. It is noticeable that baptism remained a popular religious rite for some decades after adult church attendance had begun to decline. As with all our connections between gender role and religious participation, our point is not that men could not be involved in religious rituals. It is that, by virtue of their 'secular' activity of giving birth, women had more occasion than men to be more involved with religious belief and ritual.

Some women who have given birth describe it as a modern miracle, a defining moment, and a spiritual experience.[6] We do not need to look far for less idyllic narratives of childbirth; any parenting Internet forum will furnish examples.[7] If anything, the users of the message boards advise that unrealistic expectations of a magical or miraculous birth be replaced by tempered optimism. None the less, several authors have addressed the spiritual dimension of childbirth. Susan Sered's study of giving birth, for instance, emphasizes the supernatural and miraculous element of the process for her Jewish respondents.[8] Similar research has been conducted among Mormon and Muslim women.[9] There too the participants claimed that their contact with God intensified during childbirth and directly afterwards. However, this kind of research carries little explanatory value for our task, because the women in question were all devout individuals, predisposed to read the event within a religious framework of meaning. The argument would hold more water if nominally secular women felt the presence of the supernatural during labour. Women who are already religious may intensify their beliefs as a result of childbirth and their faith may become more meaningful to them.[10] Alternatively, nominally secular women may draw on general spiritual terminology, which is not derived from any particular religious tradition, in order to describe an embodied experience as profound as childbirth. For example, Finnish women spoke of feeling more in touch with their selves and giving birth to themselves as mothers.[11] This mode of expression closely reflects the discourse of late modern spiritualities with its focus on the importance and growth of the self.

In pre-modern and early modern societies childbirth was one of the life-cycle events that was blessed by official religious rituals and surrounded by an informal web of popular folk religion and superstition. Those two things signified both its importance and its danger. The churching of women drew its celebratory power from the sad fact that in many cases the mother, or the child, or both, did not survive. In Britain in 1921 there were eighty-three deaths under the age of 1 per thousand live births. By 1999 it had fallen to just six.[12] Advances in general health, hygiene, and medical care have removed much of the danger and mystery from childbirth. The venue has shifted from the home to the clinic. And the interpretative frameworks have changed from religious to medical ones. Increasingly the only women who will see giving birth as a particularly religious or spiritual experience are those who are already religious. Others will find secular notions of significance within which to interpret it. The Jewish women in Susan Sered's study draw on a shared religious and cultural toolkit to ritualize and to some extent enchant childbirth: they wear amulets during pregnancy, seek blessing from a rabbi, go on pilgrimage, and recite psalms.[13] In other words, they resort to the supernatural in preparation for, and during, childbirth. In this sense they actively make childbirth into a religious ritual and experience; it does not become spiritual automatically. A curious aspect of Sered's study is the wide range of religious influences that informs these rituals. Jewish women use Arabic amulets and symbols, North African women consult rabbis, and East European women perform North African pilgrimage practices. In Jerusalem 'even thoroughly secular women cannot escape contact with diverse folk-religious rituals'.[14] This situation is possible only if religion (or religions) saturates a particular society and informs all spheres of life. Moreover, the ritualistic nature of childbirth among Orthodox and ultra-Orthodox Jews extends to men who take part in all the religious activities. One of Sered's striking findings is that very few of the women who performed religious rituals claimed to believe in them. Most offered a secular gloss: they chose to perform them for psychological comfort rather than out of faith in their efficacy.

Our general point is this. Traditionally, giving birth has been surrounded by religion. In the West the religious protection and celebration have gradually been reduced by a combination of decreasing danger, increased medicalization, and a decline in the proportion of the population that is disposed to see anything in religious terms. But, at any point in that secularizing trajectory, being pregnant and giving birth gave women opportunities for religious reflection and religious behaviour additional to those available to men.

Raising Children

'Every Sunday I had to recite to my mother a chapter of one of the books of the Bible. I had to learn it during the course of the week and Sunday evening, all of us, we had to say what we'd learnt without making a mistake.'[15] A whole chapter was unusual; that it was his mother rather than his father who heard his lesson was not. In most cultures women have the primary responsibility for the early care and socialization of infants. Even where the level of social development is such that early education takes place in nurseries and infants' schools rather than in the home, it is the mother who generally takes responsibility for preparing the children, taking them to and from school, and attending school events. Part of a mother's job is to explain basic religious ideas to the infants; even in pious households it is mothers who teach children to say their prayers before going to bed. Religious socialization of children remained popular for a number of generations after their parents had lost interest. There are various reasons for that. Even when the parents have lost faith in the supernatural elements of their religion, they may feel that religious instruction is a useful foundation for morality. They may feel obliged to pass on some vestige of a distinctive religio-ethnic heritage. Or they may feel that the decision to be uninterested in religion is one that their children should make for themselves.

Whatever the reasoning, in any circumstance other than both parents being thoroughly religious, the task of taking the children to church, preparing Catholic children for their first communion around the age of 8, or helping a Methodist Sunday Scholar memorize his 'turn' for the Anniversary Sunday performance almost invariably fell to mothers or, when the mother was not available, to some other female relative. For a decade or so, one of us has collected details of childhood religious experiences from the self-published biographies of non-famous people.[16] Almost without exception, it was the mother or grandmother who took the child to church or Sunday School. As churchgoing declined, the burden fell more narrowly on mothers.

Halbertal interviewed middle-class, university-educated feminist mothers about the reconciliation of their modern liberal attitudes to gender with the conservative Catholic or Jewish religious traditions of which they were part.[17] She concluded that the role of a mother is complicated by the cultural context of the religious tradition where she often faces the choice of either confusing her daughter with a mixture of traditional and modern norms, or pushing her towards the safe and clear waters of a 'one-dimensional fundamentalism'.[18] On the one hand, the mothers craved the safety of the rigid religious tradition for their daughters, but, on the other hand, they wanted to pass on the freedom to manipulate it and to choose how much of it can be resisted and challenged. Halbertal's participants raised their daughters in accordance with religious norms, because they valued 'being a good mother' more than teaching their children to resist the aspects of the tradition they considered problematic. This example suggests that, even when the women in question are not entirely supportive of the religious tradition, they may prioritize the normality of their mothering over their non-normative, feminist convictions.

Nursing the Sick and Dying

In the two gender 'roles' just discussed we have advanced a simple syllogism. Religion, both in its official and its folk forms, has much to say about, and much to do with, an important sphere of life or life event. Women either monopolize the sphere (in the case of giving birth) or dominate it (in the case of child-rearing). Hence women routinely have more contact with religious beliefs, officials, and rituals than men. Hence they have greater opportunity to become or to remain religious than men. The same logic applies to ill-health and death.

In most societies women continue to be primary, paid and unpaid, carers. In the USA, two-thirds of all cancer care-givers are women, and in 2010 women made up between 59 and 75 per cent of care-givers for individuals with a variety of such serious illnesses as cancer, brain damage, Alzheimer's, Parkinson's, and AIDS.[19] In the UK, 58 per cent of carers are female.[20] In Finland, where most of the professional and private care-givers are also women, the spiritual aspect of looking after the terminally ill has become increasingly important to the work of nurses and private carers.[21] Female participants in a Finnish study of care-givers for the dying claimed that women are naturally better at caring and at understanding grief, particularly the grief of a mother losing a child. They are also more attuned to subtleties and detail, hence better positioned to take care of the terminally ill. Some women considered their simple presence by the deathbed as almost superior to more active forms of caring and help, which they saw as insufficient, or inappropriate.[22] They also believed that they possessed 'mystical agency': a greater receptivity to supernatural grace. When a person is dying, caring takes on a more abstract meaning, because curing ceases to be an option. This type of caring necessarily centres around providing comfort and emotional support. This, in turn, evokes the traditionally feminine occupation of nursing, which historically has served as an opportunity for women to live out their Christian vocation. In the spirit of Christian caritas, nurses would be encouraged to treat their patients as spiritual as well as physical beings. In the words of Florence Nightingale, 'every woman has...at one time or another in her life, charge of the personal health of somebody, whether child or invalid— in other words, every woman is a nurse'.[23] Thus nursing as a profession and as a vocation brings together the biological and religious elements of what it means to be female. The example is important, because it gives us a clue as to the association made between femininity and religious involvement. Caring has historically been described and understood in Christian terms as a task that forms a part of the female vocation. Nursing and caring more generally are both a form of mothering, accompanied by religious or spiritual connotations.[24] Although the Christian connotations have largely disappeared in secular societies, female carers continue to bridge medicine and religion as they look after the sick and the dying and become intermediaries between doctors and chaplains. For example, the aforementioned Finnish women could be seen as taking over the job of the dismantled welfare system.[25] They fill the gap created as a result of institutional changes.

Apart from taking care of the sick and the dying in the practical sense, women also play a crucial role in creating a sense of community during times of emotional upheaval caused by death and subsequent bereavement. The 'tragedy of the inexpressive male' coupled with women's greater willingness to 'recognise, label, express and disclose feelings' creates a space for women to look after the expressive side of the bereavement process.[26] Several studies have described the gendered division of labour during periods of grief.[27] For example, in cases of a child's death, fathers tend to take care of practical aspects such as arranging the funeral and liaising with police and coroners. Mothers of deceased children, on the other hand, suspend their family responsibilities to express grief emotionally: 'wives cope by not coping.' Husbands, on the other hand, cope through engaging in practical tasks. This gendered division of grieving is consistent with the stereotype of women as the chief weepers and mourners. Also pertinent here is bonding with other women: bereaved mothers cited other mothers and female friends as the main source of expressive support. This kind of support is particularly relevant when a woman experiences a miscarriage, or stillbirth, which are both embodied experiences. Fathers in these scenarios may be sidelined in the grieving process, because they have not carried the baby. Interestingly, some bereaved mothers admitted having visited a medium to seek comfort after a child's death, and overall a much more significant proportion of women than men derived comfort from their religious beliefs. It seems that, in times of bereavement, women and men revert to very traditional gender roles, but women are more likely than men to seek solace in religion.[28]

However, on a more practical level, the old paradigm of gendered caring for the dead is changing, largely as a result of modernization. Prior to the nineteenth century, women were responsible for laying out the dead, but, with the rise of funerals as a commercial enterprise, specialized undertakers have taken over the role. In pre-industrial societies women's responsibility for caring for the dead was justified partly on religious grounds. Women were considered naturally more pious than men, and, as funeral rites were inextricable from religious tradition, it was logical that the duty of preparing the body for burial would fall to those more familiar with the realm of the sacred. The characteristics required for the task were attention to detail, care, and gentleness, and these were not the socially defined male traits. Moreover, the care of dead bodies resembled that of newborn babies: they had to be handled carefully, washed, and clothed. Hence the preparation of the dead fell easily into the category of a woman's work.

Another link was, of course, with infant mortality. Women tended to other women in labour and often witnessed the mother dying in childbirth. They thus gained experience at handling sudden death. The phenomenon of 'shrouding women' took these duties out of the home and into the wider community. 'Shrouding women' had the expertise and experience necessary to carry out the ritual of preparing the dead body, and as such the community relied on their assistance. The women themselves saw their task as a neighbourly duty, but their skills had a particular sacred status in the sense that they 'mastered the mysteries of…illness and death. They touched the untouchable, handled excrement and vomit…[and] swaddled the dead.'[29] Midwives, nurses, and shrouding women performed these tasks until the mid-1800s, when undertaking became a profession, and caring for the dead was labelled as a commercial enterprise. Where previously traditionally feminine traits had been seen as enabling the task of handling the dead, in the new system sensitivity and gentleness began to be seen as incompatible with the more technical and scientific approach to the funeral industry. In the USA, trade publications such as the *Casket* and the wonderfully named the *Embalmer's Monthly* editorialized on women's emotional and physical unsuitability for the increasingly more advanced embalming and funeral practices.[30] A century later, the end to labour market discrimination has seen women re-enter the death business, this time as paid professional undertakers and funeral directors.[31] As Charles Cowling, the author of the *Good Funeral Guide*, explained: 'This is an important job and women with their superior emotional fluency feel they can do it better. Men tend to be more buttoned up.'[32] In 1995 women accounted for 25 per cent of funeral workers in Australia. Female funeral directors are most likely to service the funerals of babies and young people as well as the funerals of women whose husbands feel more comfortable with the idea of women handling their wives' bodies. A female-run funeral company—White Lady—emphasizes the celebration of life in its philosophy.[33] It markets its services as 'ultra-feminine'. In contrast to the more tradition 'masculine' setting of dark wood panelling and mahogany office furniture, it offers a warm, frilly, and lacy environment.[34] The feminine ethos stretches to the manner in which the funeral service is carried out: the employees use a small table when dealing with the corpse, they are attentive to detail, they personalize the body as requested by the relatives, and they also provide support and an emotional crutch for anyone who appears unable to cope during the funeral. Indeed, this emotional and supportive aspect of death-work has been where a re-feminization of the industry has occurred.[35]

For all that the disposal of the body is now done by professionals, the often lengthy period of anticipating death remains the preserve of women. What free space women have gained by having fewer children is often now filled with caring for elderly parents. The thoroughly secular will not fill their bedside time pondering the meaning of life or what follows death, but those who enjoyed some sort of religious socialization in childhood may well find that task offering some encouragement to religious or spiritual speculation.

Caring

Although we have frequently used the word 'caring' to describe the work women do, the adjective also describes an attitude. We have suggested that women may be more religious than men because they have a greater part to play in areas of life where religion is especially prevalent: birth, child-rearing, sickness, and death. Thus far we have described this largely in objective terms to do with opportunity for religious reflection and contact with religious culture. Just as farmers are more likely than office workers to be tanned because they spend more time outside, women are more likely to be religious than men because they spend more time in life spheres that religion has previously dominated. We have put it in those terms because, although the consequences of women's greater connection with religion have to be imaginatively inferred, the gender differences in contact are tangible. Men might be more or less involved in the churching of women: women were always central.

We would now like to step onto less firm but equally important ground by explicitly attending to the attitudinal component of caring. Women not only perform the task of caring; they do actually care. For our purposes it does not matter whether we think that self-abnegating interest in the welfare of others comes first and explains why women have the role of carer or whether we suppose that generations of performing nurturing roles produces the corresponding attitude. What matters is that women are more likely than men to be generally solicitous and nurturing of others. Religious people will see the obvious connection. The major world religions all see themselves as religions of love. All expect that the love that God shows for his creation will be echoed in the love that we show for each other, and all place a great premium on an ethic of care for others. So women are more religious than men because they possess more of the quality found in and promoted by religion. This is not a matter of definition or tautology. The claim is not that women are more religious than men because they possess a characteristic that, because it also occurs in religion, we will redefine as religious. The case is not that all love is really religious. The claim is a causal one: because women are more caring, they are more likely than men to be attracted to a life-world that promotes a message of love and compassion. Women are more likely to be religious because this life-world resonates with them to an extent that it does not with men.

We feel somewhat uneasy with this argument and suspect that our discomfort is explained by a professional reluctance to endorse the truth claims that religious organizations make. Especially when dealing with competing religions, the social scientist adopts the posture of methodological agnosticism. As private citizens we may have our preferences, but as social scientists we cannot know which if any religion, confession, church, or congregation really has the ear of God. We report rather than endorse the claims of religions. To accept that love and compassion (rather than, for example, authoritarianism and fear) are prevailing features of Christianity or Islam and to use that as part of an explanation of some aspect of human behaviour feels a little like buying a religion's PR spiel. It seems more like religious propaganda than social science explanation.

However, this is probably an unnecessary caution. What matters in explaining social action is what the actors believe to be the case. If a significant number of nineteenth- and early twentieth-century women were attracted to the churches because they found in 'love thy neighbour as thyself' an endorsement of what they took to be an important part of their characters, then that is the explanation of their greater attachment to religion.

Changing Gender Roles

Gender relations in the West changed radically in the second half of the twentieth century. The oral contraceptive pill gave women greater control over their fertility, typical family size decreased, and increased female participation in the labour market changed gender roles and expectations for both men and women. Although women's biological ability to give birth continues to dictate their role as primary carers and transmitters of values to future generations, gender roles have become less strictly defined, because a greater proportion of women are not mothers and because mothers actively 'mother' for shorter periods of their lives. In addition, fathers now play a more active part in childcare and home-making. That change should not be overestimated.[36] Though we are constantly reminded of sociological phenomena such as 'fatherhood in transition' and the 'crisis of the breadwinner father', most fathers remain main breadwinners in fulltime and continuous employment.[37] And the majority of childcare continues to be carried out by women. In 2008, 9 per cent of UK mothers, but only 1 per cent of fathers, arranged their work to fit around school holidays. Also, 38 per cent of women with dependent children, but only 4 per cent of such men, worked part-time. As an occupation, childcare is female dominated: in Scotland, in 2005 women made up 98 per cent of pre-school education and childcare staff. Women continue significantly to outnumber men as carers, both in and outside their homes.[38]

Therefore, despite the speculations on the rise of the softer masculinity embodied by the 'new man' in the 1980s and the supposed move towards a more egalitarian model of heterosexual relationships and the increased participation of fathers in childcare, relatively traditional gender assumptions continue to structure the concept of caring, and women still tend to be cast as the obvious natural carers.[39] Caring defines feminine self-identity and women's existence, while 'not caring becomes a defining characteristic of manhood'.[40] Regardless of social class or wealth, women are likely to be responsible for both organizing care and for caring in itself.

We need to be careful about precisely what we are saying here. There has been some change in the gendered division of labour. It does not necessarily follow that, because women's roles and their concomitant attitudes explain greater religiosity, any decline in female distinctiveness in secular spheres will immediately produce a decline in female religiosity. One of the curses of social science is that patterns of behaviour can become relatively independent of their original causes. For example, women may attend church more frequently than men because they take the children for whose religious socialization they are responsible. But they may continue to attend once the children have stopped going because they find church services pleasant and rewarding. As is the case in one example we discuss in Chapter 5, they may even find a new attraction in the preponderance of women. None the less we would expect that changes in what we think are the causes of a gendered difference in behaviour would gradually and eventually result in a change in that behaviour. And this is indeed what we find. Although the rate of change and the timing of onset varies from society to society, as women become more like men in secular matters so they also become more similar in degrees of interest in and attachment to religion. For the first half the twentieth century, British churchgoing showed a growing gulf between women and men as men disaffiliated. From the 1960s onwards women followed men out of the churches.[41] That there has been some convergence suggests that changes in gender roles have been significant. That there still remains a gender difference in religiosity fits our observation that secular gender differences have softened but not disappeared.

Female or Feminine?

Clarity of exposition often requires simplification. Because doing otherwise for any length of time would make our prose even denser, we have usually talked of men and women and distinguished between biological 'sex' and sociological 'gender' only when necessary. A further important distinction is between sex or gender and the qualities that may be attributed to the two classes defined under either heading. If we distinguish between male and female, on the one hand, and masculine and feminine, on the other, it is possible to consider that men may be more or less masculine, that women can be more or less feminine, and that members of each class may to some degree possess the qualities normally associated with the other class—that is, some men may be more feminine than some women and vice versa. This still involves considerable simplification, but, if we suppose an ideal type of the feminine outlook, such as that measured by the Bem Sex Role Inventory—being emotional, intuitive, compassionate, passive, affectionate, caring—we can also suppose that it is the extent to which someone possesses this outlook, rather than gender divided into two boxes, that is related to religiosity.[42] Edward Thompson surveyed the religious beliefs and attitudes of some 350 New England undergraduates who had also taken the Bem inventory. He found that it was possessing a feminine orientation, rather than being female per se, that best explained religious belief and behaviour.[43]

As with all such research, the results are more complex than this summary suggests. For men, having a religious affiliation and a feminine outlook 'predicted variation in religiousness', but for women a feminine outlook predicted only three of the five religion variables: self-assessed religiousness, devotionalism, and religious behaviour. It did not affect either general or orthodox religious beliefs.[44] Thompson ponders possible explanations, but, without further research of this kind, the best we can say is that it seems probable that what explains women's greater interest in religion is not their biology but attitudes and experiences that are differentially distributed among women and that are to an extent also shared by some men.

Gay Men and Religion

That naturally leads us to the sensitive topic of homosexuality. Although we are not crass enough to suppose that lesbians are really men and gay men are really women, it is clear that some homosexuals possess character traits, attitudes, and orientations and, more superficially, interests and preferences that are more conventionally ascribed to the other sex. Hence we might well expect homosexuals to be closer in religious interest and involvement to the norm for the other sex. Not surprisingly, given the delicacy of the subject—in many societies homosexuality still carries a considerable stigma—there is a dearth of data on the religious preferences of gay men and women.

We do know that certain kinds of religion attract male homosexuals. Two strands of the Christian tradition have particularly drawn gay men: the Catholic Church and the 'High' or Anglo-Catholic wing of the Episcopalian Church. One plausible source estimates that 20 per cent of Catholic priests in the USA are gay in orientation and that about half of those are 'actively homosexual': well above the national average.[45] The US Episcopal Church Bishop Gene Robinson of New Hampshire said: 'If all the gay people stayed away from church on a given Sunday the Church of England would be close to shut down between its organists, its clergy, its wardens . . .'.[46]

Gay men are particularly to be found in Anglo-Catholicism. As its name suggests, this late-nineteenth-century movement was an attempt to reform the Church of England by stressing the Catholic rather than the Protestant parts of its heritage. Anglo-Catholic clergy hear confession and anoint the sick. They say prayers for the dead. They regard the priesthood as possessing supernatural powers. They believe that the bread and wine of the Eucharist really become the Body and Blood of Christ. And many encourage devotions to the Virgin Mary. Unlike Protestants, for whom correct belief and living a moral life are pretty much the sum of what is required, Anglo-Catholics lay great stress on religious ritual, which should be elaborate and aesthetically pleasing. Where Protestants will happily worship in a barn, Anglo-Catholics like ornate churches that are richly decorated and filled with the smell of incense and the sound of sacred music.

Anglo-Catholicism has always had homosexual overtones.[47] Its founder and leader before he defected to Rome, John Henry Newman, is believed by many scholars to have been a closet homosexual. He lived with fellow priest Ambrose St John for over thirty years and insisted that he be buried in the same grave as St John. Ralph Adams Cram was a leading Anglican in Boston at the end of the nineteenth century and an influential church architect in the American Gothic style. He was also actively involved in Boston's gay scene.[48] His Anglo-Catholic world was described as 'a gay white gentlemen's club . . . where religion and aestheticism come together, where worship of God mixes with reverence for beauty (in the form of music, liturgy, and sometimes choirboys)'.[49] Evelyn Waugh knew English church life well. In his classic novel of the 1930s, *Brideshead Revisited*, he has Charles Ryder, his outsider character, given this advice before going to Oxford University: 'Beware of the Anglo-Catholics—they're all sodomites with unpleasant accents.'[50] Two seminaries—Cuddesdon and Mirfield—were particularly known for attracting gay men. Bishop Wilberforce, who was generally sympathetic to the High Church movement, described the students of Cuddeson as 'too peculiar'.[51]

The following extract from one gay Christian musician's account of his socialization into this world in the north of England in the 1980s is worth quoting at length for its clear account of the appeal of ritual:

I soon realised that organists were a rare breed and very much in demand. Requests started arriving from local clergy . . . the more services I played for, the more familiar I became with the prayers, readings, psalms, and liturgy of the church. This, I am sure, was where some very solid foundations were laid as I steadily absorbed the framework of church worship through the ministry of music. Then I met Father Alan. He unashamedly poached me from my deputizing duties at a neighbouring church, and within weeks my understanding of worship had been notched up several gears as I was introduced to the glory of High Church ritual done superbly well. And not only did the worship style reach deep down inside me, but I was thrilled to be invited regularly to the gin parties in the Rectory where famous Anglo-Catholic clergy would attend with their boyfriends, and hold court among the new initiates of this delightfully camp club. At this time I was in my mid-twenties, learning about being gay... and learning quite a lot about a very rarified section of the Church of England...After about a year as deputy organist, altar server, and 'in' friend of the gay clergy at this Anglo-Catholic basilica, I was invited to move house and become a lodger in a Rectory somewhat nearer to my place of work. Through various social encounters, the priest had become a dear and sincere friend, it really suited my personal circumstances to accept his offer, and I spent 12 very happy months sharing the Rectory with him.[52]

Interesting though this phenomenon is, it gives us little help in understanding why women are more religious than men, because, although we can trace a link from femininity to a certain type of male homosexuality to this style of religion, there is a fundamental break between the interests of gay men and women. The aesthetics of Anglo- and Roman Catholicism may attract women and 'feminine' men, but those men are presumably also attracted by ritualistic Christianity's traditional hostility to women. So we are unlikely to learn much about women's religiosity by detailed study of this particular association beyond the argument made by historians such as Callum Brown and Leon Podles that many Christian churches from around the middle of the nineteenth century became increasingly unattractive to men precisely because they became 'feminized'.[53]

If the religious preferences of homosexuals are to illuminate the ties between femininity and religiosity, we need to know more about the religious beliefs and behaviour of homosexuals at large rather than of those who have elected to join a particular religious movement. The only such source we can find is a detailed analysis of some 10,000 respondents to the US General Social Survey (GSS) between 1991 and 2000. The GSS asked for the sex of sex partners over the previous five years. It also asked about religious beliefs and behaviour. Hence Darren Sherkat was able to compare the scores on four religion items—church attendance, frequency of prayer, having abandoned a childhood religious affiliation, and believing that the Bible is the 'actual or inspired word of God'—for six groups: heterosexual, bisexual, and homosexual men and the same for women. The results show the predictable lead for heterosexual women. They also show that 'gay men are more avid religious participants than male heterosexuals and other non-heterosexuals, and are similar to female heterosexuals in their rates of religious participation'.[54] Sherkat's tentative explanation of his results involves the notion of risk: the topic of the next chapter.

Conclusion

Unsurprisingly, given the complexity of the issue, our conclusion to this discussion of gender roles and attitudes is tentative. Some elements of the division of gender roles are patently conventional; one at least has a solid biological basis. There is no physical reason why men should not play an equal part in the care of the elderly, but only women give birth. The 'secular' gender roles have religious consequences. In deeply religious cultures, those consequences are deliberate: religions have much to say about birth, child-rearing, and death, and place on women ritual obligations that reinforce their commitment to the faith. But even in semi-secular cultures, so long as there is any active religious culture, women's greater involvement in key life stages will bring them into greater contact with religious beliefs, officials, and rituals and will give them more occasion to reflect on the religious or spiritual significance of those life stages.

We have also identified a congruence of interest between the caring and nurturing attitudes that are associated with women's roles and a major (but by no means the only) theme of most religious traditions. The distinction between role and attitude took us to research that tried to identify the religious effects of feminine and masculine orientations and to the religious preferences of homosexuals. Though there is little such work, it does suggest that what explains women's greater interest and involvement in religion is not being female as such but being more feminine. Precisely what aspects of being feminine are relevant will be pursued in Chapter 7.

7

Risk

Introduction

The idea of risk was famously introduced into the discussion of religious belief by the seventeenth-century French mathematician and philosopher Blaise Pascal. In Note 233 of his posthumously published *Pensées*, Pascal suggests that, although reason cannot prove the existence of God, reasoning through the possible costs and rewards would lead the reasonable man to wager that God does exist. The logic is this. If we live as if there is no God, and we are wrong, we suffer eternal damnation. If we live as if there is a God and we are wrong, we lose nothing more than some transient pleasures. If we live as if there is a God and we are right, we win eternal salvation. While Pascal's wager was sensible in the monotheistic culture of seventeenth-century Catholic France, its value in the modern world of multiple Gods seems less obvious: which God would you choose? We will return to that after considering an interesting explanation of female piety that links gender to faith via the idea of risk aversion.

The previous chapter considered various versions of the theory that the roles women play and the attitudes that inform such roles either make women more disposed to be religious or give them greater contact with religious rituals and beliefs. This chapter starts from the other end, by considering the possibility that the focus of attention should be men's irreligion, not women's religion. As discussed at the end of the previous chapter, Daniel Sherkat suggested that the gender difference in religiosity might be explained, not by the positive features of femininity, but by the negative features of masculinity. Men are more likely than women to take risks and to bet the wrong way in Pascal's wager.

Risk Aversion

Patterns of criminal and deviant behaviour give one very good reason for thinking that there is some systematic connection between gender and risk-taking. In most societies and settings, men are vastly more likely than women to commit crimes and to deviate conspicuously from important social norms. In 2002 in the USA, men were nearly ten times more likely than women to commit murder.[1] In England and Wales in 2006 between 82 and 94 per cent of all offenders convicted or cautioned for serious crimes such as violence against the person, criminal damage, robbery, and burglary were male.

Of course, as with all social patterns, some of the apparent difference in the commission of criminal and deviant acts may be a function of our expectations shaping what we see and how we define it. If we expect crime to be largely a male pursuit, we may overlook those acts of women that, had they been carried out by men, would have been classified as crimes. Or we may see them but classify them in some more benign fashion. That point has often been made with regard to suicide statistics. As women conventionally commit suicide by methods (such as poisoning) that are ambiguous enough to be interpreted as accidents, it is possible that the expectation that men are more likely than women to kill themselves generates its own supporting evidence through selective interpretation of ambiguous cases. However, even with due allowance for selective labelling, there is no doubt that the vast majority of serious crimes are committed by men.

There is an obvious substantial connection between crime and deviance and personal piety. In most cultures both the legal codes that define crime and the general norms that define deviance are heavily influenced by the dominant religion. Hence the Godly will also be law-abiding and conformist. Furthermore, the dominant religious culture of any society tends to support the status quo, so that, even if there is no specific theological reason for supporting a particular law, the Godly will generally be on the side of law and order.

However, a more subtle connection can be made through the notion of risk. Those who commit crimes run the risk of being caught and of being punished. Some career villains might view periodic punishment as an unavoidable tax on their chosen profession, but most presumably hope to get away with their crimes. Hence those who commit crimes are risk-taking, while those whose timidity (rather than conscious commitment to legality) discourages them from actions that would otherwise be attractive are 'risk averse'.

Risk preference was first introduced into the discussion of religious preferences by Alan Miller and John Hoffman.[2] They explain the gender gap by three elements. The first two—feminine qualities acquired through socialization and women's structural location in society—were the subject of the previous chapter. The third one is risk. That men and women apparently differ in their willingness to take risks could be explained by biology or by socialization. Biologists would argue that the male propensity to take risks is caused by such features of physiology as muscle mass and by a heightened need for stimulation. Although sociologists would not rule out some underlying physiological origins, they point to the way that children are socialized. Girls are discouraged from such 'boyish' behaviour as playing aggressively, tree-climbing, and roaming outdoors and encouraged in domestic arts and crafts and gentile pursuits such as music and dance.

In order to make their case, Miller and Hoffman measure the risk preferences of a sample of college students by asking them to rate their attraction to 'adventure-seeking'. They find that 'risk preference is a significant predictor of religiosity' and that adding it to a model predicting religiosity that includes gender, race, rurality, and mother's and father's level of education (an index of social-class background) reduces the effect of gender by about 40 per cent. That is, some of the explanatory work previously being done by gender is better done by risk preference. And it is a significant predictor of religiosity for both males and females.[3] Miller and Hoffman see risk as only one factor mediating religiosity, which should be taken into account, but not necessarily prioritized. Risk aversion is simply another feminine trait 'typically associated with increased religiosity'.[4]

Rodney Stark pushes the argument much further. Over a very long career Stark has produced a number of theories of religion. His early work with Charles Glock was within the secularization paradigm explained in Chapter 9, but what his last two have in common is the assumption that being religious is the default human condition.[5] With William Sims Bainbridge, he produced an elaborate argument that can be summarized as follows.[6] Because people always want more than they can get, they will always be in the market for compensators, which can be either explanations for why they have not achieved the desired rewards or promises that the rewards will eventually be forthcoming. Because religions can invoke the supernatural, they are better than secular belief-systems at producing compensators. For example, they can explain the lack of rewards by the ineffable will of the Almighty or by defects in a previous life and they can promise rewards in a next life or in an afterlife. As we saw with the example of evangelical Protestant healing in Chapter 5, religion can offer more powerful remedies than secular therapy. So the demand for religion should be high and stable. This remained the underlying assumption of Stark's subsequent body of 'rational choice' or 'supply-side' theory, which in a wide variety of interesting ways tries to show that differences in the levels of religiosity are not, as the secularizationists think, a consequence of social changes that make religious ideas more or less plausible. That would entail variation in 'demand'. Rather, they are a consequence of changes in the 'supply' of religion.[7] What is important for our purposes here is that Stark believes irreligion to be rare.

Stark's address of the gender differential in religion starts by demonstrating, as we did in Chapter 1, that, if women's heightened religiosity is not universal, it is very close to it. He cites the data from the 1995–6 World Values Survey of forty-nine Western and eight non-Western societies to show that in all instances women outnumber men on most, if not all, religiosity measures. Women are more likely than men to consider themselves religious, to derive comfort and strength from religion, to pray, to believe in an afterlife, and to believe in God.[8] Stark is dismissive of previous attempts to explain the gender differential. In particular he is critical of the use of socialization, because he believes the notion to be too broad.

However, if socialization can be conceptualized and measured more rigorously, then perhaps its explanatory potential can be salvaged. If socializing women into traditional gender roles makes them more religious (because it reinforces the traditionally feminine traits associated with religious behaviour), those women who reject the patriarchal model should be closer to males on the religiosity scale. As there are more of such women in modern egalitarian liberal societies than in traditional cultures, the gender gap in religiousness should be smaller in the former than in the latter.[9] Miller and Stark test these hypotheses, using a cross-national and inter-religious sample. Their findings are quite striking. Gender differences in religiosity are greater in nations where single motherhood is more approved of, abortion is more common, and the socialization of women is more liberal. 'Contrary to expectations, where female socialization is less traditional, the effect of gender on religiousness is actually greater', and they are surprised to find 'a strong and consistent inverse relationship between traditional socialization and gender differences in religiousness'.[10]

As ever, Stark's work is thought-provoking, but it need not be persuasive. One obvious problem is the 'ecological fallacy': assuming that all subsidiary parts of a large unit severally share the characteristic of the unit. America as a whole is wealthier now than in 1990, but not all Americans will have become richer at the same rate and some may well have become poorer. One has only to consider the differences in social attitudes between southern California and South Carolina to appreciate that giving a single 'traditional socialization' score to countries may be misleading. It is quite possible for a society that overall has relatively modern attitudes to contain extremely traditional subgroups. Indeed, the former can cause the latter. The primary cause of the rise of the new Christian right in the USA in the late 1970s was apparent liberal domination of the culture. For Miller and Stark's inverse correlation of traditional gender socialization and the gender gap in religiosity to mean what they want it to mean, it would have to be the case that the same people were being sampled in both measures. That is, that the men and women who were most different in religiosity were also those who had been raised with the most patriarchal attitudes. Their research design does not rule out the possibility of the conflict between liberals and conservatives encouraging each to exaggerate their differences.

A second weakness is that cross-national comparison is illuminating only to the extent that the dependent variable (the effect) and the independent variable (the supposed cause) are the only differences in play in the comparisons. And here they are not. The popularity of religion per se in any society is not considered. This seems a strange omission, when plain reasoning tells us that the popularity of something as important as religion in any social subgroup will in part be a product of its overall popularity and not just for the tautological reason that overall popularity is an aggregate of popularity with men and with women. Because Stark does not believe in secularization, he does not consider that the gender gap may change as religion declines. But that is roughly what we find in Britain. Over the course of the twentieth century the gender gap in British religion first expanded as men disaffiliated and then contracted as both men and women converged on indifference.

A third problem with the general argument is that it seeks a single cause of women's heightened religiosity. Stark asserts: 'any phenomenon that occurs in many and very different social and cultural settings necessitates explanations that are equally general, which tends to rule out most social and cultural factors.'[11] We see no reason to accept that as a general axiom of social science and less reason to accept it in this case. Given that there are only three possible states in our 'effect'— women being more religious than men, men being more religious than women, and the two genders being the same—it seems quite possible that any one of the three may have a variety of causes.

Finally, we see as somewhat limited the value of operationalizing 'socialization' as a process of transmitting values that can be assessed by asking adults questions about particular attitudes. It is difficult to express this clearly, and our hunch may be even harder to test, but, as we noted in the previous chapter, part of the gender gap in religiosity may result from the inadvertent part that secular gender roles play in providing opportunities for acquiring or reinforcing religious beliefs. Stark could argue that the sorts of survey questions used to identify traditionalists in his survey data will at least loosely tap the same phenomenon, but that is not terribly persuasive. Consider just one illustration of the complexities involved. Even in modern egalitarian societies, the care of frail and elderly relatives usually falls to women. Even thoroughly modern women may find themselves taking their mothers to church. We do not want to take the complexity argument to the point of implying that social science explanations are untestable and we respect the ingenuity of Miller and Stark's attempt to test the effects of socialization, but we do not accept that their tests exhaust the possibilities.

Having (in our view prematurely) given up on socialization, Stark opts for risk as the explanation of the gender gap on the grounds that he cannot think of anything else sufficiently general and, for the same reason, he opts for hormones as the explanation of different attitudes to risk. He assumes that most people are religious and that male irreligion is a form of risk-taking to be explained by the same sort of biological mechanisms that explain why some men so value instant gratification that they find it difficult to control their impulses. As with crime so with irreligion. It is the testosterone that explains the behaviour of the same minority (primarily but not exclusively male) who cannot 'inhibit their impulses, especially those involving immediate gratification and thrills' and who reject religion.[12]

As Stark himself acknowledges and we noted in the previous chapter, attempts to explain complex and diffuse patterns of social action by features of human biology do not have a good track record. It may well be, for example, that the oxytocin released in the female body within an hour of giving birth influences the bonding experience between the mother and the newborn baby.[13] High levels of oxytocin in women might make them more emotionally attuned to others, hence more empathic and less likely to engage in violent behaviour, but there are so many other factors that go into the development of our personalities and relationships that it is hard to see how oxytocin or any other hormone can usefully explain adult behaviour. We do not deny the importance of biology. We only note that, as the basis for explaining complex adult human behaviour (as distinct from, say, the baby's clutching for the breast), biology runs into two difficulties. First, there is far too much variation in the behaviour of people with a common biology. Second, there is too great a gulf between what biology might explain and the human choices that interest us. Testosterone level in men may be experimentally associated with aggression, but there are so many other cultural and situational encouragements to, and inhibitions on, aggression and so many different ways that aggression can be channelled (many of which are highly valued) that testosterone no better explains crimes of violence than did Lombroso's head shapes and dragging knuckles.

Socialization and Risk Combined

If we do not share Stark's view that socialization has been eliminated, it is possible to go back to the Miller and Hoffman position of supposing that risk aversion has a social rather than a biological origin. An example of such an approach is Jessica Collett and Omar Lizardo's argument that risk preference is a product of family background. They divide households into two types: patriarchal and egalitarian. In the former type, men possess authority because of their position in the workplace outside the home. As a result, mothers in such families reproduce the patriarchal model at home. Girls in these households will be subject to more scrutiny and control than boys, leading them to become more risk averse. In egalitarian households, on the other hand, gender differences in the degree of risk aversion will be less significant or non-existent. Parental class and position in the family home can be measured by both parents' socio-economic status, and results indicate that, as the socio-economic status of the mother increases, the daughter's religiosity decreases. Therefore, a purely physiological explanation of gender difference in religiosity does not hold. If it were the case that the gender gap in religiosity was purely down to physiology, the difference would remain constant and unaltered by childhood environment.[14] Instead, as girls are exposed to gender-egalitarian socialization, they become less risk averse, more like boys, and less religious as a result.

What Is Risky about Irreligion?

One can often be drawn deep into the minutiae of academic arguments and lose sight of the foundational premisses. It is worth noting that the risk debate, like Stark's rewards-and-compensators theory and his rational-choice approach to religious behaviour, are much more popular with US than with European sociologists. Just as Pascal's wager seemed clever and convincing in seventeenth-century France, the idea that irreligion is dangerous may be plausible to Americans but foreign to most Western Europeans. When we discuss the risk hypothesis with our undergraduates, they find the argument hard to comprehend, because the idea that anything is at stake in being irreligious appears entirely alien to them.

Two possible meanings of the proposition that irreligion is dangerous need to be distinguished carefully. In the discussions above, the risk is divine punishment. Like Pascal's gambler, the person who chooses not to believe in God is risking the loss of heaven and the gain of hell. But that makes sense only if one believes in such a God. That is, irreligion is conceivably risky only for those who believe, and so attitudes towards risk cannot explain belief. It is possible to envisage a useful application of the idea, but it is very narrow in scope. In England in the Middle Ages, asking people to swear an oath on the Bible to tell the truth was effective, because Christianity so pervaded the entire culture that even hardened criminals might hesitate to test the proposition that there was no God. Where a shared religion is so powerful that few will dissent from it and fewer still will be entirely confident in that dissent, then risk aversion might well explain conformity. But its explanatory value declines rapidly as irreligion becomes more common.

The second meaning has similarly narrow application, but it applies to a rather different situation. Irrespective of one's personal beliefs, one may hesitate openly to defy religious conventions. Here what is at risk is not divine approval but the approval of other people. Either out of respect for the sensitivities of others or out of self-interest—they might need their help some day—non-Christian farmers in Wales in the 1950s were reluctant to harvest on a Sunday for fear of offending Christian neighbours. In 2010 all three major British political parties had leaders who were not committed Christians.[15] It is difficult to imagine any similar US politician making the same admission without career damage.

Because Stark supposes that being religious is the natural or default human condition, he elides these very different circumstances and supposes that timidity will generally be associated with religiosity. What we are suggesting is that religious risk is an issue only for people in thoroughly religious societies and that social disapproval is a similarly narrow concern, this time to be found at one point on the transition from thoroughly religious to fairly secular.

To keep this discussion simple, we have thus far treated religiosity as a singular property that societies can have in greater or less abundance. We have treated religious and secular societies as if they were the extreme ends of a single scale. However, the matter is more complicated. First, we need to attend to specific proportions within any religious belief system. The cost of unbelief will clearly vary with the content of what it is that is not believed. If individuals (whether religious or not) do not believe in the afterlife, they will not be concerned with posthumous punishment and, logically, they will not consider irreligiosity as risky, regardless of their gender. This is one of the theoretical weaknesses of Stark and Miller's argument.[16] Low levels of religious activity are not inherently risky, unless we include individuals' beliefs about the afterlife into the analysis. If women are indeed less prone to risk-taking, then female believers in the afterlife should be more religious than their male counterparts. Moreover, the levels of religiosity for female and male non-believers should be equally low if the afterlife ceases to be an issue. A study by Marie Roth and Jeffrey Kroll, for example, found that women and men who believe in the possibility of punishment in the afterlife were more similar in their levels of religiosity than non-believers of both genders. This, in turn, demonstrates that risk preference does not determine levels of religiosity among men and women, because even women who do not believe in hell display higher levels of religious activity than male non-believers.[17]

There is also a more subtle issue to do with the attitude of the dominant religion towards the 'reach' or application of its principles. The secularization of the West has not only entailed a decline in the number of people who believe in supernaturalist religion; it has also involved a signal change in the nature of much religious belief. Traditionally the religious culture of the West has been exclusive, dogmatic, authoritarian, and doctrinaire. It has supposed that there is a single God with a single truth that applies to all people, whether they like it or not. Most Western churches are now much more ecumenical, inclusive, liberal, and tolerant in their beliefs. Many have responded to the increasingly diverse nature of the religious culture by adopting a form of relativism. They suppose that what they believe is 'true for them' but need not apply to anyone else. The price of liberty to enjoy one's own religion in peace is permitting others the same privilege. The consequence is that, even among peoples of faith, not sharing a particular religion (or not having any) can no longer be seen as 'risky'. Stark himself recognizes that point when he distinguishes 'high-risk' and 'low-risk' types of religion, but he does not follow through. If the twentieth century has seen not only the decline of religion but also the replacement of much high-risk religion by low-risk alternatives then the value of the notion of risk as an explanation of religious preferences declines to the point of redundancy.

To be fair to the notion of risk, we want to add one last consideration. It may have been a throwaway remark, but, in defending their suggestion that people's religious preferences may be shaped by their attitudes to risk, Miller and Hoffman include a mention of Bronislaw Malinowski's anthropological classic *Argonauts of the Western Pacific*.[18] The Trobriand Islanders that Malinowski studied fished in two very different contexts. When they fished in the lagoon, where the waters were relatively calm, the men did not resort to fishing magic. But before fishing in the potentially treacherous open seas, they performed various rituals as protection against hazards over which they had no more practical control. Invoking the supernatural was the last-resort response to dangerous situations for which the fishers had no technical this-worldly solutions.

This may seem like an example of religion controlling risk, but it is irrelevant to Miller and Hoffman's concern with explaining why some people are more religious than others because the Trobriand Islanders did not divide into believers and unbelievers. They all believed, and they consensually drew on their shared religious culture to solve practical problems as appropriate. It was the fishing in the open sea, not a lack of belief, that was risky.

Conclusion

There is certainly something intuitively plausible about the notion that men are more likely to be attracted to risk-taking than women. We need only note the gender composition of mountaineers, sky-divers, and professional fighters, on the one hand, and members of book clubs, sewing circles, and cookery clubs, on the other, to see that men are more likely than women to find pleasure in the dangerous and the potentially painful. And, as with every other gender difference, it is tempting to forget the sociological distinction between sex as a biological given and gender as a social construct. It is perhaps surprising that a sociologist of Stark's distinction should so readily reject social explanations in favour of the biological, but we can appreciate the intuitive plausibility of biological explanations of risk aversion.

However, as the above discussion has demonstrated, what seems plausible does not stand up to detailed scrutiny. And, even if it were undoubtedly the case that women were more timid or cautious than men, this would not tell us anything about religious preferences in societies where the dominant religious tradition had weakened to the point where it is not obvious that there is any particular risk attached to being irreligious.

Risk-preference theory offers an interesting alternative explanation to the question of women's greater religiosity, and its authors certainly stimulated a debate on the possible connections between risk, gender, and religious proclivities. However, while thought-provoking, the explanations offered have not furthered our understanding of feminine and masculine attitudes to religion.

8

Ways of Life

Introduction

Conventionally, the various things that we could mean when we describe people as religious are grouped under three headings: identity, belief, and behaviour. We want to know if people see themselves as religious, if they hold religious beliefs, and if they do what their faith requires. That third box can usefully be divided. Especially when trying to estimate the extent to which people in the Christian tradition are religious, the behaviour in question is overtly concerned with religion narrowly defined: going to church, praying, or reading religious texts. But religions may proscribe or prescribe a very wide range of behaviour not immediately connected with religion: diet, dress, interpersonal behaviour, sexuality, and attitudes to work, for example. Although pious people of most faiths will object to the distinction implied in these labels—they will say everything is primary—let us call these primary and secondary religious behaviour.

Hardly surprisingly, these four facets of 'being religious' tend to go together; when we survey people we find that responses cluster. For example, there are not many people who insist that they are strong Christians but do not hold conventional Christian beliefs and never attend church. The alert reader will notice that the previous sentence stops short at primary religious behaviour. It does not include the fourth facet of living the religious life or secondary religious behaviour. Care needs to be taken here to avoid casually insulting Christians, but there is not a lot of distinctive behaviour that the Christian faith mandates for everyday life. In part that reflects the success of Christianity in shaping the general culture of Christian societies in its image. In contrast, Islam and Judaism have a great many behavioural require-

ments. We can see the point if we compare the Christian's Ten Commandments with the Muslim's shariah and the Jew's Leviticus.

Classically Jews recognize 613 *mitzvoh* or commandments as listed
by the twelfth-century rabbi and philosopher Maimonides: 365 instructions to refrain from certain acts and 248 positive commandments:
Wikipedia has a handy list.[1] Many of the *mitzvoh* are now literally
irrelevant: it is hard to see how the temptation to 'offer peace to
Ammon and Moab while besieging them' could arise or require heroic
resisting. Some are now unwise: there are just too many places that the
Jews would have to torch if they took seriously the command to burn
a city that has turned to idol worship. But there are still very many
rules concerning personal dress, demeanour, and diet. Muslims similarly have a large number of instructions for everyday life given to
them in the Quran or extrapolated from stories of the Prophet's life.

All religions have an orthodoxy or a notion of correct beliefs and all
have an orthopraxy or a notion of correct action, but it is the case that
major religions differ in the relative weight of these two fields. Christianity, especially in its Protestant forms, lays great stress on orthodoxy:
salvation rest primarily on believing certain things, which are conveniently summarized in short creeds or statements of belief. Evangelicals
like to talk of their 'walk with the Lord', but there is little agreement
on behavioural requirements beyond those rules that are common to
decent folk the world over. Islam and Judaism are orthoprax religions.
Clearly one has to have the beliefs, or most of the actions would seem
silly, but there is a lot of behaviour.

We introduce these distinctions because they allow us to draw attention to an important point mentioned previously but not dwelt upon.
Determining whether the gender gap in religiosity is universal or just
very common—which has considerable consequences for its explanation—requires that we be able to measure and compare religiosity in
non-Christian religions and cultures. The first of our four facets of
religion can be applied cross-culturally; we can ask everyone some version of the question 'How important is your religion to you in living your life?' There are a few scholars who argue that to talk of
'religion' as a sphere distinct from the rest of life is a modern Western
practice (part of the Enlightenment 'project') that properly postmod-
ern sensitivities should disdain. We have discussed this at length elsewhere.[2] It is enough for our purposes here to note that, as the success
of World Values Survey demonstrates, in practice most people in

most religious cultures have little difficulty understanding or sensibly answering questions designed to tap religious identification or belief.

The problem with the third and fourth facets of religion—primary and secondary religious behaviour—lies not in measuring them. For that one simply needs extensive knowledge of the religion in question. Rather it lies in comparing the results in each field cross-culturally and in finding the right balance of the two fields. Regularly gathering together for worship has been the central act of religious solidarity for Christians for centuries, and church attendance data fit closely with other measures of religious interest. Regularly attending the temple or *gurdwara* may be less important than domestic religious ceremonies to Hindus and Sikhs. And, if our purpose is to derive a single measure or sense of religiosity so that we can answer such questions as 'Are the Egyptians more religious than the Americans?', we need to balance the weight given to primary and secondary religious behaviour. Egyptians may score higher on the latter than the former; with Americans it will be reversed.

All of the above is intended to bring us to this point: it is difficult to estimate a gender gap in religiosity for orthoprax religions, because different obligations may be set for men and for women, both deliberately and accidentally. The *mitzvoh* that forbid men and women to wear each other's clothing are gendered in their intent. The very many Jewish dietary requirements are in theory universal, but in practice they are impositions on women, because women do most of the food purchasing, preparation, cooking, and serving. Women may score lower than men on primary but higher than men on secondary religious behaviour. Hence the universality of gender differences in religiosity may be difficult to establish with certainty.[3]

In this chapter we will discuss some aspects of Muslim and Jewish women's religion. In part we are concerned to show the complexity of the lived religious life. In part we are motivated by the concern that informed Chapter 5: to show the rationality beneath what may seem like self-defeating choices. A third interest is to demonstrate the importance of secondary religious behaviour and thus illustrate our caution about underestimating women's religiosity. Finally we introduce another partial answer to the book title's question: in some settings women are more religious than men because they are required to be responsible for the religious commitment and morality of other people.

Muslim Women in Britain

Britain's Islamic communities have received a considerable amount of attention in the first decade of the twenty-first century. A significant number of studies have mapped the various ways in which Muslim women experience marriage, family life, education, labour market, the relationship between ethnicity and identity, and attitudes to veiling. However, religious attitudes and practices, although implicit in all of the above themes, are rarely the focus of research. In this section we will address the question of how Muslim women in the West, and in modernizing Islamic countries, practise, experience, and use religion in ways that set them apart from men.

Often, when Islam is discussed publicly in the UK, gender relations and the treatment of women in Muslim communities are used to highlight the potential problems in the relationship between Muslims and the secular mainstream. British Muslims are often frustrated with being labelled as outsiders and with their lifestyles being contrasted with traditional British values.[4] In particular, the status of Muslim women is used as an index of the extent to which Islamic values and behaviour are compatible with the British way of life. In such public discussions, Muslim women are often treated as an internally uniform group. However, British Muslims (or their parents or grandparents) are divided by tradition—Sunni or Shia—and by sectarian preference. They come from the Indian subcontinent, the Middle East, the Far East, and North Africa. They speak an array of different languages and they are further divided by distinctly different economic, educational, and cultural backgrounds.[5]

Such differences structure to a large extent the relative social mobility of Muslim women. Ethnic and cultural background shape women's access to education and employment. For example, a recent study of the impact of marriage on work patterns shows that women of Pakistani and Bangladeshi heritage who were born or raised in the UK are much more likely to be economically active than those who came to the UK as adults, possibly for marriage.[6] The barrier to entering the labour market is not the husband's explicit disapproval on religious grounds, though that is often part of the general community background; rather it is the woman's obligations towards young children and her relative lack of education. Furthermore, that the lives of

Turkish women, or Asian women whose families came to Britain via East Africa, are markedly less conservative than those of women from Bangladesh shows that the cultural mores of the heritage community may be more important than any Islamic rules regarding knowledge and education. Although the numbers of Pakistani and Bangladeshi women entering higher education have increased slightly, their presence at universities is still considered at odds with their cultural background. Consequently, educated women from these backgrounds may be viewed as rebellious and atypical.[7] Ironically, disabilities may be compounded by secular agencies that, with the best intentions, stereotype individuals according to what they assume are Islamic views on appropriate gender roles. For instance, there is a tendency for school careers advisers to steer Muslim girls towards subjects and careers traditionally considered feminine.

Research based on the national UK Labour Force Survey shows that highly educated professional South Asian women reject arranged marriage and instead either co-habit with their partners, or remain single.[8] On the other hand, qualitative studies of British Muslim women argue that education and professional success makes them more, not less, culturally and religiously aware.[9] The key lesson is that Islam, like Christianity, comes in a wide variety of forms. More generally, these discussions demonstrate that social reality is always more complex than we would like it to be. However, people are highly adept at simplifying the world around them for practical purposes, which is why the dominant Western image of Muslim women continues to featured 'heavily veiled, secluded wives, whose lives consist of little more than their homes, their children, and the other women in the harem or immediate kinship circle'.[10]

Despite the rather pessimistic picture of the plight of Muslim women painted by the media, increasing numbers of Western women convert to Islam. The overall numbers of converts, female and male, remains relatively small: between 100,000 and 120,000 at the start of the twenty-first century.[11] According to the British Muslims Monthly Survey, female converts outnumber male converts by approximately two to one; in the USA the ratio is around four to one.[12] Many British women reportedly convert for the purpose of marriage, but even if this is not the driving force behind their conversion most make their initial contact with Islam through interpersonal contact with believers. Female converts cite a variety of reasons for embracing Islam, but one of the

most common factors is their dissatisfaction with the secular expectations placed on British women: a sentiment that echoes the reported
stories of American converts or returnees to evangelical Christianity,
Orthodox Judaism, and conservative Catholicism collected by academ-
ics in the 1990s.[13] They feel pressed to become 'superwomen' who
embody contradictory traits. An ideal woman is expected to be dynamic
yet passive, professionally ambitious yet a perfect wife and mother, and
respectable yet sexually desirable. Although attracted to Islam by its
simple resolution of these dilemmas, female newcomers to Islam seem
to retain the secular view of gender relations: they did not embrace
Islamic attitudes to gender unconditionally. Most do not support radical
moves such as the introduction of the Sharia law in Britain, for example. As one female convert explains: 'I am not impressed by so-called
Muslim countries. They seem to repress women into second-class citizens.'[14] Interestingly, female converts also cite the eclipse of community
and the devaluation of family life in contemporary Britain as reasons
for their defection to Islam (where both are highly valued).[15]

Overall, in 2008 there were at least 800,000 Muslim women in Britain.[16] The post-Second World War arrivals are believed to have been
isolated, homebound, and forced to rely on male family members to
mediate the wider society. While it may be true that these women
remained in the private sphere, their activities extended beyond those
of homemakers. Many worked from home as machinists for the textile
industry, which allowed them to contribute to the household budget.[17]
Like any other migrant group, Pakistani Muslim women in the 1960s
and the 1970s, and Bangladeshi Muslim women in the 1980s, organized informal networks of support, which reduced the sense of alienation in the new social context and served as a resource for dealing with
practicalities of daily life. More significantly, these groups also taught
women Islam through collective readings of the Quran in private
homes. These, in turn, gave rise to women-only Quran study circles.
The fact that they were both female-organized and female-led made
them particularly relevant and empowering. More importantly, they
were soon extended from meetings confined to the domestic sphere to
public spaces, such as community centres and even mosques, which
increased their visibility and social significance. Another permutation
of this kind of activity were the emerging Muslim self-help organizations. They actively encouraged literacy and English-language skills to
enable migrant women's fuller participation in public life. Not only

did these initiatives invite criticism from the males in the community but they also faced practical challenges, such as the lack of funding from the state that allocated priority to men's organizations. More politicized Muslim women's organizations sprang up in the 1980s and 1990s. For example, Women against Fundamentalism was created specifically in reaction to the Rushdie Affair, whereas the Muslim Women Talk campaign aimed at creating a bridge between Muslim women and governmental bodies in the aftermath of the London bombings in 2005.[18] The An-Nisa Society, founded in 1985 in London, is a group run by women 'for the welfare of Muslim families'. The focus is on what we could call the relational aspects of Islam such as community relations, youth, education, and raising awareness of Islam in the UK and beyond.

In theory Islam deems men and women equal, and Muslim women should be able to exercise as much religious agency as men. But the religious lives of Muslim women are shaped to a large extent by the normative patterns specific to their respective heritage communities, and in practice men and women are expected to be pious in different ways. While men are expected to attend the mosque regularly, women are not. If we measured religiosity only by primary religious behaviour, Muslim women would appear far less religious than their Muslim male and their female Christian counterparts. In Britain, women are allowed into mosques, but their presence is problematic. The wish to keep men and women separate made their participation particularly awkward in the 1960s and 1970s, when many mosques were small converted houses. More recent purpose-built mosques have reserved spaces and prayer facilities for women. This allows them to participate in worship but not always to see or hear what goes on in the main prayer hall, which inevitably affects the quality of their religious experience.[19] Women are often assigned small and secluded areas, which gives the impression that female worship is accorded less importance. None the less, Muslim women are not entirely passive in the face of this marginalization. Alternatives to traditional forms of worship—such as religious study circles—have sprung up in the bigger cities in Britain. Many also provide access to women-only sporting facilities, education, and employment opportunities.[20]

Women's participation in mosques has become politicized. Since the 2005 London bombings, the government has promoted the female presence in Muslim places of worship as part of its anti-terrorist strategy.

The *Good Practice Guide for Mosques and Imams* states that 'education and awareness needs to increase amongst Mosque committees and imams on the importance of providing space and facilities for women'.[21] The document implies that this step towards greater gender equality will make the social group in question more civilized.[22] Muslim women are expected to de-radicalize their communities and close the gap between Muslim and British ways of life.[23] The unspoken assumption is that Muslim women welcome such liberation from the male pressure of their culture, which makes them the key to the successful integration of Islamic communities into Britain. Their greater participation in the mosque life would counter the influence of radical Islamism. The interesting feature of this government interest is that it is predicated on a largely untested assumption: that Muslim women are generally more religiously moderate and liberal than their fathers, husbands, brothers, and sons. Sadly we know very little about gender differences in religious beliefs and attitudes within British Islam. Almost all the research on Muslim women in Europe has been based on qualitative studies of small groups. Nationally representative large-scale surveys such as the British Social Attitudes survey have too few members of religious minorities in the sample to be informative, and those surveys that do boost non-Christian numbers generally do not ask detailed and sensitive questions about religious beliefs. The best we can say is what is presented in Table 1.3: that Muslim women in Britain are slightly more likely than Muslim men to claim to be 'practising' their faith.

We do know that, as was the case with conservative Christian households, the Muslim household is defined as a feminine space where women lead in the transmission of cultural and religious values. As religious rituals, such as washing before prayer, then praying before daily activities, are built into daily life, young children learn them from their mothers, many of whom remain at home throughout the day. We also know that Muslim women's participation in the labour market continues to be influenced by men who have both secular and secondary religious behaviour concerns. As the male breadwinner should be able to provide, a working wife undermines her husband. The religious lifestyle issue is proximity to non-family men. In conservative interpretations, women must be shielded from close contact with male strangers. In part this is to prevent sexual impropriety; in part it is because such contact is itself sexual impropriety. Muslim women themselves take these risks into consideration when deciding on appropriate jobs. Working in a shop, for example, is less morally questionable than driving a taxi.[24]

The emphasis on the strict gendered division between private and public is highly relevant with regard to female involvement in mosque activities. The issue of women's presence in mosques becomes even more complex if religious associations are exempt from gender equality laws. In Norway, for instance, this is the case for churches and mosques, but at the same time both institutions belong in the public sphere and should thus be held accountable for their exclusion of women.[25] In Pakistani and Moroccan mosques in Oslo, women have been given separate prayer rooms (fitted with a PA system so they can hear the imam), although in some cases they literally 'earned' their space by selling their jewellery to contribute to the cost of the building.[26] For Pakistani and Moroccan women in Norway, the mosque is an important site of cultural transmission. As migrants living in a non-Islamic state, they need to create ways of reinforcing cultural and religious values. In their home countries they had relatives, neighbours, and communities, which made the process of maintaining religious heritage happen organically. However, in Norway their houses are too small to accommodate large numbers of women for informal prayer and support meetings, so they use public spaces, such as mosques. Ironically, the only way of gaining in-depth knowledge of their own religion and culture is to go outside the home and seek out other women in the same position. Their presence in the mosque enables these women to create leadership positions for themselves by becoming Islamic teachers of children and other women. For example, one of the participants in Line Nygahen Predelli's study of Norwegian mosques 'leads the women's group and is a Quran teacher in her mosque'.[27] This situation is a Muslim version of Brasher's 'gendered sacred canopy' discussed in Chapter 5: Muslim women are part of the mosque and accountable to the imam, but they self-govern and create their own subsystem of religious meaning.

Muslim Women in the Non-Western Context

Outside the UK, new forms of Islamic religiosity are developing in countries where Islam itself is undergoing profound transformations as a result of political and economic shifts. Lara Deeb's study of the emergence of 'public piety' among Lebanese Shia provides an excellent example of Muslim women's role in reinventing religious expression and practice in their communities.[28] Women are central to this process because female morality and religiosity are often understood as representative of (and responsible for) the wider collective. Deeb's study describes a situation where Islam is reformed to fit modern attitudes and ways of life. In this context, public piety implies 'understanding and practising Islam "correctly"; sacrificing one's time, money and life to help others; and supporting the Resistance against Israeli occupation'.[29] Underlying these principles is a strong belief in both spiritual and material progress. By spiritual progress, Lebanese Shias mean the aforementioned public piety and the task of authenticating Islam. Spiritual and material progress go hand in hand, because authenticated Islam stimulates a move away from Islamic tradition, which is seen as backward and ignorant. Practising the modern version of Islam involves engaging consciously with religion and its place in one's life. Direct access and interpretation of the sacred texts enables the process and helps to develop religious knowledge. This form of Islam is intrinsically modern; to its adherents, it is civilized and progressive and has the added bonus of spiritual superiority over the secular West. The concept of public piety, and in particular its highly gendered expression, provides a good example of Muslim women's religiosity that takes place outside the mosque, yet still in public spaces. Visible demonstration of faith validates a woman's 'morality and membership in the community'.[30] This form of religiosity, dictated by the circumstances and the history of the Islamic community in question, puts women at the centre of public displays of piety, which hitherto was a sphere largely reserved for men.

A few words of clarification are necessary here. The Lebanese Shia are a politically and economically marginalized group, caught up in an international conflict and faced with Western notions of what it means to be modern. Deeb's interviewees see religion as inseparable from daily life and public piety, by extension, as proof of their modernity. They distinguish between traditional Islam—automatically performed and taken for granted—and authenticated Islam: a conscious accomplishment that stresses the importance of religious clothing, prayer, and religious activism in the community. For women, this distinction between traditional and modern Islam is crucial. Deeb's women thought their parents and grandparents unquestioningly accepted the inherited religious tradition but had little awareness of true religion. In contrast, their own authenticated Islamic practice is supposedly informed by deep knowledge and understanding.

In the light of all of the above, public piety becomes 'women's jihad'.[31] Shia women admire such religious figures from the past as Sayyida Zaynab, who was the daughter of Ali and granddaughter of Mohammad but more importantly was a woman who fought for God. She exemplifies spiritual strength, and her actions set moral guidelines for pious women. In attempting to follow Zaynab in their daily and seasonal religious practices, women also fulfil gendered social expectations as the ones responsible for the morality of men and children. Shia women in Lebanon face an easier task than Pentecostal women in Colombia, because their husbands are already Muslim. However, they are still the ones who remind their husbands to perform religious duties such as fasting and praying. They set high standards of religious behaviour for themselves and for other women. As the commended form of piety is public, making comparisons becomes relatively straightforward, because one can see what other women are wearing and whether they work in the community to improve other people's lives. Pious women press others to 'conform to Islamic dress code by teasing, comments, pointed storytelling, and praise of the hijab'.[32] Dressing in accordance with the Islamic rule is not half as important as community work, however. Community service has become one of the main channels for expressing piety, to the extent that to some women it is as significant as prayer. Charity work and volunteering are not new in the sense that both constitute forms of *sadaqah* (charitable giving), but in the past acts of charity were performed only on special occasions, such as Ramadan, so they were not always visible. In this sense, the new publicly visible forms of charity operate very much like a sociological experiment in collective monitoring and management of what economists call 'free-riding': enjoying the benefits of communal effort without contributing proportionately. It is relatively simple to determine who contributes on a regular basis and thus fulfils the religious duty at the same time as working towards material progress of their community.

To return to a theme of Chapter 6, women are expected to volunteer largely because they are held to possess the qualities that make them natural carers. Female volunteering is also politicized, because it becomes the feminine way of resisting Israeli occupation while at the same time preserving one's femininity and moral status. Volunteering organizations operate as a second home for many women who gain an opportunity to participate in public life without compromising their domestic duties. Obviously, this puts additional pressure on Shia women, many of whom already perform a double shift of running the household and working. In a sense, their situation is similar to that of Western women who often juggle work and home life. This pressure is magnified further by the fact that Lebanese women display their piety by a successful performance in three spheres: the home, professional work, and volunteering. The better they are at juggling multiple commitments, the more they are publicly seen as praising God. This leads to situations where many women get up extremely early to cook, or stay up late to perform chores they do not have the time for during the day. As Deeb comments, 'faith contributed to tirelessness of many volunteers, as energy and efficiency were viewed as gifts from God'.[33] This emphasis on multi-tasking as a daily expression of piety also affects the negotiation of gender relations. While some husbands feel neglected as a result of their wives' volunteering work, others (especially younger ones) appreciate it, not least because it enhances their own piety by proxy. One woman's husband told her: 'If I'm not doing my duty, what you do should cover both of us.'[34] The notion of women performing piety on behalf of men is by no means restricted to Islam. We find the same gender division of religious labour in Catholicism. In Polish Catholicism, women are chiefly responsible for preserving religious rituals, and female members of the family and local community keep practices alive beyond the institution of the Catholic Church. Polish women attend church and pray much more often than men; they also own more religious paraphernalia and sacred objects: medallions, crosses, and religious icons.

In Lebanon, men do good works simply by facilitating women's volunteering. Young women often agree to marriage on the condition that they continue to volunteer, and more and more men agree. While raising awareness of the importance of community work among men appears successful on the whole, men do not entirely believe that women could run a voluntary association. As a female volunteer said: 'They think that when women gather we just gossip or fight.'[35] Traditionally, femininity tends to be associated with irrationality and laziness in the eyes of Lebanese men. But female volunteers see personal self-improvement coupled with community work as the form of religiosity that set them apart from traditional Lebanese women. They put a lot of energy into empowering poor women through education, so that the latter feel more at ease in the public sphere and are able to participate more fully in public life, without compromising their femininity or piety.

The way in which these women organize their lives very much resembles the logic of the Protestant ethic and its emphasis of living one's life entirely for the glory of God. The mechanism of social scrutiny that women engage in through gossip, judgement, and criticism of other women ensures compliance to the model of public piety and also creates the kind of anxiety that afflicted the Puritans. The women who manage to multi-task are nicknamed 'sisters-superwomen'. Their success is attributed mainly to the fact that they limit 'useless' pursuits such as socializing. Thus piety at home and in the public sphere is often achieved through personal sacrifice, which in turn enhances its value in the eyes of others. Pious women claim that, if understood and applied correctly by men, the authenticated version of Islam could solve many problems caused by patriarchy. To them, being a good Muslim means participating in all spheres of life without being judged on the basis of their gender. These women are not interested in liberating themselves individually but are more concerned with being able to practise a 'pious and moral lifestyle', unobstructed by patriarchal norms.[36] The wider importance of women's role in the Shia community is that women's material and spiritual progress testifies to the emergence of the Shia modern religiosity, and, what is more, it is indispensable to it.[37] Perhaps it is this sort of communal and public religiosity coupled with the sense of religious responsibility in pioneering a new form of Islamic religiosity that motivates such eager and committed religious involvement on the part of Shia women.

Women Reinterpreting Religion

We would like to pick up briefly a point we made in Chapter 5 regarding women in Western societies who opt for particularly conservative versions of their faith. We suggested that such choices are, somewhat ironically, a consequence of the freedom permitted by a nominally secular, liberal, and individualistic culture. This idea also applies to any discussion of migrant Muslim women's religiosity in the West.

Regardless of the degree of assimilation into, or interaction with, the host society, these women are sooner or later exposed to non-Muslim codes of behaviour in the workplace, education, or the media. Unless a group chooses to protect their culture and values and isolate itself in the manner of Exclusive Brethren, or the Amish, its members will inevitably come into contact with norms and values that differ from, or directly contradict, their own. Several Muslim feminists, in a similar way to feminist Christian theologians, have mapped the strategies of textual interpretation that Muslim women may and do apply in their reading of the Quran.[38] Women can make Islam their own by a selective and highly critical reading of the text. Our point is that such practices are possible for Muslim women who live in secular countries, but the story is much more ambiguous if we look at Iran, Afghanistan, or Saudi Arabia. A Catholic girl, brought up in a strongly religious household in a culture where Catholicism is constantly reinforced as the only valid religion and the Bible is interpreted by priests, is unlikely to think her way out of the dominant religious discourse without being exposed to alternatives. Likewise, a Muslim woman in an Afghan village is in no position to decide to study the Quran and reinterpret the *hadiths* for the purpose of self-development. Even if the Taliban were not actively constraining schooling for girls, most Afghanis are so thoroughly socialized into a very traditional Islam that, even if the idea of adapting Islam enters her universe of meaning, it will appear inappropriate or blasphemous. A flexible attitude to piety is most likely to emerge in the context of religious diversity or secularity.

A helpful example here is provided by Raana Bokhari's study of Gujarati Sunni Muslim women in Leicester, which focuses on their engagement with *Bihishti Zewar* (*Heavenly Ornaments*), a nineteenth-century didactic manual and one of the seminal texts in reformist Islam.[39] The book was originally intended for upper-class Muslim women in India, but subsequently the text was extended to include men and Muslims elsewhere. It is now a key textbook in the Gujarati-run *madrassahs* for girls in England. The female participants in the study are members of the Muslim Gujarati community in Leicester, which Bokhari describes as 'self-sufficient' in terms of community structures, yet 'a mix of both British and Indian' in terms of cultural influence.[40] As it stands, *Bihishti Zewar* would not be seen as emancipatory by feminist scholars. Its author, Ashraf Ali Thanawi, describes women as idle, talkative, messy, disorganized, and out of control. However, he also emphasizes women's moral equality with men.[41] The key aspect of this text is its emphasis on religious reform as detached from the state and as individually monitored self-improvement. The author's aim was to furnish Muslim women with Islamic knowledge. The prescriptions in the text concern women's participation in the public sphere. Thanawi believed that women had no place in the mosque, or any other public space, and should refrain from leaving home unless absolutely necessary. The text was written in the period when India was under the British rule, and many reacted against the colonial power by engaging in a search for a true Indian identity by means of stressing religious observance.[42] The Deobandi School was at the forefront of the resistance to the British Raj in their work towards empowering Muslims through their own tradition. The small town of Deoband became known as divinely authenticated by the Prophet and a place where an empowering and reformist version of Islam was taught. This marked Muslims as separate from, and morally superior to, the British.

In the Gujarati community, women veil completely by covering their hands, feet, and face. As Bokhari herself admits, it seems to an outsider that these women are 'silent and removed from the public'.[43] All the female interviewees studied *Bihishti Zewar*, but their attitudes and use of the text varied greatly. Some used it as a practical manual for everyday matters, but not as a source of spiritual knowledge. Others criticized it for its lack of relevance to Muslim women's lives in Britain. Others still challenged the advice on women's withdrawal from the public sphere. Aisha said: 'we forget that when Thanawi was writing, the homes were buzzing with life and women weren't isolated. But in England, you'd be cut off if you stayed at home.' Another woman, Salima, commented:

on the bits about your religion, I think he's very good, but on women, he's derogatory... Things have to be applicable in your environment. Like it's normal to hold hands with your husband in England when you're out and about, but not in India. So I leave bits out... You can't live according to the Indian subculture 100 years ago.

The text is used for practical purposes but it does not inform women's spirituality. Salima's spiritual life was informed by a careful selection of elements compatible with modern times and her cultural location. She said: 'we can access more information now... Now you know you can question things...'.[44] The women also proposed their

own distinct definitions of public space. For some, public meant anywhere outside the home, while for others it depended on other people
being present. For example, the sheer presence of male strangers marked
the gathering as public space. Overall, the Gujarati women emphasized
the usefulness of ritual chapters over cultural requirements aimed at
female Muslims. *Bihishti Zewar* is used by the Gujarati community as an
expression of collective identity, but the women in the study adjust
their use of it to the context and redefine the notions of spirituality and
public space for themselves while still using the traditional text.

This example is crucial, because it demonstrates a version of creative
interpretation that is also commonplace among Christian women in
the West. In the USA, evangelical women adhere to conservative religiously mandated social mores while actually leading liberated lives,
complete with careers and egalitarian marriages. Modernity enables
them to engage in reinterpretation and re-evaluation of nominally
conservative religious resources. Under the right circumstances,
Muslim women act in the same way.

Veiling and Visibility

We do not wish to reproduce the debate on veiling that has already
been covered in great detail elsewhere.[45] None the less, as dress forms
a crucial tool for asserting and displaying religious affiliation as well as
the degree of piety among Muslim women, we wish to draw attention
briefly to the ways in which women use dress to 'do religion' in different cultural contexts. In some, Islam is the dominant religion, while in
others it is one of many. In some contexts adopting the veil is a choice,
in others it is not. The key point is that, when women are in a position
where they can exercise a choice, their actions tell us a lot about their
attitude to religiosity; it is a public statement about the place and relative importance of religion in their lives.

The question of veiling needs to be discussed in the context of
migration. Several studies of young Muslim women in Britain clearly
show that the third generation of migrants face a very different social
reality from the one their parents did. Young Muslim women prioritize
religious over ethnic identity in order to validate and legitimize the
women's claims of Islam.[46] These strategies, however, can be employed
only by the middle and upper classes, and second- or third-generation

UK-educated migrants. A lot of young Muslim women know more about Islam than their parents.[47]

Approaches to religious dress vary drastically among young Muslims, and attitude shifts are often dictated by socio-political events. A small minority deliberately adopt a conservative version of their parents' religious dress in order to make a point about their religion and heritage. Their choices are not always welcomed by the parents and grandparents, who prefer a more accommodating attitude to the surrounding society. Young women who opt for the *niqab*, for example, risk criticism from their family members and risk reducing their chances of finding a husband in the Muslim community.[48] Here, we are faced yet again with the issue of visibility. For some Muslim women in the West, the act of displaying their religion through everyday attire amounts to a spiritual and a political statement, albeit one that potentially exposes them to hostility and aggression in the public sphere. Unlike their parents and grandparents, these women feel they have to preserve their religion and cultural heritage through dress. Muslim girls as young as 16 can be aware of the danger of losing their religion and culture. 'If we're not good at it ourselves, how are we going to teach children?', one teenager commented.[49] In a country where Islam is a minority religion, religious practice needs to be externalized in order to be meaningful. For Muslim women living in Sweden, for example, the Swedish insistence on religion being private and publicly invisible is amusing and strange. As Sadia, the chair of the Young Muslims' association in Stockholm, summed it up: 'but what good is faith... if you cannot see it?'[50] Similarly, some young Muslim women in Britain express their piety by wearing the *hijab*: 'I was passionate about being a Muslim and I wanted people to see me as a Muslim.'[51] That passion often arises when women realize for the first time the symbolism of veiling for Muslim identity. An Australian medical doctor recalls donning the veil after her pilgrimage to Mecca in the late 1980s.[52]

While veiling enables women in the West to display their religion publicly, in other parts of the world opting for explicitly religious clothing may signify 'a quest for individual and societal moral renewal'.[53] The leaders in such moral renewals tend to come from upper-middle-class, economically privileged backgrounds, but the bulk of the followers are urban middle- and lower-middle classes. In Mali, Muslim women set up Quran study groups and women-only worship circles. Membership in such groups and donning the veil qualifies these women as real Muslims. Appropriate religious clothing not only expresses but also achieves modesty, femininity, and religious virtue.

The subject of morality and dress points to one universal feature that can be found in all religions. All faiths grapple with the issues of sex and sexuality, and in the majority of cases there is a strong tendency to control this aspect of human life. As most religions remain strongly patriarchal, women are subject to stricter sexual control than men. Among other things, secularization weakens religion's control of public issues, such as politics, economy, and law. The churches play little or no role in influencing governmental decisions in the West. Likewise, Muslims living in the West are less concerned with distinctive Muslim teachings on such macro issues as politics or the economy. However, the private sphere of family and intimate relations is the last field that religions give up. It is also a powerful one, because it touches on the most intimate and sensitive aspects of people's lives. This is why gender segregation and control of female sexuality are such integral elements of any fundamentalist agenda. As Martin Riesebrodt demonstrates, the need to monitor and domesticate women's sexuality was central to the rise of both Protestant fundamentalism in the 1920s and Iranian Islamic fundamentalism in the 1980s. In New York and Tehran fundamentalists obsessed about the detrimental effects of public display of the female body on male morality. Both regarded women as temptresses who were responsible for men's sexuality.[54] When women are cast as moral agents whose behaviour testifies to their own and men's religiosity, they are pressed into sexually conservative behaviour that is associated with greater religiosity. John R. Straton, a leading New York Baptist in the late nineteenth century, was concerned with sexual morality to the point that he suggested a national costume for American women to protect modesty and propriety.[55] Thus we have another layer of gendered religious division of labour: women maintain religiously mandated conservative sexual mores. We will return to this point while discussing Orthodox Jewish rules with regard to gender and prayer.

Jewish Women and Rituals: Doing the Right Thing

Like Islam, Judaism is an orthoprax religion that places great importance on secondary religious behaviour and very different requirements on men and women. For example, the fact that Jewish men report greater synagogue attendance than women tells us little about overall gender differences in religiosity.[56] Worldwide, Jewish women score either the same or lower than men on all markers of religiosity—attendance, denominational loyalty, belief in God, belief in life after death—except for prayer. However, the lower levels of primary religious behaviour will usually be more than compensated for by extensive secondary religious behaviour. For the women concerned, religion frequently constitutes an essential part of their daily routine, so they do not necessarily separate the sacred from the profane in the same way that men do. In the case of Jewish women, it is worth looking at what they define as religious practices central to their lives.

In Judaism, food is infused with particular religious significance. Its selection and preparation are organized strictly around religious principles and prescriptions. Historically, women were solely responsible for ensuring that the family meals were kosher and carried the burden of preparing food for the Sabbath. Cooking and feeding people, both family members and guests, is an extension of caring practices, but, more generally, it provides a sense of security and orderliness in the relationship with the supernatural. In Judaism, in particular, the role of food and women in the creation and maintenance of Jewish identity was and continues to be so important that it has been labelled 'kitchen Judaism' by some writers.[57] Hence, for example, for elderly Jewish women in Jerusalem feeding poor people, the food they cooked was 'the greatest *religious* act that a woman (not a man) can perform'.[58] Susan Sered illustrates the superiority of the feminine way of expressing religiosity with a story that she heard from a number of those she studied. A rabbi and his wife both helped a poor family on a daily basis, but, while he gave them money, she cooked for them. The women argued that the wife was more righteous, and thus religious, because homeless people would not have the kitchen to cook the food they bought in, so the rabbi's charity was useless. These women fed those in need because 'God wants them to'.[59] The act expresses religiosity in the way that enhances their personal relationship with God. Making sure that the food is handled in the kosher manner performs the same religious function for these women. Cooking and handling food in accordance with religious rules are laborious tasks and carry heavy responsibility. Moreover, food serves as a tool for expressing religious sentiments and knowledge through ritual. Sered's research participants observed religious holidays differently from men. For men, the Sabbath meant mainly rest, prayer, and religious study; for women, it meant preparing and then serving food to others. The gendered division of labour was noticeable in the synagogue, where the women's gallery was deserted on Friday nights. Similarly, on Saturday mornings women would stay behind to prepare the meal to be served after their husbands' return from synagogue. The only females who could take time out of the Sabbath preparations were widows and unmarried girls.[60] These Jewish women saw their culinary preparations as central to religious holidays because of the special role they played in them. Not only did they have the expertise to carry out the food rituals, but they also considered themselves the proper guardians of law and tradition who wielded the creative power over religious customs. Their husbands were mere participants; they were the ones who made things happen.[61] Interestingly, they also had a very clear definition of what constitutes a religious woman. They understood proper religiosity as moral behaviour in relationships with other people: practising charity, honesty, help, and kindness. A Jewish man may be pious, pray, study the Torah, and be wise, but he can still be a bad person and hurt others. But, for women, religiosity does not stop at the door of the synagogue but is expressed through and defined by appropriate interpersonal conduct.[62]

Some religious customs and rituals can be even more hidden from view and thus more open to manipulation, which complicates the question of the degree of women's religiosity even further. Probably one of the most intimate, invasive, and controversial rules derived from Talmud concerns rituals around menstruation. *Niddah* refers to the laws of ritual purity and immersion, and the term designates the state of impurity a woman remains in for the five days of menstrual flow and seven days afterwards.[63] Sexual intercourse and physical closeness between husband and wife are prohibited during that time. On the final day, the woman goes to the *mikveh* (a 'purification pool'), where she ritualistically cleanses herself in order to be able to resume sexual relations with her husband. Jewish feminists deem the practice oppressive and degrading for women, but women's own interpretation and use of the ritual vary wildly. Certainly, observance of *niddah* is a religious practice fraught with issues for Orthodox Jewish women in modern societies. Coupled with the use of contraception, it can cause problems for observant women. However, it is important to note that, despite potentially being an invasive ritual, *niddah* also allows Orthodox

Jewish women to exercise choice within both their marriage and their religious practice. The *halakhic* ban on physical contact with the husband, the compulsory internal checks to determine whether *niddah* is over, and the requirement to seek advice from a rabbi all add up to the source of frustration, anger, and suffocation for many women. Those women who find the *niddah* profoundly problematic do not leave their religious tradition but try to find ways of circumventing it by, for example, seeking out a lenient rabbi, or skipping rabbinic advice altogether. Many others find this religious obligation beneficial and an intrinsic part of their religious lifestyle, albeit one that does not necessarily make sense. One woman explained that, having taken on the laws upon marriage, she felt 'a great amount of happiness because I knew I was doing the right thing'.[64] Moreover, unlike other religious customs and rituals, *niddah* is women's responsibility, and it is through observing it properly that Jewish women comply with the religious law and act as religious agents. The checks are between them and God—nobody else knows the truth, which makes personal piety all the more important and real. Perhaps the most empowering element of *niddah* for Orthodox Jewish women is that it gives them a legitimate reason to suspend sexual relations with their husbands. The law creates a space for women that is religiously sanctioned and removes the guilt aspect of refusing to have sex but also enhances the quality of the marriage when the couple are reunited. Extrapolating from this, some women would delay their visit to the *mikveh* in order to exercise sexual power, or simply as a form of birth control. As the woman is entirely in charge of this religious custom, she can use it in order to exercise control over her and her husband's sexuality. In other words, in religions where practices encompass and govern all aspects of everyday lives, women's piety can sometimes be put to work for practical purposes, even though the driving force is a patriarchal religious custom.

Conclusion

At first sight, Islam and Judaism seem to threaten our starting assumption that women generally are more religious than men. As our tentative explanations of the gender gap are social rather than biological (or the biological is heavily filtered through social roles and expectations) and therefore permit cultural variation, we do not need all women in

all societies to be more religious than men. But, given the generality of
the causes we have so far advanced—women's more intimate and frequent association with birth, illness, and death; women's concern for
the health of the body; women's responsibility for child-rearing and
early education, the expectation that women will be more caring than
men—even our approach would be threatened by the existence of
large religious cultures in which men were patently more pious than
women.

Fortunately this is not what we find in Islamic and Jewish societies.
The key is the difference between orthodox and orthoprax religions.
In the latter, religiosity is expressed much more in secondary religious
behaviour—in actively supporting religiously mandated rules for food
preparation and consumption and in bearing the burden of sexual
propriety, for example—than in such elements of primary religious
behaviour as attending temple or mosque. It is too broad a topic to
explore fully here, but one consequence of the spread of the individualism and egalitarianism inherent in modernization is the challenge to
the traditionalism of orthoprax religion. One response to that challenge is to scale back the plethora of secondary religious behaviour
requirements and to shift attention to the other three facets of religion.
An example of that is liberal Judaism in the United States, which in
many respects is now very similar to a mainstream Protestant denomination. Another response to modernization is rejection, but that rejection contains elements of what it rejects. Fundamentalism is generally
less a demand to return to the religious forms of the past (which are
often criticized as being ritualistic in the wrong sense) than a radical
reworking of the past that, like the European Protestant Reformation
of the sixteenth century, requires individuals actively to live their faith
rather than to go through the motions and rely on the overall religiosity of the community. Women in orthoprax religions, especially those
who now find themselves in largely secular societies, have to find new
ways of living out their faith, and in this chapter we have discussed a
few such examples.

One theme of the chapter that has consequences for our primary
question is the expectation that women will be responsible for the
spiritual well-being of men. In some religious cultures—pre-Reformation Christianity, for example—religious merit that was earned by
such primary religious acts as saying prayers could be 'transferred' from
the godly to the ungodly. In Islam and Judaism, women support men's

religiosity through their responsibility for the plethora of secondary religious requirements: the religious elements of everyday life. The word 'sacrifice' comes to mind. It is especially appropriate for the burden of ensuring sexual continence. It is women whose freedom of movement, dress, and association is curtailed in order to prevent men being tempted into sin. It would be unfair to assume that pious women invariably suffer as a result of their religiously motivated actions. None the less, it is clear that, while women strive for the right to practise religion in ways that maximize their enjoyment of the sacred, they often do so on behalf of others, less spiritually capable or less eager to perform their religious obligations.

9
Secularization

Introduction

If we have achieved nothing else, we have demonstrated the difficulty of answering what seemed at the start to be a simple question. Much of the complexity stems from the fact that we are exploring a changing relationship between two phenomena that have themselves been changing. The power of religious institutions and the nature of religious belief and ritual vary with time and place, as do the social consequences of gender. Even the most physical aspect of being female is hardly a given. Members of communitarian sects such as the Amish and the Hutterites marry young, do nothing to restrict fertility, and have large families. Among their American neighbours, it is now common for women to avoid pregnancy altogether, to give birth to their first child late in life, or to give birth to few children. Same biology: different biological consequences. In addition, what any culture makes of childbirth varies enormously. We should not suppose parents of the eighteenth century to be entirely heartless, but there is a discernible difference in the emotional energy that parents invest in their offspring when pregnancy is common but survival rates are low and in our circumstances of low fertility and high survival rates. And, beyond behaviour and attitudes related to child-bearing and child-rearing, there are very obviously large social differences in the rights, responsibilities, and roles attached to gender.

All that is commonplace. What should be noted for our purposes of trying to explain apparent differences in male and female attitudes to religion is that both ends of our causal connection—being female and being religious—have been markedly altered by modernization. The rise of the industrial liberal democracies of the West has been accompanied by systematic, regular, and thus far unreversed changes in both the status of women and the nature and status of religion.

This chapter presents a brief explanation of secularization: the decline in the power, prestige, and popularity of religion in the vast majority of modern industrial liberal democratic societies of the West. It will demonstrate that, although the causes of that decline are universal, the impact is uneven, because the social forces in question bear unevenly on different social categories. This is, of course, a gross simplification that will offend the historians of any particular time and place, but it is not misleading. In essence we will divide the life-world into public and private spheres and argue that the effects of secularization are felt first in the public sphere—that is, they are felt earlier and more strongly by men than by women.[1]

Feminist Scholarship and Male Bias

Before we present our summary explanation of secularization, we will address and rebut a dull but important argument about the effects of male chauvinist bias on sociological treatments of secularization. Feminist scholarship has made an important contribution to the social sciences by pointing out that women's lives often differ from those of men, that such differences have been systematically neglected in the social sciences, and that paying attention to them may improve our understanding. However, accepting those claims leaves the question of what attitude we should adopt to 'pre-feminist' explanations of social phenomena. Should we dismiss Weber and Durkheim because they failed to ask all the right questions? Some scholars believe the secularization paradigm to be misleading because its main progenitors did not attend to gender differences. For example, an American feminist glosses the secularization theory of religious change as follows:

The story, generated by elite white European male scholars tells their understanding of the displacement of powerful state churches by secular authorities in the public realm, with a subsequent loss of status for the men who continued to lead those churches at all levels, and at the same time a migration of men like themselves out of the churches...the secularization story is told from the vantage point of the unmarked mainstream, whose religion is mapped onto the dominant culture...in telling the story of secularization in terms of decline, we tell a partial story of elite white men.[2]

This is a complex claim. By suggesting that 'telling the story of secularization in terms of decline' is just one option among many, it rejects the fact of secularization. It also offers an explanation of why male sociologists have got it wrong.

It is certainly true, as we have argued at length elsewhere, that secularization is much more than just decline.[3] But the fact of decline is unarguable. However we measure it, every index of interest in, and the power of, religion in the industrial liberal democracies of the West shows decline. Even in the USA, where decline started much later than in Europe, regular churchgoing is down from 40 per cent of the population in the 1950s to around 20 per cent in 2010. But, quite independently of that, the explanation of why commentators got it wrong (if indeed they did) is unconvincing. That Marx, Weber, and Durkheim were white Europeans is beyond contest, although, as almost all Europeans of their era were white, their colour is unremarkable. That they were part of the elite is contentious. That their views are in some sense explained by their loss of status and that the secularization paradigm is solely or even primarily the work of members of dominant churches is patently false. Many church leaders noted and were concerned about the decline of their churches, but that tells us nothing about sociological commentators on secularization.

If one was really interested in developing a biographical treatment of the sociology of secularization, one would better begin by noting the prevalence of outsiders, often émigrés and displaced persons, who had an awkward and marginal relationship to power. Such leading lights of the Scottish Enlightenment as Adam Smith, David Hume, and Adam Ferguson were at best lower middle class. Lords Monboddo and Kames were not aristocrats; they were self-made lawyers who acquired their apparently aristocratic titles on being raised to a particular level in the court system. Max Weber was wealthy, but his liberal politics and his periodic bouts of mental illness made him a somewhat marginal figure in German public life. Karl Marx was the son of a Jewish convert who spent most of his life in exile and who was marginalized both by his politics and by his poverty. Émile Durkheim was also by origins an outsider: his family were Jews. The early part of his career was precarious, and he ended his days marginalized in a right-wing France by his liberal opinions.

The elite and establishment depiction becomes even less sustainable if one moves to the post-1945 contributors to the secularization paradigm. Ernest Gellner was born in Paris to a middle-class Jewish family from Bohemia: people whose state, the Austro-Hungarian Empire, had been dissolved in 1918. He was educated in Prague, in an English-language school, before his family moved to England. He studied at Oxford but fought with a Czech emigré unit when he joined the army and after the war returned to Prague to study before being again made stateless by the Communist takeover. David Martin's father was a taxi driver, and the origins of Bryan Wilson, Roy Wallis, and James Beckford were equally humble. Even the male part of the explanation is true only for that period of European academic life when most scholars of every discipline were male. And the depiction of the consequences of social background for the key ideas is as inaccurate as the account of social background. Some versions of the secularization story may be 'told from the vantage point of the unmarked mainstream', but, as we will see, an important part of the explanation of secularization concerns the impact of subordinate and peripheral religious movements arguing against the privileges of established churches.

However interesting this soap opera treatment of the history of sociology might be, it is irrelevant. What features of their biography, social or idiosyncratic, led Adam Ferguson to his essay on the *Origins of Civil Society* or Karl Marx to his *A Contribution to the Critique of Hegel's Philosophy of Right* tell us nothing about whether their observations are accurate and their conclusions sound. What matters is the clarity of arguments and the quality of the evidence that can be adduced for and against them. Unless we believe that social science is unusually vulnerable to distortion by the interests of its promoters, we need think no worse of it for having male progenitors than we do of physics or trigonometry.

One critic of the secularization paradigm has asserted that 'the gender-blind approach which has long characterised the sociology of religion not only ignores gendered difference but assumes the masculine point of view is normative'. She adds: 'Because they take the male experience to be normative, the narratives of secularisation under discussion assume that modern men and women are affected in exactly the same way.'[4] Neither of these assertions is necessarily true, and the use of 'normative' is misleading. As we are not doing moral philosophy, norms (in the sense of rules for proper behaviour) are irrelevant. What matters is the 'normal' in the statistical sense, and, in trying to estimate how influential or popular religion was in England in 1800 as compared to 2000, a 'point of view', masculine or otherwise, is neither here nor there. Historians may argue about the accuracy and validity of the 1851 Census of Religious Worship, but we see no evidence that female and male historians differ systematically in their treatment of that or related sources.

Rather than take the fact that Weber, Durkheim, and others often wrote in generalities that paid little attention to differences of gender (or of class and region and ethnicity) as proof that their core ideas are mistaken, we will sketch the secularization paradigm and demonstrate not only that it is quite compatible with an appreciation of gender as an important social variable, but also that it predicts the gender differences in religiosity that we seek to explain.

Explaining Secularization

We do not need to suppose that the agricultural feudal societies of Europe in the Middle Ages were entirely populated by observant well-informed Christians to appreciate that there has been a considerable decline in the power, popularity, and persuasiveness of religion and that this change, which we conventionally call secularization, has some non-accidental relationship with modernization. This view is generally more popular with European scholars, where the decline of religion has been more rapid, than it is with Americans, but even in the United States there has been a marked decline in the power of religious institutions and in popular involvement in the churches. Furthermore, even many US critics of the secularization paradigm accept the validity of those of its elements concerned with the public status and coercive power of religion.[5]

The primary purpose of the secularization paradigm is to identify those elements of modernization that accidentally and inadvertently combine to weaken the power of religious institutions and to create the social space for indifference to religious beliefs. Our starting point for understanding modernization is the shift from animate to inanimate forms of productive power. The medieval ploughboy used an ox and his own strength; the modern farmer directs a machine powered by fossil fuels. The increasing use of inanimate sources of power made the societies of the West increasingly wealthy. As they prospered, they became more complex, and their structures changed in ways that had implications for religion.

Structural Differentiation and the Marginalizing of Religion

One element of modernization is structural or functional differentiation. Society and social life fragment as specialized roles and institutions are created to handle specific features or functions previously combined in one role or institution.[6] The family was once a unit of production as well as the institution through which society was reproduced. With industrialization, economic activity became divorced from the home. It also became increasingly informed by its own values. At work we are supposed to be rational, instrumental, and pragmatic. We are also supposed to be universalistic: to treat customers alike, paying attention only to the matter in hand. The private sphere, by contrast, is taken to be expressive, indulgent, and emotional. We would criticize as discriminatory the welfare clerk who favoured his co-religionists, but we would be equally critical if he treated his own children no differently from other children.

There are many consequences of functional differentiation and increased specialization. For religion, the primary one is the church's loss of functions to secular institutions. Education, health care, welfare, and social control either have become the preserve of new secular institutions or, if religious bodies continue to provide them, are increasingly subject to secular norms and standards. This has two secularizing effects. The narrowing of activities reduces the status of religious institutions and it reduces their reach, so that, irrespective of their orientation to religion, people simply have less contact with the churches and are thus less subject to religious influence. The modern US megachurch with its array of ancillary social activities is an attempt to regain some of that relevance, but it differs from its pre-modern ancestor in offering what are essentially optional leisure activities.

Social Differentiation

As society fragments, so do the people. The precise mechanics are complex, and some of the effects are paradoxical. Economic growth, especially in the industrialization phase when the large 'manufactory' displaced the craft workshop, created an ever-greater range of occupation and life situations that challenged the fixity of hierarchy on which feudal societies depended. In feudal societies, masters and servants lived cheek by jowl. Such proximity was possible because the gentry had no fear that the lower orders would get ideas 'above their station'. They had sufficient confidence in the principle of hierarchy for different grades of food to be served to people of different status at the same table. As class structures become more fluid and complex, and as the idea of hereditary inequality becomes more difficult to defend, we see geographical distance increasingly replacing social distance. As confidence in the division of people into 'estates' or 'stations' wanes, together-but-patently-unequal is replaced as the model of social organization by theoretically-equal-but-separate. Increased literal distance between status groups is accompanied by increased clustering of people of similar status.[7] This exaggerates, of course, but one can picture an evolution from an economy where every family makes its own clothes, to one where every village has its tailor, to one where clothes are made by large numbers of workers in a factory.

The details need not concern us beyond the general observation that the plausibility of a single moral universe in which all people have a place depends on the social structure being stable. With new social roles and increasing social mobility, communal conceptions of the moral and supernatural order fragmented. As classes became more distinct, they became more distinctive. The consequences for religion depend on whether the dominant tradition of Christianity is Protestant or Catholic. Martin noted a major effect of the Reformation when he wrote that 'the logic of Protestantism is clearly in favour of the voluntary principle, to a degree that eventually makes it sociologically unrealistic'.[8] Belief-systems differ greatly in their propensity to fragment. The Catholic Church claims that Christ's authority was passed to Peter and then fixed in the office of Pope. It claims control of access to salvation and the right to decide disputes about God's will. If those claims are accepted, the Church is relatively immune to fission. As to depart from Rome goes to the heart of what you believe as a Catholic, such departures are difficult. Tensions are sublimated until they provoke extreme upheavals, such as the French Revolution. Thus, as Catholic countries modernized, they split into the religious and the secular: so in the twentieth century Italy, Spain, and France had conservative Catholics traditions and powerful Communist parties.

Protestantism was vulnerable to schism because it rejected institutional mechanisms to settle disputes. Asserting that everyone can equally well discern God's will invited schism. Tradition, habit, respect for learning, or admiration for piety provide some cohesion and thus restrain division, but they do not prevent it. The Reformation produced not one church purified and strengthened but competing perspectives and organizations, which map roughly on to the material circumstances of those who are attracted to them. The great pyramid of pope, bishops, priests, and laity both mirrored and justified the social pyramid of king, nobles, gentry, and peasants. Independent small farmers, skilled workers coming together in craft guilds, or the rising business class preferred a more democratic religion; hence their attraction to such Protestant sects as the Presbyterians, Baptists, and Quakers. We will return to the consequences of religious diversity shortly.

The Rise of Individualism

One of the master features of modernization, visible in a great many changes, is the growing importance of the individual as against the organic community. The Reformation was not the only source of individualism, but it gave it a powerful boost. The pre-Reformation Christian Church represented the entire people to God, and its officials did religious work on behalf of the population at large. It was possible for religious merit to be transferred from the godly to the less godly. Prayers could be said for the dead. The wealthy left large sums of money to fund post-mortem religious activity on their behalf, but even the most humble left what they could to fund others to pray for their souls. By removing the special status of the priesthood and the possibility that religious merit could be transferred, the Protestant Reformers asserted what was implicit in early Christianity: that we each had to answer for ourselves to God. That is, we were all equal in the eyes of God. That equality initially lay in our sinfulness and our responsibilities, but the idea could not indefinitely be confined to duty. Equal obligations eventually became equal rights.

If the sixteenth-century Reformation inadvertently encouraged individualism by making salvation a personal rather than a communal property, we need to explain why the egalitarian notion that we are all in some sense equal remained confined for so long to the narrow field of salvation. The explanation lies in the increasing complexity of social relations. Economic development brought change and the expectation of further change. And it brought occupational mobility. As it became more common for people to better themselves, it also become more common for them to think better of themselves. However badly paid, the industrial worker did not see himself as a serf.[9] The serf occupied just one role in an all-embracing hierarchy and that role shaped his entire life. A tin-miner in Cornwall in 1800 might be oppressed at work, but in the late evening and on Sunday he could change clothes and persona to become a Baptist preacher: a man of prestige. Such alternation marks a crucial change. As social status became more task-specific, it became possible for people to occupy different positions in different hierarchies.[10] That in turn made it possible to distinguish between social roles and the people who filled them. Roles could still be ranked and accorded very different degrees of power or status, but the people behind the roles could be seen as in some sense equal. As we can see in the slow expansion of the franchise, powerful interests constrained the egalitarian ideal: the right to a say in how one was governed spread only slowly from the grandest landowners to male householders to all adult men and eventually to all adults. In racially divided societies, there was a further lag in accepting that all races should be accorded the same rights, but this does not change the fundamental point that modernization was accompanied by an increasingly egalitarian individualistic ethos.

Far more could be said about this, but individualism is a vital part of the secularization story because it eventually became the right to choose what Gods to worship and that freedom had a powerfully corrosive effect on the dominant faith. Individual liberty could produce waves of religious revival as enthusiastic personal commitment replaced dull conformity, but it also opened the way for indifference and secularity.

The Decline of Community

Societalization is the term Bryan Wilson gives to the way in which 'life is increasingly enmeshed and organized, not locally but societally'.[11] If social differentiation and individualism are blows to small-scale communities from below, societalization is the attack from above. Close-knit, integrated, communities gradually lost power and presence to large-scale industrial and commercial enterprises, to modern states coordinated through massive, impersonal bureaucracies, and to cities. This is the classic community-to-society transition delineated by Ferdinand Tönnies.[12]

The effects of this for religion are sometimes compressed into the proposition that the move from the country to the town and the city was accompanied by a decline in piety. In a longer version of this story we would here discuss the many exceptions to the proposition and note the ways in which cities allowed and encouraged new forms of voluntary association religion, but there is a basic truth in the rural–urban contrast.[13] There is a crucial difference between a single religious culture that is so stable and reinforced in so many ways that it is taken for granted and one that is knowingly chosen from a variety of alternatives. The parish church of the Middle Ages baptized, christened, confirmed, married, and buried all the villagers. Its calendar of services mapped on to the seasons. It celebrated and legitimated local life. In turn, the world view it represented drew strength from being frequently reaffirmed by the local people. In 1898 almost everyone in the rural Aberdeenshire village of Daviot celebrated the harvest by bringing tokens of their produce to the church. In 1998, a very small number of people in the village (only one of them a farmer) celebrated by bringing to the church vegetables and tinned goods (many of foreign provenance) bought in a supermarket that is itself part of a multinational combine. Instead of celebrating the harvest, the service thanked God for all his creation. Broadening the symbolism of the celebration solved the problem of relevance but at the cost of direct contact with the lives of those involved. When the all-embracing community of like-situated people working and playing together gives way to the dormitory town or suburb, there is little left in common to celebrate. There is also little persuasive power. The notion of community is now often romanticized so that its coercive elements are forgotten, but coercion—formal and informal—is essential to the maintenance of belief-systems. The medieval parish church rewarded conformity (by, for example, distributing alms to the deserving poor) and punished dissent (for example, by requiring sexual deviants publically to confess their sins), but equally as important was the low-level everyday coercion of gossip and critical judgement.

The increasing fragmentation of society and the decline of the community reduced the plausibility of any single overarching moral and religious system and thus allowed competing religions. While they may have had much to say to private experience, they could have little connection to the performance of social roles or the operation of social systems because they were not society-wide. Religion retained subjective plausibility for some, but lost its objective taken for granted-ness. It was now a preference, not a necessity.

Social and Cultural Diversity

Diversity created the secular state. Modernization brought with it increased cultural diversity in three ways. Peoples moved and brought their language, religion, and social mores into a new setting. Second, the expansive nation state encompassed new peoples. Third, especially common in Protestant settings, economic modernization created classes that created competing sects. Hence the paradox: at the same time as the nation state was trying to create a unified national culture out of thousands of small communities, it was having to come to terms with increasing religious diversity. The solution was an increasingly neutral state. The idea of having one legally established state church to which all subjects or citizens should belong was abandoned altogether (the United States) or was neutered (the British case). While freedom from entanglements with secular power allowed churches to become more clearly spiritual—to concentrate on their core task—their removal from the centre of public life reduced their contact with, and relevance for, the general population. The increased secularity of the public sphere did not prevent people maintaining voluntary religious associations, but it did mean a significant loss of propaganda.

There is an important subsidiary point that we should stress here. Some scholars take the French Revolution example of avowed secular-ists attacking the power of religion as the dominant model for explain-ing the growth of the secular state.[14] That is appropriate for Catholic and Orthodox countries, but in most Protestant countries the increas-ing neutrality of the state and the public sphere was actually driven by minority sects and denominations anxious to protect themselves from state coercion. This is an important point, because, if the secularity of the modern state is the product of conscious work by secularists, it is a straightforward power struggle between two competing teams, and we could imagine an alternative outcome. If we recognize the role of Protestant dissenters in reducing the power of the religious establish-ment, we also see that this change as a 'functional requirement' for peace in a religiously diverse context that accepts the egalitarian principle. That is, it is an essential operating principle for modern societies.

Increasing religious diversity also called into question the certainty that believers could accord their religion.[15] Ideas are most convincing when they are universally shared. The elaboration of alternatives provides a profound challenge. Believers need not fall on their swords when they find that others disagree with them. Where clashes of ideologies occur in the context of social conflict or when alternatives are promoted by stigmatized or subordinate people who need not be seriously entertained, the cognitive challenge can be dismissed.[16] None the less the proliferation of alternatives removes the sense of inevitability. When the oracle speaks with a single clear voice, it is easy to believe it is the voice of God. When it speaks with twenty different voices, it is tempting to look behind the screen. Believers may respond to the fact of variety by supposing that all religions are, in some sense, the same. Another possibility (and they are not incompatible) is to confine one's faith to a particular compartment of social life. With compartmentalization comes privatization: the sense that the reach of religion is shortened to just those who accept the teachings of this or that faith, As Luckmann puts it:

This development reflects the dissolution of one hierarchy of significance in the world view. Based on the complex institutional structure and social stratification of industrial societies different 'versions' of the world view emerge ... With the pervasiveness of the consumer orientation and the sense of autonomy, the individual is more likely to confront the culture and the sacred cosmos as a 'buyer'. Once religion is defined as a 'private affair', the individual may choose from the assortment of 'ultimate' meanings as he sees fit.[17]

Thus far we have been concerned with variations on the general theme that the changes in the social structure that we gloss as 'modernization' brought increased liberty in the field of religion. We now turn to the changing plausibility of religious ideas.

Science, Technology, and Self-Confidence

Critics of the secularization paradigm misrepresent it by elevating science to a central position: 'it is science that has the most deadly implications for religion.'[18] A zero-sum notion of knowledge, with rational thought and scientific knowledge conquering territory from religion and superstition, was carried into sociology by Auguste Comte and Karl Marx among others, but it is not part of the modern secularization paradigm. We recognize that modern people are quite capable of believing untruths and hence that the decreasing plausibility of any one body of ideas cannot be explained simply by the presence of some (to us) more plausible ones. The crucial connections are more subtle and complex than those implied in a science versus religion battle and rest on more nebulous consequences of assumptions about the orderliness of the world and our mastery over it.

More important than science was the development of effective technologies. Religion is often practical. Holy water cures ailments and prayers improve crop quality. Modern technology secularizes not by showing religion to be false but by reducing the occasions on which people have recourse to religion: displacement rather than refutation. Farmers need not stop praying to save their sheep from maggots, because an effective sheep dip becomes available, but in practice most do. The more that we gain effective control over areas of life, the fewer are the occasions on which religious solutions seem the most persuasive. A perfect example can be seen in the contrasting response of the Church of England to the Black Death of 1348–49 and the HIV/AIDs 'gay plague' of the 1980s. In the first case, the Church tried to deflect God's wrath by arranging weeks of fasting and special prayers. In the second, it called for more government investment in medical–scientific research.

More generally, as Martin puts it, with the growth of science and technology 'the general sense of human power is increased, the play of contingency is restricted, and the overwhelming sense of divine limits which afflicted previous generations is much diminished'.[19] In traditionally religious world views, people are insignificant specks of dust. For Christians, humankind has, since the expulsion from the Garden of Eden, consisted of pitiable, worthless, and sinful creatures who are redeemed only by the undeserved love of an all-powerful God whose divine providence must always be a mystery to us. That relative scale of importance fits well the experience of most people in most times and places until the modern era. We may be deluding ourselves, of course, but modern people do not share the fatalism or what we could now call the 'low self-esteem' of our ancestors. What previous societies regarded as fate, we see as problems for our governments to solve by the rational application of knowledge. This change does not prevent people being religious, but it does explain why we are no longer much attracted to religions that stress sin and divine punishment. Science and technology have not made us atheists, but the underlying rationality and the subtle encouragement to self-aggrandisement make us less likely than our forebears to entertain the notion of a powerful divine force external to ourselves. It explains why most Christian churches in the West have given up hell, why erratic providence has been replaced by a predictable beneficence, why the tyrannical God has been replaced by the wise and kindly father figure, why the point of worship is now this-worldly therapy rather than the placating of an angry God, and why some people find the self-religions of New Age spirituality an attractive option.

Toleration, Relativism, and Indifference

The Christian Church of the Middle Ages was firmly authoritarian and exclusive in its attitude to knowledge. There was a single truth, and it knew what it was. Increasingly, social and cultural diversity combines with egalitarianism to undermine all claims to authoritative knowledge. While compartmentalization (the idea that my God rules my private life but need not rule the lives of others or my engagement in the public sphere) can serve as a holding operation, it is difficult to live in a world that treats as equally valid a large number of incompatible beliefs, and that shies away from authoritative assertions, without coming to suppose that there is no one truth. Diversity is particular undermining when it appears in the family. The socio-psychological effects of alternative faiths can be held at arm's length when the adherents of those alternatives either are literally distant or can be blackened with some shared invidious stereotype. So long as all of 'us' are Baptists and we know that Catholics are illiterate welfare scroungers, we can remain confident in the rectitude of our religion. But when our relatives marry Catholics and we discover that they are pretty much like us, it becomes increasingly difficult to insist that what is true for us must also be true for everyone else. The tolerance that is necessary for harmony in diverse egalitarian societies weakens religion by forcing us to live as if we could not be sure of God's will. A remarkable example of the problem is inadvertently given by the Bolton Interfaith Council, which, in a pamphlet encouraging people to walk around various worship sites in the city, has pages on 'What Christians believe', 'What

Muslims Believe', and 'What Hindus Believe', which present all three faiths as if they were equally correct. It is difficult to imagine how any young resident of Bolton who was looking for a spiritual home could be recruited to any version of the three traditions by such relativism.

The consequence, visible from the mid-nineteenth century in liberal democracies, is a decline first in the commitment of, and then in the number of, church adherents. The change was slow because it was largely generational. A majority of people tended to maintain the faith they acquired from their parents, but each generation of parents worked less hard to ensure that their children were socialized in the faith. If all faiths (and none) offer a road to God, and if there is no hell for heretics, then there is no need to ensure the transmission of orthodoxy.

The above is a highly compressed summary of the argument that a variety of economic, social, political, and cultural changes combine to change fundamentally the status and nature of religion in the modern world. We need to add one final point. Arguing from a wide variety of premises (including the belief that humans are genetically programmed to be religious), many scholars accept most of the above and yet deny that the liberal industrial democracies of the West have become more secular. They argue that change is not the same as decline and that in various ways—'believing but not belonging', vicarious religion, implicit religion, alternative spirituality—people are really as religious as ever they were. There is nothing wrong with that argument other than a complete absence of supporting evidence. The evidence of the decline of Christianity is abundant. There is no evidence that alternatives come anywhere close to being of the scale required to fill the gap left by that decline. Between 1851 and 2001 the proportion of the population of England and Wales that attended church fell from around 50 per cent to around 5 per cent: a 45 percentage point gap. On the most generous definitions, both field studies and surveys suggest that no more than 2 per cent of the population is engaged in practices associated with alternative or holistic spirituality.[20]

Which Elements are Gendered?

Having presented a rather breathless summary of the secularization thesis, we can now consider to what extent elements of it are 'gendered'. It is important to distinguish two quite different meanings of that term that are often elided. We need to consider first to what extent elements of the secularization thesis are likely to be mistaken because they do not consider men and women separately. Second, we need to consider to what extent correctly identified social changes bear differently on men and women.

Those observations concerned with societal and social structure (for example, functional differentiation, social differentiation, the decline of community) operate at a degree of abstraction that makes reference to particular subpopulations unnecessary. It is hard to see how the proposition that the growing autonomy of specific spheres such as the economy and the polity reduces the remit and thus the influence of the church would be altered by attention to gender (or any other major demographic division). Likewise for the social–psychological claim that being exposed to positive social interaction with carriers of different religious perspectives creates problems of certainty and conviction for the believer. The proposition may be wrong, but, unless we suppose that men and women differ in close-mindedness and dogmatism, it is not wrong because it fails to distinguish between them. It is similarly difficult to see what distortion occurs by treating as a universal the claim that science and technology reduce occasions for resort to religious solutions. The illustrations that we could draw from the life experiences of women and men will be different, as would be the examples we would draw from different social classes, but the key principle—that religion loses authority as the range of events for which it offers the best solution decreases—seems genuinely universal. That scholars such as Martin and Wilson consistently use male pronouns for humankind may offend the modern spirit and may even indicate certain blind spots, but, rereading their work, we find no reason to suppose that a greater sensitivity to gender (or to class or race or ethnicity) would have changed their arguments.

It is more fruitful to pursue the second sense of 'gendered': to consider to what extent the social forces that produce secularization bear differently on men and women. This is actually much more difficult than one might suppose: first, because causation in general is difficult to establish for highly complex changes over long periods of time and, secondly, because the lives of men and women are normally so closely intertwined that, even if the initial impact on men and women is different, the effects will almost immediately be passed from one to the other.

As an example of the first problem, consider religion's loss of functions. It seems entirely plausible that Christianity was more persuasive in the Middle Ages than in the late nineteenth century, because the church's wider range of responsibilities and activities in the early period gave it a greater presence in most people's lives, but it is very difficult to see how we prove that to be the case when the loss of functions was extremely slow and uneven. We can 'test' various parts of the assertion by staged comparisons; for example, comparing the popularity of the Catholic Church in Ireland (which was still the main provider of health care and education) and the Presbyterian Church in Scotland (which was not) in 1900. But there are so many other differences between the two settings that the best we can say of such comparisons is that the results are entirely compatible with the secularization thesis. Similarly with Martin's point about increased mastery over fate. Although as an imaginative experiment we might be able to associate different classes of people with different levels of fatalism, Martin's claim actually concerns nebulous assumptions that permeate entire cultures. His account seems to fit the very different attitudes to life of modern people and their pre-industrial ancestors, but it is difficult to see how we would pin it down sufficiently to test it.

The second problem is the casual way that gender differences in work or in social influence are assumed to produce different world views. That men and women in a patriarchal society have different rights and responsibilities does not mean that they do not talk to each other. A large population of adults living alone is a novelty. Until recently most people lived in or with couples, much of their life experience was common, and the rest was the subject of discussion. Because this is a rather sensitive subject ,we will be irritatingly precise about what we mean here. We do not mean that eighteenth-century marriages were partnerships of equals; we mean only that many of the objective features of life such as wealth, residence, and status were shared, that conversation between the sexes was common, and hence that husbands and wives and parents and children shared many beliefs and attitudes. So social changes that affected men would also affect women and vice versa. Consider the increased toleration of religious dissent that accompanied the growth of religious diversity. The repeal of the various legal disabilities imposed on dissenters in Britain obviously benefited men more particularly than women in that it was male dissenters who were excluded from holding certain civil positions by virtue of their faith; women were excluded by virtue of gender. But the resultant improved social status and wealth of male dissenters benefited their entire families.

Furthermore, the long-term effects of experiences are rarely confined to just the person who has them, because people translate experience into ideas and share them with others. Consider the young man in a religiously divided society who falls in love with and marries a woman from the other faith. Initially he alone has a good reason to replace his culture's disdain for 'them' with a new tolerant outlook, but he can persuade family and friends of the virtues of the new orientation. That people who have different 'social' locations and different experiences can communicate means that the fit between material interests and attitudes is always loose. It is especially loose in the case of gender, because in most settings men and women live together in a web of ongoing conversation and interaction. In brief, it need not follow that, because some parts of life are gendered, men and women will possess gendered religious outlooks.

All of this may seem like an admission that many social science ideas simply cannot be tested. Naturally we would not go that far, but we do recognize that demonstrating causal connections between naturally occurring changes in the real world (as contrasted, for example, with the experiments of the psychologist's lab) is often immensely difficult and that the best we can do is show that overall patterns are compatible with particular explanations.

Finally we turn to general gender patterns of religiosity and their compatibility with the secularization thesis. Not surprisingly, we find a good fit. The universality of the secularization thesis is amply supported by the fact that, although men generally give up religion before women, once the process of decline has begun the trajectories are similar and the end result is much the same. There may be a lengthy middle period when ambiguously religious men tolerate or even encourage their spouses' greater religiosity in a household division of religious labour, but the majority of men and the majority of women in liberal democracies are not now religious (nor, we might add for completeness, spiritual). That is, we do not have to explain different outcomes; we only have to explain different timings. What needs to be explained is why men fall away from religious observance before women.

Contrary to those scholars who argue that the secularization thesis needs to be altered to accommodate gender, we believe that this pattern is precisely what the thesis specifies. The first site of secularization is the public sphere. It is there that economic rationality first encouraged religious differentiae to be overlooked; then procedural rationality imposed notions of fairness. Scottish Presbyterian mineowners and iron masters of the nineteenth century might privately have preferred Protestant to Catholic workers, but economic rationality caused them to employ the cheapest labour, and in some cases economic interest so obviously trumped religious preference that Catholic Irish labourers were brought to Scotland to break the power of the nascent trade unions. The imposition of bureaucratic rationality on the world of work required that government clerks treated people in a universalistic fashion, attending only to the matter in hand. At the start of the American Civil War freed slaves who joined the Union army were paid less than white soldiers, but the combination of equity and rationality won out, and by the end of the war they were paid the same. The private sphere, of which the family and the home were the primary site, was exempted from such rationalization. In the mid-nineteenth century, when employers were finding it difficult to defend religiously discriminatory hiring, no one thought ill of a family that hired only co-religionists as domestic servants or that required servants to attend the family's church, even if they belonged to a different denomination. Even now, when religious discrimination is expressly outlawed in the public sphere, it is thought perfectly proper for religious people to wish to marry only those who share their faith.

We could multiply illustrations, but the point seems largely uncontroversial. Until relatively recently men had greater involvement than women in the public sphere. Women were less likely than men to work outside the home. If they did, they were less likely to work full-time or to work in large-scale enterprises outside the immediate neighbourhood. Men were also much more likely to occupy civic and public positions that required them to deal rationally and bureaucratically with people of diverse religious backgrounds. Men were much more likely than women to travel widely, to serve overseas in the armed forces, or to administer distant imperial possessions. In the late nineteenth century, County Durham collieries employed Protestants and Catholics; Irish immigrants were particularly known for their skills in sinking the initial pit shafts. Especially when attending church and school took them to opposite ends of the village, English Methodists and Irish Catholics might practise a degree of residential segregation, and the wives and children might socialize primarily with their own. That might allow the families to continue to view 'the others' in terms of negative stereotypes. But the men and women differed in one crucial respect: colliers of all religions and none worked together in life-supporting interdependence in the pit. The division of the life-world into relatively distinct spheres initially insulated women from many of the secularizing forces that bore on the public sphere. That the same division was accompanied by the general principle that the public sphere should be increasingly religiously neutral while the home should be the primary site for religious edification and socialization seems to explain why secularization should have impacted on men earlier and to a greater extent than on women.

The same point can be made about what Wilson called societalization or the decline of community. Although the process is general, it bears first on industrializing centres and their edges. Hence in the twentieth century the most religious and traditionally religious parts of most modern states are the remote geographical peripheries: the American south and the Scottish highlands and islands, for example. And it impacts first on men. An example from rural Wales will illustrate the point. The village of Llansantffraid Glyn Ceiriog lies close to the border with England, but the geology gave it an introverted character. It was economically self-sufficient. Most men worked in agriculture or in quarrying. And it remained Welsh-speaking after neighbouring settlements had become Anglophone. In the nineteenth century it had a strong evangelical chapel culture. In 1905 the settlement at the end of the valley, Llanarmon, had three chapels with a regular attendance of 234 from a population that was barely higher. Shortly before Ronald Frankenberg began his fieldwork in the early 1950s, the quarry closed and village life changed dramatically. Most men left the village every morning to work in towns in England. Most women remained in the valley. While the men developed friendships with work colleagues outside the valley, their wives continued to regard each other as their primary reference group. They visited each other in their homes and they met and talked at the local shops and in their conversations they monitored each other's behaviour and criticized those who fell short of chapel standards. For the men, the village became a residential dormitory; for the women it remained their entire social world.[21] We cannot prove that the greater integration of the men folk into the wider British culture was the cause of their earlier defection from chapel-going, but it seems certain to have played some part. It is certainly the case that when we compare four similar Welsh parishes we find that levels of religiosity remained highest in those most isolated from the cultural mainstream.[22]

Women and Modernization

Modernization was accompanied by secularization. It was also accompanied by a profound change in the status of women. The precise timings varied by country, region, and class, but the later nineteenth and twentieth centuries saw women gradually acquire first formal rights (such as the right to stand for political office and to vote) and then comparable social status. The two world wars were a profound encouragement to an assumption of equality, as was the increasing availability of effective contraception and growing desire of couples to reduce family size. Women increased their presence in the paid labour force and in higher education. The change were not easy or readily accepted, but by the end of the twentieth century the essential equality of men and women was widely taken for granted and most states had adopted laws to prevent discrimination on the grounds of gender.

As the lives of women became more like the lives of men, so their attitudes to, and involvement in, religion converged. On the basis of large-scale survey data from the 1980s, De Vaus and McAllister concluded that women in full-time work 'are less religious than those out of it and have a broadly similar [religious] orientation to males'.[23] Data on a large number of European countries from the first decade of the twenty-first century show that working women (at 34 per cent) were markedly less likely than housewives (at 47 per cent) to describe themselves as 'highly religious'.[24]

Conclusion

It is impossible to discuss religion in modern industrial liberal democracies without talking about secularization. Although scholars continue to argue over the relative weight of various causes of change, the major contours of change are indisputable. Without wishing to get bogged down in debates about the way they are related, we can distinguish three broad themes.

First, the state has become increasingly secular. The modern state is not theocratic. Where state or national churches remain, they are, like the monarchies with which they are often associated, shadows of their pre-modern selves. Crucially, citizens no longer suffer disabilities for worshipping the wrong God or none. The modern language of human rights allocates rights to people irrespective of their faith, and modern governments usually seek to avoid what the American courts call 'excessive entanglement' with religion.

Second, the loss of power that religious institutions experienced as a result of the state becoming increasingly neutral has generally been accompanied by a marked decline in the proportions of populations that are self-consciously religious. That is, membership of religious institutions and involvement in organized religious activities—from attending church to holding family prayers—has declined.

Third, there has been a marked shift in the self-understanding of religions, as people who remain involved in organized expressions of religion have become increasingly assertive and selective in what they will believe. The large churches have become increasingly liberal and tolerant and reduced the demands for loyalty they make of their members and adherents. The same principles of assertiveness and selectivity can be seen in the world of contemporary spirituality beyond the traditional religions. Those people who remain interested in religion or spirituality generally act as knowing consumers rather than as loyal followers.

In thoroughly religious societies, there may be gender differences in religious duties and obligations, but there are no discernible differences in underlying attitudes and beliefs. We can explain that with three observations. First, the culture of the seriously religious society is so permeated by religious assumptions that they shape consciousness. Second, constant interaction with believers will repair (or repress) the rare doubter. Men and women may experience the world differently. But interaction between men and women, especially within families, will ensure that there is no great difference in how people think of the divine and the supernatural. Third, to the extent that people do differ in their enthusiasm for religious rituals, the pressure to conform will ensure compliance.

This third point is important. The precise details of how it operates will vary from culture to culture, but one of the marks of how seriously a society takes any practice is the extent to which it requires conformity. The requirement could come from the state, as in the nineteenth-century Swedish law that required government ministers to be members of the national church, or it could come from informal social expectations. In the Edwardian era a middle-class man would be expected to lead his family to church, and his absence would be regarded as dereliction of family obligation as much as neglect of religious duty. Today a husband is expected to accompany his wife to hospital, to court, and to the funeral of her close relatives. If a couple is invited to a party as a couple and one declines to attend without a suitable excuse, that would be counted as an insult to the other. However, we do not expect couples to share leisure interests. Partners are not faulted for failing to attend sporting events or book clubs.[25] One of the clearest signs of the early stages of secularization in Christian societies is the shift of churchgoing from the category of activities that, irrespective of personal preferences, require joint attendance, to the realm of the entirely optional. One of the clearest signs of the late stages of secularization is that even most women no longer go to church.

The same point can be made from another direction by considering marriage partner selection. One mark of the importance of any particular characteristic is where it figures on the list of features one seeks in a spouse. Jane Austen's mother characters wanted to know wealth but they also wanted to know breeding. One of the surest signs of the declining relevance of religion in the modern world is the increasing proportion of people who marry 'out' of their heritage religious community. And one of the surest signs of the insignificance of much contemporary spirituality is that a potential spouse sharing an interest in yoga or meditation is on a par with him or her liking the same kind of music: it is good to have interests in common but it is not a deal-breaker.

To summarize, the disaffiliation from the churches that is one major facet of secularization starts with men. For over a century, from at least the 1850s to the 1960s, women form an increasing proportion of churchgoers. And then they too start to fall away. As other gender differences decline, and as religion becomes less persuasive, the differences in male and female interest in religion also decline.

10

The Sum of Small Differences

Introduction

It is wise to be clear about the limitations of our work. Even in the natural sciences, where experiments, designed to eliminate many variables and simplify what is observed, can be frequently repeated to produce a large body of findings, it is often very difficult to demonstrate that one thing is caused by another. As the Latin tag 'post hoc ergo propter hoc' ('after this therefore because of this') reminds us, that one thing follows another does not necessarily mean that the first causes the second: the ordering may be coincidence or both may have some other unknown cause. What we can do in the social sciences often falls woefully short of what the physicist or chemist can do in the laboratory. Psychologists can create artificially simple experimental situations but, even when these produce relatively clear conclusions, they often tell us little about the naturally occurring social world precisely because they are artificially simple.

Sociologists trying to explain some naturally occurring phenomenon generally pursue two lines of enquiry in tandem: we search for regularities in large bodies of information about patterns of behaviour and we try to construct a plausible account of why someone in this or that situation, who holds certain beliefs or values or attitudes, would act in this way rather than that. That is, we search for a correlation between two measures and then try to ensure that we are not making the 'post hoc ergo propter hoc' mistake by finding in actors' accounts of what they are doing the material that would allow us to construct a plausible interpretation of the discerned pattern.

While proving that something is the case is very difficult, it is easier to show that it is unlikely to be so: either the evidence does not fit or the implied motive model makes little sense.[1] For example, the proposition that all people are innately religious might have been plausible in 1800, but there are now so many people in the West who do not hold supernatural beliefs, who have no involvement with religious organizations, and who describe themselves as 'not religious' that, even if we can bring some of them back into the fold by arguing that, unbeknownst to themselves, they are really religious, we will still have enough non-religious people to defeat the universal claim. Similarly, we can demonstrate that some explanations imply a model of human behaviour that is so implausible we would never apply it to ourselves. The economist's assumption that people constantly seek to 'maximize utility' often produces implausible claims. Rodney Stark, for example, argues that clergy who are paid from state taxes rather than congregational donations will prefer small congregations to large ones because that means less work for the same pay.[2] Would we apply the same logic to ourselves and say that university professors prefer their courses to be unpopular because that allows utility maximizing? We doubt it. Together disconfirming evidence and sound reasoning can always help eliminate the unlikely explanation.

A further difficulty, which dogs this study, is overdetermination: a single event may apparently have many causes, and, as we cannot experimentally manipulate our subjects, we have little chance of ranking causes in order of efficacy or of dividing them into such useful categories as necessary and sufficient conditions.

However, we should not be too dismal about the prospect of sociological explanation. There are many features of human behaviour that make it vastly more difficult to study than the expansion of metals: one obvious difficulty is that our raw material possesses degrees of self-awareness and degrees of freedom that allow it to change. The metallurgist need not entertain the possibility that a bar of iron may learn from being repeatedly heated and change its rate of expansion. But sociologists have two distinct advantages over natural scientists. We can in various ways interrogate our subjects: we can interview them, read their diaries and letters, or strike up conversations that allow us subtly to probe. And we share many of the characteristics of our subjects. When people tell us that they stopped going to church because they were too busy, or did not like the new pastor, or found the church building too cold, we can plausibly consider that really they have lost faith but that they feel a little guilty about it and do not want to hurt the feelings of church people and so are obfuscating. We do not have to be ex-Christians to understand that obfuscation. We need only have been in some similar situation: having to explain why we keep avoiding a friend's musical or sporting performances, for example. That we share a common humanity with our subjects often allows us to render meaningful a very wide variety of experiences.

The point of this brief aside on the philosophy of social science is to provide something of an apology for the lack of certainty in the previous chapters. The question 'Why are women more religious than men?' is easy to pose; it is difficult to answer definitively, but in that it differs little from most questions about naturally occurring human behaviour. The question needs to be broken down into smaller segments and each pursued by a variety of research methods. Different methods will often produce conclusions that are difficult to reconcile. In the end, the best we can usually do is suggest that some explanations are more plausible than others.

Small Differences

With these qualifications and apologies duly entered, we can now attempt a succinct answer to the question 'Why are women more religious than men?'. Our first, and perhaps most important, conclusion is that, though the question can be posed as if it concerned a single unitary social fact, it is actually an amalgam of different social facts, each with its own small explanation, some of which overlap and reinforce each other. That is, the causes of gender differences in religiosity differ with time and place.

Lagged Effects of Secularization

The social forces that weakened the plausibility and power of religion in modern industrial liberal democracies had their first and greatest impact on the public sphere. To the extent that the explanation of secularization sketched in the previous chapter is plausible, we have also accidentally explained why it is initially men who leave the churches and who lose interest in religion first. As the other consequences of modernization include the erosion of traditional gender roles, greater egalitarianism, and increasing similarity of the lifestyles and life chances of men and women, this effect is by and large temporary. The difference in religiosity between men and women in England or Sweden in the late nineteenth and early twentieth centuries is a consequence of time lag.

Vicarious Religion, Respectability, and Patriarchy

Patriarchy is an important element of the explanation. In many societies and settings, women are more religious than men because men wish them to be so and have a variety of forms of social pressure that can be used to encourage or ensure female conformity. This would explain heightened female religiosity in religious societies, but at first sight it seems redundant in the semi-secular societies that show the strongest gendered pattern of religious adherence. Why, in Manchester in 1960, where most men were patently not religious, should men press women into remaining religious? It seems counter-intuitive that men should encourage women to hold beliefs that they no longer hold and to engage in ritual activities that they no longer believe to be effective. There is no mystery about most divisions of labour: masters force slaves to work for them, because the fruits of such labour are unarguably real. Religion is different, in that it is pointless if you do not believe in it. If there is no God, there is no point in men pressing their wives to worship him. If there is a God, they had better worship him too.

This is actually a misleadingly 'Reformed Christian' way of framing the question, and we need to qualify it by recognizing that most of the world religions (including the Catholic and Orthodox strands of Christianity), to varying degrees, permit a religious division of labour because they allow that religious merit can be transferred. A degree of bet-hedging is possible. I may not be sure enough of the existence of God to worship him, but I may be happy to encourage my believing spouse to say prayers, light candles, or makes sacrifices on my behalf.

But, even where the secular man does not hope to gain religious merit through the piety of his spouse, he may still hope to gain social credit. Particularly in the early stages of secularization, being religious may still carry a large number of socially positive connotations. Especially if the ruling classes continue to be religious, there may still be residual social kudos attached to religion. Secondly, if religion is strongly associated with morality, non-religious people may feel obliged to describe themselves as 'Christian', even if they never attend church or do anything that demonstrates an active Christian commitment. In such circumstances, irreligious or only very weakly religious men may well encourage their wives to do religion on their behalf. We saw this in the example of Protestant terrorists in Northern Ireland taking pride in the fact that their wives were good God-fearing women who raised the children right.

That the churches have for centuries enjoyed the position of monopoly provider of moral teaching has created an extremely strong link in the popular mind between religion and morals. Even some parents who reject the historical and supernatural claims of their culture's dominant religion may feel that their obligation to raise their children to be ethical and moral agents gives a good reason for some religious socialization. Given the traditional gender division of roles, that task is more likely to fall to the mother than to the father. The pious father will lead his family in prayer and to worship. The avowedly atheistic father will prevent his children falling into the clutches of the God-botherers. But, for all levels of belief between those two extremes, a household division of religious labour will rest on and thus reinforce women's involvement in religion.

The Control of Sexuality

Religion is intimately associated with the control of sexuality. Because it is often a source of tension and conflict and because parentage often has important implications for inheritance, almost all societies show a strong interest in controlling sexual activity. Who can do what, when, and with whom is the subject of powerful social mores, and these are usually legitimated by being given divine justification and underpinning. Although the high theory of most religions places an equal burden on men and women to control their urges, in almost every society women make the sacrifices that are involved in such control. The fourth item in the following equation from Ayatollah Hojatoleslam Kazem Sedighi may be unusual, but the ordering of the first three is commonplace: 'Many women do not dress modestly, lead young men astray, and spread adultery in society, which increases earthquakes.'[3] It is women who must be confined indoors or camouflaged. We say 'women make the sacrifices' rather than 'men oppress women', not because we are shy of using the language of coercion but because force is required only when socialization has failed. In worlds where a particular religious culture is established and unchallenged—rural England in 1600, rural Ireland in 1800, or Arabia in 1850—everyone will be so successfully socialized into its norms that women will conform 'naturally'. Even when gendered norms are challenged, many women may willingly embrace their subjugation: the Obedient Wives Club in Malaysia is an example.[4] Only when the norms are under serious challenge is violence or the threat of violence required to enforce them.

But women are not always passive. There are many times and places where women have used religion as a socially acceptable reservoir of reasons to avoid sex and the repeated pregnancies that it used to cause. As we saw in Chapter 2, many women found positive secondary benefits in Protestant movements (secondary that is to the primary purpose of salvation): the religious ideal of purity may have been a burden to some, but it was an escape route for others. In Chapter 5 we noted the appeal to Latin American women of Pentecostalism: it offered an alternative to the culture of machismo. In Chapter 8 we found Orthodox Jewish women using religious precepts to regulate male sexual demands.

Secular Gender Roles

It is important to distinguish this point from the previous two points, which were primarily concerned with men's encouragement of women's religious behaviour. Here we are concerned with secular sexual divisions of labour and their somewhat coincidental association with religion. In most societies, women are allocated a number of tasks that coincidentally keep them closer to religion than men. Life is often viewed as something miraculous, for which a religious response is appropriate itself. Death raises vital issues about the nature of life and the destination of the person (or soul) after the death of the body. Organized religion is very largely concerned with birth and death. For obvious reasons, women in all societies are much more involved than men in childbirth; in many cultures they are also much more involved in the management of death. We do not suppose that women are consequently more disposed than men to think on higher things (though we leave open the possibility that they might be). Our point is the mundane and more observable one that, the more people associate with the clergy, take part in religious offices, and attend church, the more likely they are to become or remain religious, and the secular division of gender roles brings women into the orbit of organized religion more often. The same point holds if we think of the culture of 'folk' religion that used to surround childbirth and death: for secular reasons, it was a women's world.

Along with roles come attitudes. We are not suggesting that only women or that all women are caring, but we observe that, in almost all hitherto-known societies, women are much more involved in the nurture of others, and that this work is accompanied by a difference in attitude. Women are generally more caring than men. Of itself that would not explain why women are more religious. Again we are suggesting a thinner and more roundabout connection. Prior to the rise of the welfare state, religious institutions were the primary providers of care for the poor, the elderly, the sick, and the infirm, and religious values were a primary source of encouragement to charity and philanthropy. Even in semi-secular societies, religious institutions and religious people provide a great deal of social and personal care. An infirm and elderly lady of our acquaintance who had outlived all her friends had only two regular visitors: an elder of the church she used to attend and a younger female neighbour who took her hot food every day on the self-deprecating grounds that 'I'm cooking for the family anyway and there's always something left over'. That the young woman's attitude brought her into contact with and made her familiar with the attitude of the religious official may well explain her sympathy for the local church. Put more systematically, we are suggesting that women's greater sympathy for organized religion may in part result from their 'lay' caring attitudes coinciding with the professional attitude of the churches. That one spends time caring for others will not make one religious (either in reality or by definition), but it is the basis for recognizing something in common. This is a small gender difference, but then our general approach to explaining gender differences in religiosity is that we are seeking the cumulative effect of small differences.

The Body, Illness, and Health

Our initial interest in health and the body was sparked by the para-religious phenomenon of holistic spirituality. As we argued in Chapter 4 a good deal of what is often presented as a new form of religion is better described as an interest in physical and psychological well-being. It was only when assembling the material for the earlier chapters that we appreciated the extent to which concern for diet, exercise, and bodily discipline have long been part of the appeal of religious reform movements. We avoided being drawn too far into the mammoth task of explaining why dominant notions of masculinity should make health-seeking behaviour (unless it coincidentally involves combat) a sign of weakness. We simply note that women are more likely than men to be interested in self-help activities to promote good health and that, in addition to explaining a large part of women's involvement in the world of holistic spirituality, this may also explain some of the appeal of such movements as Seventh-Day Adventism and Christian Science.

Conclusion

Much of this study has been deliberately inconclusive. For the reasons sketched at the start of this chapter, firm conclusions about big questions are hard to come by in the social sciences. In so far as we have a firm and brief answer to the question posed in this book's title, it is as follows. We have not inserted at all the obvious places the qualification that circumstances will be different for members of religio-ethnic minorities. We can cover that with the general observation that, in so far as migrants to the West from more traditionally religious cultures and their descendants become better assimilated in every other respect, their religious lives will also become more like those of the generalized actors we have in mind in the following summary.

1. There is nothing in the biological make-up of men and women that of itself explains the gendered difference in religiosity that, if not exactly universal, is extremely widespread.

2. The essentially different role of women and men in reproduction directs women more than men to the social role of carer and thus creates the lattice on which complex gendered divisions of labour can be created, sustained, and elaborated. The role of carer and primary responsibility for socialization of the young keep women closer than men to organized religion, make more attractive belief in the afterlife, and sustain attitudes that find expression in the broader cultural worlds of contemporary spirituality.

3. The role of religion in the control of human sexuality gives men an interest in pressing women to adhere closely to the dominant religious culture. It may also give women who find male sexual demands oppressive a good reason to embrace and promote personal piety.

4. Because dominant notions of masculine toughness militate against attention to physical and psychological health, interest in bodily purity—peripheral in more mainstream religion but central to many new religious movements and to holistic spirituality—attracts women more than men.

5. But the largest part of the answer is simply time lag. Men were generally affected earlier than women by the secularizing forces that reduced the plausibility of religious beliefs and turned religious rectitude from a necessary condition for citizenship into a personal preference. Religion's loss of power, popularity, and prestige in the modern world has been slow and uneven. In semi-secular cultures, religion retains enough social prestige and heritage heft to give those who are ambivalent reasons to retain some sort of residual attachment. That, for the reasons given above, women are more likely than men to be religious (or spiritual) is reinforced by a gendered household division of religious labour.

Although we can imagine a personal calculus that would make this a permanent condition—a sort of vicarious Pascal's wager in which the ambivalent or uninterested man finds nothing objectionable in his spouse being religious—the cultural context of the Western world is changing in a way that makes it much more likely that the graphs of male and female religiosity will converge as they approach zero. In 1900 more than half the population of most Western societies had some active church attachment. In 1950 most European and American children were socialized in education systems that taught the essential truth of the Christian faith and between 20 and 60 per cent of children also attended church or Sunday School. With church attendance rates around the 10 per cent mark in many European states and Sunday Schools attended only by the children of the faithful, being uninterested in religion no longer carries any social stigma. Hence the greater religiosity of women is now more of a freely chosen personal preference than an expression of women compensating for men in some household division of religious labour. To return to points 3 and 4 above, the decline of the churches means that whatever interest remains in controlling sexuality or in achieving bodily purity will find secular expressions. To return to point 2, the social changes that have weakened organized religion in the West have also reduced some of the differences in life circumstances of men and women. Enough women are now free of the social roles that coincidentally brought them into the orbit of organized religion to destroy the web of expectations that disposed them to be more favourable, as a class, to religion.

Notes

CHAPTER I

1. We are grateful to David Voas for calculating, using church-based data for 2005, 2007, and 2008, a baptism estimate for England of 22% or 33%, depending on whether one takes those baptized in the first year of infancy or those baptized at any age up to 12.
2. C. Brown, *The Death of Christian Britain* (London: Routledge, 2001), 168; D. Voas, 'Intermarriage and the Demography of Secularization', *British Journal of Sociology*, 54 (2003).
3. Data kindly provided by the office of the Registrar-General for Scotland.
4. We are grateful to Tony Glendinning for help in analysing the results of the 2001 Scottish Social Attitudes survey. The Conservative Protestant category had only twenty-four people in it; hence one should be cautious of making too much of this.
5. C. Field, 'Zion's People: Profile of English Nonconformity', *British Religion in Numbers* <http://www.brin.ac.uk/news/?p=299> (accessed 7 May 2010).
6. P. E. Scott and A. Gelder, *Church Life Profile 2001: Denominational Results for the Methodist Church* (London: Churches Information for Mission, 2002).
7. P. L. Sissons, *The Social Significance of Church Membership in the Burgh of Falkirk* (Edinburgh: Church of Scotland, 1963), 56.
8. C. Field, 'Gender Audit Report, Scottish Episcopal Church', *British Religion in Numbers* <http://www.brin.ac.uk/news/?p=355> (accessed 9 May 2011).
9. Field, 'Zion's People'.
10. C. Brown, *Religion and Society in Twentieth-Century Britain* (London: Pearson Education, 2006), 182–3.
11. BBC, *Religious Broadcasting and the Public: A Report of a Social Survey of Differences between Non-Listeners and Listeners to Religious Broadcasts* (London: BBC, 1955), 18.
12. P. Brierley, *Religious Trends*, v (London: Christian Research Association, 2005). J. Ashworth and I. Farthing, *Churchgoing in the UK* (London: Tearfund, 2007) <http://news.bbc.co.uk/1/shared/bsp/hi/pdfs/03_04_07_tearfundchurch.pdf> (accessed 9 Jan. 2009).

13. D. Davis, C Watkins, and M. Winter, *Church and Religion in Rural England* (Edinburgh: T and T Clark, 1991), 214.

14. ABC Television, *Television and Religion* (London: University of London Press, 1965), 28.

15. Mass Observation, *Puzzled People: A Study in Popular Attitudes to Religion, Ethics, Progress and Politics in a London Borough* (London: Victor Gollanz, 1947): 21.

16. Davis et al., *Church and Religion*, 253.

17. Data from International Social Survey Programme (ISSP) surveys of 1991, 1998, and 2008 provided by David Voas.

18. A. Porterfield, 'Women's Attraction to Puritanism', *Church History*, 60 (1991), 196.

19. B. E. Lacey, 'Gender, Piety and Secularization in Connecticut Religion, 1720–1775', *Journal of Social History*, 24 (1911), 800.

20. R. S. Lynd and H. M. Lynd, *Middletown: A Study in Contemporary American Culture* (New York: Harcourt, Brace and Company, 1928), 355, 529.

21. A. L. Winseman, 'Religion and Gender: A Congregation Divided', *Gallup*, 3 Dec. 2002 <http://www.gallup.com/poll/7336/Religion-Gender-Congregation-Divided.aspx?version=print> (accessed 8 Sept. 2010).

22. A. Keysar, 'Who Are America's Atheists and Agnostics?', in B. Kosmin and A. Keysar (eds), *Secularism and Secularity: Contemporary International Perspectives* (Hartford, CT: Institute for the Study of Secularism in Society and Culture, 2007), 33–9.

23. G. H. Gallup, 'Why are Women More Religious than Men?', *GPNS Commentary*, 17 Dec. 2002 <http://www.gallup.com/poll/7432/why-women-more-religious.aspx> (accessed 17 Sept. 2010).

24. C. Woolever, D. Bruce, K. Wulff, and I. Smith-Williams, 'The Gender Ratio in the Pews: Consequences for Congregational Vitality', *Journal of Beliefs and Values*, 27 (2006), 25–38.

25. Keyser, 'Who Are America's Atheists and Agnostics?', 36.

26. B. A. Kosmin and A. Keyser, *American Religious Identification Survey ARIS 2008 Summary Report March 2009* (Hartford, CT: Trinity College, 2009), 11.

27. J. Wilson and D. E. Sherkat, 'Returning to the Fold', *Journal for the Scientific Study of Religion*, 33 (1994), 154.

28. M. Hill and R. Bowman, 'Religious Adherence and Religious Practice in Contemporary New Zealand: Census and Survey Evidence', *Archives de sciences sociales des religions*, 30 (1985), 91–112.

29. *National Church Life Survey 2001* <http://www.ncls.org/default.aspx?sitemapid=30> (accessed 10 Feb. 2011).

30. S. King-Hele, 'The Dynamics of Religious Change: A Comparative Study of Five Western Countries', Ph.D., University of Manchester, 2010. We are grateful to Dr King-Hele for permission to cite her data.

31. A. Dubach, 'The Religiosity Profile of European Catholicism', in M. Rieger (ed.), *What the World Believes* (Gütterslöh:Verag Bertelsmann Stiftüng, 2009), 509.

32. E. Pace, 'Catholicism in Italy: The Soft Secularization in a Post-Ideological Society', in D. M. Jerolimov, S. Zrinščak, and I. Borowik (eds), *Religion and Patterns of Social Transformation* (Zagreb: Institute for Social Research, 2004), 93.

33. K. Niemelä. 'Between East and West—Finnish Religiosity from an European Perspective', in D. M. Jerolimov, S. Zrinščak, and I. Borowik (eds), *Religion and Patterns of Social Transformation* (Zagreb: Institute for Social Research, 2004), 112.

34. R. Inglehart, M. Basanez, and A. Moreno, *Human Values and Beliefs: A Cross-Cultural Sourcebook* (Ann Arbor: University of Michigan Press, 1998), tables V175 and V176.

35. G. Davie, *Religion in Modern Europe: A Memory Mutates* (Oxford: Oxford University Press, 2005), 66.

36. A large body of WVS data is helpfully summarized in R. Stark, 'Physiology and Faith: Addressing the "Universal" Gender Difference in Religious Commitment', *Journal for the Scientific Study of Religion*, 41 (2002), 495–507.

37. S. Bruce, 'A Practical Definition of Religion', *International Review of Sociology*, 21 (2011), 105–18.

38. P. Heelas and L. Woodhead, *The Spiritual Revolution* (Oxford: Blackwell, 2005), 94.

39. IPSOS-MORI, '*Schotts's Almanac* Survey on Belief' <http://www.ipsos-mori.com/Assets/Docs/Archive/Polls/schottsalmanac2.pdf> (accessed 8 Mar. 2011).

40. YouGov, 'Life after Death Poll for ITV's *This Morning*, 8–11 October 2004' <http://today.yougov.co.uk/sites/today.yougov.co.uk/files/YG-Archives-lif-itvTM-LifeAfterDeath-041013.pdf> (accessed 9 Apr. 2010).

41. IPSOS-MORI, '*Schott's Almanac*'.

42. YouGov. 'Life after Death'.

43. G. Gorer, *Exploring English Character: A Study of the Morals and Behaviour of the English People* (New York: Criterion Books, 1955), 267. His survey showed 4% of women but only 2% of men 'regularly' followed advice in horoscopes.

44. L. Grant, 'New Age Ninnies', *Independent*, 27 June 1993.

45. P. Norris and R. Inglehart, *Sacred and the Secular: Religion and Politics Worldwide* (New York: Cambridge, 2004), 70.

46. P. Laslett, *The World We Have Lost* (London: Routledge, 2002).

47. R. Whiting, *The Blind Devotion of the People: Popular Religion in the English Reformation* (Cambridge: Cambridge University Press, 1989), 70.

48. D. Voas and A. D. Crockett, 'Religion in Britain: Neither Believing nor Belonging', *Sociology*, 39 (2005), 11–28.

49. E. Katz and P. Lazarsfeld, *Personal Influence* (New York: Free Press, 1955).

50. J. Lofland, *Doomsday Cult: A Study of Conversion, Proselytization and Maintenance of Faith* (Englewood Cliffs, NJ: Prentice-Hall, 1966).

CHAPTER 2

1. Mass Observation, *Puzzled People: A Study in Popular Attitudes to Religion, Ethics, Progress and Politics in a London Borough* (London: Victor Gollanz, 1947), 21.

2. See the Wikipedia entry for Muhammad al-Mahdi <http://en.wikipedia.org/wiki/Muhammad_al-Mahdi> (accessed 12 Aug. 2011).

3. D. Berger, 'On the Spectrum of Messianic Belief in Contemporary Lubavitch Chassidism', *Yated Ne'eman* (Israel), 14 July 2008, 18, 21–2 <http://chareidi.shemayisrael.com/archives5766/pinchos/olubavtchpnc66.htm> (accessed 23 Oct. 2010).

4. E. D. Andrews, *The People Called Shakers* (New York: Dover, 1963), 12.

5. Andrews, *The People Called Shakers*, 66.

6. Andrews, *The People Called Shakers*, 92.

7. Robert Burns to James Burness, 3 Aug. 1784: quoted in J. Train, *The Buchanites from First to Last* (Edinburgh, Blackwell, 1846; Memphis: General Books reprint-on-demand, 2010), 26–7.

8. Train, *Buchanites*, 32.

9. J. H. C. Harrison, *The Second Coming: Popular Millenarianism 1780–1850* (London: Routledge and Kegan Paul, 1979).

10. There is a helpful guide to Joanna Southcott writings at <http://www.btinternet.com/~joannasouthcott/books.htm> (accessed Dec. 2010).

11. Details of the case, along with Bateman's skeleton, can be found at the Thackray Museum in Leeds.

12. Her pregnancy was actually an advanced case of dropsy or edema—that is, fluid retention.

13. J. Smith, *Octavia Daughter of God: The Story of a Female Messiah and her Followers* (London: Jonathan Cape, 2011), 72.

14. Smith, *Octavia*, 99.

15. Smith, *Octavia*, 100.

16. Smith, *Octavia*, 190.

17. E. G. White, *A Sketch of the Christian Experience and Views of Ellen G. White* (1851), from the Wikipedia entry for Ellen G. White <http://en.wikipedia.org/wiki/Ellen_G._White> (accessed 2 Feb. 2011).

18. E. G. White, *Retrospection and Introspection* (Cambridge: Cambridge University Press, 1915), 24–5.

19. Matthew 9: 2–7.

20. M. B. G. Eddy, *Science and Health with Key to the Scriptures* (Boston: A.V. Stewart, 1910), 367. On women in the Shakers, Spiritualism, Christian Science, and Theosophy, see M. F. Bednarowski, 'Outside the Mainstream:

Women's Religion and Women Religious Leaders in Nineteenth Century America', *Journal of the American Academy of Religion*, 48 (1980): 207–32.

21. R. Stark, W. S. Bainbridge, and L. Kent, 'Cult Membership in the Roaring Twenties: Assessing Local Receptivity', *Sociological Analysis*, 42 (1981), 140.

22. The idea that there were races that pre-dated God's creation of Adam and Eve was for a while popular as a way of reconciling the Christian creation story with the racist division of the world into peoples of varying degrees of worth and with Darwinian notions of evolution.

23. Stark et al., 'Cult Membership', 140.

24. R. Pearsall, *The Table-Rappers* (London: Book Club Associates, 1972), 217.

25. R. Stark, 'Physiology and Faith: Addressing the "Universal" Gender Difference in Religious Commitment', *Journal for the Scientific Study of Religion*, 41 (2002), 495.

26. S. Bruce, 'Puritan Perverts: Notes on Accusation', *Sociological Review*, 33 (1985), 47, 63.

27. Smith, *Octavia*, 181–95.

28. For a good general account, see C. Campbell, 'The Easternization of the West', in B. R. Wilson and J. Cresswell (eds), *New Religious Movements: Challenge and Response* (London: Routledge, 1999), 35–48.

29. R. Wallis, *The Elementary Forms of the New Religious Life* (London: Routledge and Kegan Paul, 1984). Because it serves our current interests, we are using only his original contrast of world-affirming and world-rejecting religions (as presented in his inaugural lecture at The Queen's University of Belfast) and leaving aside the middle category of 'world-accommodating' that he added for this book-length version.

30. L. Dawson, 'Who Joins New Religions and Why: Twenty Years of Research and What We Have Learned', in L. Dawson (ed.), *Cults and New Religions: A Reader* (Oxford: Blackwell, 2003), 123.

31. It is worth remembering that all social phenomena may have idiosyncratic features. The unusually large proportion of men in the Brahma Kumaris in Australia in the 1970s was a consequence of one very effective male member recruiting his friends and colleagues.

32. S. Fuller and J. L. Martin, 'Women's Status in Eastern NRMs', *Review of Religious Research*, 44 (2003): 354–69.

33. See the Wikipedia entry for the Transcendental Meditation movement <http://en.wikipedia.org/wiki/Transcendental_Meditation_movement> (accessed 8 Nov. 2010).

34. S. Tipton, *Getting Saved from the Sixties* (Berkeley and Los Angeles: University of California Press, 1992), 103.

35. E. Burke Rochford, *Hare Krishna Transformed* (New York: New York University Press, 2007), 55.

36. E. Puttick, 'Women in New Religious Movements', in B. R. Wilson and J. Cresswell (eds), *New Religious Movement* (London: Routledge, 1999), 141–62.

37. Rob Balch, personal communication, 3 Dec. 2010.
38. W. Cadge, 'Gendered Religious Organizations: The Case of Theravada Buddhists in America', *Gender and Society*, 18 (2004), 777–93.
39. Tipton, *Getting Saved from the Sixties*, 182.
40. R. Wallis, 'Inside Insight', *New Humanist*, 5 (1979), 94; B. Cathcart, 'Rear Window: Arianna Stassinopoulos', *Independent*, 16 Oct. 1994.
41. P. Heelas, personal communication, 8 Dec. 2010.
42. E. Barker, *The Making of a Moonie: Brainwashing or Choice?* (Oxford: Basil Blackwell, 1984), 206–7.
43. V. Lanternari, *The Religions of the Oppressed* (New York: Alfred A. Knopf, 1963).
44. Dawson, 'Who Joins New Religions', 123.
45. W. Cross, *The Burned-Over District: The Social and Intellectual History of Enthusiastic Religion in Western New York, 1800–1950* (Ithaca, NY: Cornell University Press, 1982), 178.

CHAPTER 3

1. R. Pearsall, *The Table-Rappers* (London: Michael Joseph, 1972), 70.
2. See the Wikipedia entry for the Fox sisters <http://en.wikipedia.org/wiki/Fox_sisters> (accessed 3 Mar. 2011).
3. A. Conan Doyle, *The History of Spiritualism* (New York: G. H. Doran and Co., 1926).
4. B. Goldsmith, *Other Powers: The Age of Suffrage, Spiritualism and the Scandalous Victoria Woodhull* (London: Granta, 1998), 139.
5. Conan Doyle, *History*, ii. 146.
6. J. Steinmeyer, *Hiding the Elephant* (New York: Arrow, 2005), 95–6.
7. H. Houdini, *A Magician among the Spirits* (Cambridge: Cambridge University Press, 2002), 1924), p. xx.
8. Pearsall, *The Table-Rappers*, 228.
9. R. B. Davenport, *The Death Blow to Spiritualism* (New York: G. W. Dillingham, 1888), 76.
10. The Wikipedia entry for the Fox sisters <http://en.wikipedia.org/wiki/Fox_sisters> (accessed 3 Mar. 2011).
11. *New York Herald*, 9 Oct. 1888.
12. Goldsmith, *Other Powers*, 187–95. The same can be said for Woodhull's healing powers. Although she participated in her father's cynical snake-oil schemes (one of which caused the death of a patient and led to her sister being charged with manslaughter), she believed in her own powers of magnetic healing.
13. Calculated from data on the Association of Religion Data Archive <http://www.thearda.com/Denoms/families/index.asp> (accessed 7 Aug. 2011).
14. J. Hazelgrove, 'Spiritualism after the Great War', *Twentieth Century British History,* 10 (1999), 404–30; P. Brierley, *Religious Trends*, ii, and *Religious Trends,*

v (London: Christian Research, 2003, 2005); T. Walter, 'Mediums and Mourners', *Theology*, 119 (2007), 94.

15. B. Martin, 'The Spiritualist Meeting', in D. Martin and M. Hill (eds), *A Sociological Yearbook of Religion in Britain*, iii (London: SCM Press, 1970), 146–61.

16. Martin, 'The Spiritualist Meeting', 147.

17. Martin, 'The Spiritualist Meeting', 149.

18. R. L. Moore, 'The Spiritualist Medium: A Study of Female Practitioners in Victorian America', *American Quarterly*, 27 (1975), 202.

19. M. Gaskill, *Hellish Nell: Last of Britain's Witches* (London: Fourth Estate, 2001), 114–15.

20. I. M. Lewis, *Ecstatic Religion: A Study of Shamanism and Spirit Possession* (New York: Routledge. 2003).

21. Goldsmith, *Other Powers*, pp. xiii–xiv. Moore, 'Spiritualist Medium', makes the same point.

22. R. Stark, W. S. Bainbridge, and L. Kent, 'Cult Membership in the Roaring Twenties: Assessing Local Receptivity', *Sociological Analysis*, 42 (1981), 140.

23. G. K. Nelson, 'The Membership of a Cult: The Spiritualists National Union', *Review of Religious Research*, 13 (1977), 174.

24. G. Gorer, *Exploring English Character* (New York: Criterion Books, 1955), 253.

25. D. Davies and A. Shaw, *Reusing Old Graves: A Report on Popular British Attitudes* (Crayford, Kent: Shaw and Sons, 1995), 26–7.

26. G. Gorer, *Death, Grief and Mourning in Contemporary Britain* (London: Cresset Press, 1965), 167.

27. Gorer, *Exploring English Character*, 258.

28. See suicide.org <http://www.suicide.org/suicide-statistics.html> (accessed 1 July 2011).

29. Office of National Statistics, 'Trends in Suicide in England and Wales, 1982–96', *Population Trends*, 92 (Summer 1998).

30. A. Varnik, K. Kolves, C. M. van der Felz-Cornelis, A. Marusic, H. Oskarsson, A. Palmer, T. Reisch, G. Scheerder, E. Arensman, E. Aromaa, G. Giupponi, R. Gusmao, M. Maxwell, C. Pull, A. Szekely, V. Perez Sola, and O. Hegerl, 'Suicide Methods in Europe: A Gender-Specific Analysis of Countries Participating in the "European Alliance Against Depression"', *Journal of Epidemiology and Community Health*, 62 (2008), 545–51.

31. J. C. Diggory and D. Z. Rothman, 'Values Destroyed by Death', *Journal of Abnormal and Social Psychology*, 63 (1961), 206.

CHAPTER 4

1. For the Unification Church, see <http://www.religioustolerance.org/unificat.htm> (accessed 10 Apr. 2011).

2. S. J. Palmer, *Moon Sisters, Krishna Mothers, Rajneesh Lovers: Women's Roles in New Religions* (Syracuse, NY: Syracuse University Press, 1994), 90.

3. Figures supplied by the Registrar-General for Scotland. The totals may be artificially depressed by the fact that the census forms were completed on behalf of all members of a household by a single 'household reference person', usually the oldest male, who may have chosen to overlook a young family member's deviant religious identity. But, even if we doubled the numbers, they would remain trivial.

4. P. Heelas and L. Woodhead, *The Spiritual Revolution: Why Religion is Giving Way to Spirituality* (Oxford: Blackwell, 2004), 6.

5. For the Order of Critical Believers, see <http://criticalbelievers.proboards. com/index.cgi?board=ufoealien&action=display&thread=4639> (accessed 2 July 2011).

6. C. D. Bader, F. C. Menken, and J. O. Baker, 'Who Believes in UFOs and Extraterrestrials?', *Paranormal America* (The Association of Religion Data Archives) <http://www.thearda.com/paranormal/index.asp?s=ufo> (accessed 13 June 2011).

7. T. Hartmann, and C. Klimmt, 'Gender and Computer Games: Exploring Females' Dislikes', *Journal of Computer-Mediated Communication*, 11 (2006), article 2 <http://jcmc.indiana.edu/vol11/issue4/hartmann.html> (accessed 1 July 2011).

8. For a good illustration of esoteric physics, see <http://www.bibliotecap-leyades.net/archivos_pdf/esoteric_physics.pdf> (accessed 1 July 2011).

9. Heelas and Woodhead, *Spiritual Revolution*, 94–5.

10. M. Hamilton, 'An Analysis of the Festival for Mind–Body–Spirit, London', in S. Sutcliffe and M. Bowman (eds), *Beyond New Age: Exploring Alternative Spirituality* (Edinburgh: Edinburgh University Press, 2000), 1999.

11. D. Houtman and S. Aupers, 'The Spiritual Revolution and the New Age Sender Puzzle: The Sacralization of the Self in Late Modernity (1980–2000)', in K. Aune, S. Sharma, and G. Vincent (eds), *Women and Religion in the West: Challenging Secularization* (Aldershot: Ashgate, 2008), 114.

12. J. de Hart, *Zwevende Gelovigen: Oude Religie and Nieuwe Spiritualitiet* (Amsterdam: Uitgeverij Bert Bakker, 2011). Interestingly de Hart believes that the gender difference in contemporary spirituality largely disappears once one controls for the difference in religiosity more conventionally defined. The difference between that and our finding that the gender difference holds even when one controls for conventional church background and belief may be a result of the way in which he defines and measures spirituality.

13. D. E. Sherkat, 'Tracking the Other: Dynamics and Composition of "Other" Religions in the General Social Survey, 1973–1996', *Journal for the Scientific Study of Religion*, 38 (1999), 551–60.

14. Heelas and Woodhead, *Spiritual Revolution*.

15. P. L. Berger, B. Berger, and H. Kellner, *The Homeless Mind: Modernization and Consciousness* (Harmondsworth: Penguin, 1974). Heelas and Wood-head, *Spiritual Revolution*, 167–8 n. 9.

16. L. Woodhead, 'Why So Many Women in Holistic Spirituality?', in K. Flanagan and P. Jupp (eds), *A Sociology of Spirituality* (Aldershot: Ashgate, 2007), 117.

17. Woodhead, 'Why So Many Women . . . ?', 119–20.

18. Furthermore, the 'spiritual' is likely to be exaggerated in those responses because a disproportionate number of completed questionnaires came from practitioners and group leaders rather than from rank-and-file or one-off participants. See D. Voas and S. Bruce, 'The Spiritual Revolution: Another False Dawn for the Sacred', in K. Flanagan and P. Jupp (eds), *A Sociology of Spirituality* (Aldershot: Ashgate, 2007), 43–62.

19. Heelas and Woodhead, *Spiritual Revolution*, 91.

20. On this point the two principal investigators of the Kendal project disagree. Woodhead stresses problem-solving; L. Woodhead, '"Because I'm worth it": Religion and Women's Changing Lives in the West', in K. Aune, S. Sharma, and G. Vincent (eds), *Women and Religion in the West: Challenging Secularization* (Aldershot: Ashgate, 2008), 157. Heelas thinks this an unbalanced assessment of a group of people who were above-averagely content with life.

21. T. Glendinning and S. Bruce, 'New Ways of Believing or Belonging: Is Religion Giving Way to Spirituality?', *British Journal of Sociology*, 57 (3), 399–413.

22. Woodhead, 'Why So Many Women . . . ?', 120.

23. E. Sointu and L. Woodhead, 'Spirituality Gender and Expressive Selfhood', *Journal for the Scientific Study of Religion*, 47 (2008), 260.

24. T. G. Foltz, 'Women's Spirituality Research: Doing Feminism', in N. Nason-Clark and M. J. Neitz (eds), *Feminist Narratives in the Sociology of Religion* (Walnut Creek, CA: AltaMira Press, 2001), 89–98. Not surprisingly, more mainstream neo-paganism in the USA has a less skewed gender base. A 1990s survey suggested it was 57% female; D. L. Jorgensen and S. J. Russell, 'American Neopaganism: The Participants' Social Identities', *Journal for the Scientific Study of Religion*, 38 (1999), 325–38.

25. The Women of Wisdom Foundation, see <http://www.womenofwisdom. org> (accessed 8 Mar. 2011).

26. Sacred Journeys <http://www.sacredjourneys.com> (accessed 2 June 2011).

27. Patricia Dancing Elk-Walls <http://www.sacredhealingwomen.com> (accessed 7 May 2011).

28. Brighde's Blessing Retreat with Kathy Jones, Thursday, 31 Jan.–Sunday 3 Feb. 2008. Four-day non-residential retreat <http://www.kathyjones.co. uk/retreats/bridie_retreat.html 2008> (accessed 2 June 2011).

29. Woodhead, 'Why So Many Women . . . ?', 124.

30. Pampering 4 Life <http://wellnessindustry-bunny.blogspot.com/2011/04/ divine-healing-spirituality-and-your.html> (accessed 3 July 2011).

31. Soul Pampering <http://www.soulpampering.com/about.html> (accessed 3 July 2011).

32. *Clapham and District Newsletter*, 70 (Apr. 2011).
33. W. H. Courtenay, 'Constructions of Masculinity and their Influence on Men's Well-Being: A Theory of Gender and Health', *Social Science and Medicine*, 50 (2000), 1386.
34. Courtenay, 'Constructions', 1389.
35. R. O'Brien, K. Hunt, and G. Hart, '"It's Caveman Stuff, but that is to a Certain Extent how Guys Still Operate": Men's Accounts of Masculinity and Help Seeking', *Social Science and Medicine*, 61 (2005), 503–16.

CHAPTER 5

1. L. Isherwood, *Introduction to Feminist Theology* (Sheffield: Sheffield Academic Press, 2001).
2. e.g. J. Brink and J. Mencher, *Mixed Blessings: Gender and Religious Fundamentalism Cross Culturally* (London: Routledge, 1997).
3. B. E. Brasher, *Godly Women: Fundamentalism and Female Power* (New Brunswick, NJ: Rutgers University Press, 1998), 13.
4. Brasher, *Godly Women*, 137.
5. R. M. Griffith, *God's Daughters: Evangelical Women and the Power of Submission* (Berkeley and Los Angeles: University of California Press, 2000).
6. Griffith, *God's Daughters*, 75.
7. Griffith, *God's Daughters*, 155.
8. Brasher, *Godly Women*, 35.
9. Griffith, *God's Daughters*, 113.
10. Griffith, *God's Daughters*, 85.
11. Griffith, *God's Daughters*, 39.
12. C. Manning, *God Gave Us the Right: Conservative Catholic, Evangelical Protestant and Orthodox Jewish Women Grapple with Feminism* (New Brunswick, NJ: Rutgers University Press, 1999).
13. E. W. Ozorak, 'The Power but not the Glory: How Women Empower Themselves through Religion', *Journal for the Scientific Study of Religion*, 36 (1996): 17–29.
14. Ozorak, *The Power*, 25.
15. D. R. Kaufman, *Rachel's Daughters: Newly Orthodox Jewish Women* (New Brunswick, NJ: Rutgers University Press, 1991).
16. Y. Yadgar, 'Gender, Religion, and Feminism: The Case of Jewish Israeli Traditionalists', *Journal for the Scientific Study of Religion*, 45 (2006), 364.
17. See also L. Davidman, *Tradition in a Rootless World: Women Turn to Orthodox Judaism* (Berkeley and Los Angeles: University of California Press, 1993).
18. Kaufman, *Rachel's Daughters*, 10.
19. David Martin was one of the first sociologists of religion to draw attention to the Pentecostal phenomenon in his work. See in particular D. Martin, *Tongues of Fire: Pentecostalism in Latin America* (Oxford: Basil Blackwell, 1991), and D. Martin, *Pentecostalism: The World their Parish* (Oxford: Basil Blackwell, 2002).

20. Pew Forum on Religion and Public Life, 'Overview: Pentecostalism in Latin America', 5 Oct. 2006 <http://pewforum.org/Christian/Evangelical-Protestant-Churches/Overview-Pentecostalism-in-Latin-America.aspx> (accessed 1 Aug. 2011).
21. E. E. Brusco, *The Reformation of Machismo: Evangelical Conversion and Gender in Columbia* (Austin, TX: University of Texas Press, 1995).
22. E. P. Stevens, 'Marianismo: The Other Face of Machismo', in A. Pescatello (ed.), *Female and Male in Latin America* (Pittsburgh, PA: University of Pittsburgh Press, 1973), 90–101.
23. Brusco, *The Reformation*, 97.
24. Brusco, *The Reformation*, 117–18.
25. Brusco, *The Reformation*, 125.
26. Brusco, *The Reformation*, 137.
27. M. Frahm-Arp, *Professional Women in South African Pentecostal Charismatic Churches* (Leiden: Brill, 2010).
28. Frahm-Arp, *Professional Women*, 153.
29. Frahm-Arp, *Professional Women*, 160.
30. Frahm-Arp, *Professional Women*, 222.
31. Frahm-Arp, *Professional Women*, 218.
32. Frahm-Arp, *Professional Women*, 234–5.
33. Frahm-Arp, *Professional Women*, 255.
34. Frahm-Arp, *Professional Women*, 258.

CHAPTER 6

1. C. Shea, 'The Nature–Nurture Debate Redux', *Chronicle Review of Higher Education*, 9 Jan. 2009 <http://chronicle.com/article/The-Nature-Nurture-Debate/33480> (accessed 7 July 2011).
2. C. Lombroso with G. Lombroso-Ferrero, *Criminal Man, According to the Classification of Cesare Lombroso* (New York: G. P. Putnam and Sons, 1911).
3. T. Laquer, *Making Sex: Body and Gender from the Greeks to Freud* (Cambridge, MA: Harvard University Press, 1990).
4. J. Butler, *Gender Trouble: Feminism and the Subversion of Identity* (London: Routledge, 1999). In the light of Butler's influence, it is worth noting that she is a philosopher and expert on literary fiction rather than a social scientist.
5. *The Thankes Geuing of Women after Childe Birth, Commonly Called the Churchyng Of Women* <http://users.ox.ac.uk/~mikef/bcp1552.html> (accessed 3 July 2011).
6. A. Oakley, *From Here to Maternity: Becoming a Mother* (Harmondsworth: Penguin, 1981).
7. A particularly popular and influential UK website is <http://www.mumsnet.com>.
8. S. Sered, 'Childbirth as a Religious Experience? Voices from an Israeli Hospital', *Journal of Feminist Studies in Religion*, 7 (1991), 7–18.

9. L. C. Callister, 'The Meaning of the Childbirth Experience to Mormon Women', *Journal of Perinatal Education*, 1 (1992), 50–7; L. C. Callister and I. Khalaf, 'Culturally Diverse Women Giving Birth: Their Stories', *Science across Cultures: The History of non-Western Science*, 5 (2009), 33–9.

10. L. C. Callister, 'Spirituality in Childbearing Women', *Journal of Perinatal Education*, 19 (2010), 16–24.

11. L. C. Callister, K. Vehvilainen-Julkunen, and S. Lauri, 'Giving Birth: Perceptions of Finnish Childbearing Women', *American Journal of Maternal and Child Nursing*, 26 (2001), 28–32.

12. Office for National Statistics, 'Childhood, Infant and Perinatal Mortality: Stillbirth and Infant Death Rates by Age at Death 1921–1999' <http://www.statistics.gov.uk/StatBase/xsdataset.asp?More=Y&vlnk=3209&All=Y&B2.x=66&B2.y=6> (accessed 9 Jan. 2009).

13. Sered, 'Childbirth', 189.

14. Sered, 'Childbirth', 189.

15. J. Seabrook, *Working-Class Childhood: An Oral History* (London: Gollanz, 1982), 35. The speaker was remembering his childhood before the First World War.

16. This may be a peculiarly British phenomenon, but, since the invention of the word processor and the opening of census records, there has been a surge in popularity of family history and of 'ordinary' people composing self-published memoirs, usually of poor but doggedly cheerful childhoods.

17. T. Hartman Halbertal, *Appropriately Subversive: Modern Mothers in Traditional Religions* (Cambridge, MA: Harvard University Press, 2002).

18. Halbertal, *Appropriately Subversive*, 159.

19. Caregiver Hope <http://caregiverhope.com> (accessed 10 June 2011); see also Family Caregiver Alliance, *Factsheet: Selected Caregiver Statistics, 2010* <http://www.caregiver.org/caregiver/jsp/publications.jsp?nodeid=345> (accessed 7 Jan. 2011).

20. Carers UK <http://www.carersuk.org> (accessed 10 Jan. 2011).

21. T. Utriainen, 'Agents of De-Differentiation: Women Care-Givers for the Dying in Finland', *Journal of Contemporary Religion*, 25 (2010), 437–51.

22. Utriainen, 'Agents', 442.

23. F. Nightingale, *Notes on Nursing* (New York: D. Appleton and Company, 1860).

24. Utriainen, 'Agents', 448.

25. Utriainen, 'Agents', 449.

26. J. Duncombe and D. Marsden, '"Workaholics" and "Whingeing Women": Theorising Intimacy and Emotion Work—The Last Frontier of Gender Inequality?', *Sociological Review*, 43 (1995), 152; G. Riches and P. Dawson, 'Communities of Feeling: The Culture of Bereaved Parents', *Mortality*, 1 (1996), 143–61.

27. e.g. N. James, 'Emotional Labour: Skill and Work in the Social Regulation of Feeling', in L. McKay, K. Soothill, and K. M. Melia (eds), *Classic Texts in*

Healthcare (Oxford: Butterworth-Heinemann, 1998); M. S. Stroebe, 'New Directions in Bereavement Research: Exploration of Gender Differences', *Palliative Medicine*, 12 (1998), 5–14.

28. Riches and Dawson, 'Communities of Feeling'.
29. L. Ulrich, *A Midwife's Tale: The Life of Martha Ballard Based on her Diary, 1785–1812* (New York: Vintage Books, 1990), 47.
30. R. Pringle and J. Alley, 'Gender and the Funeral Industry: The Work of Citizenship', *Journal of Sociology*, 31 (1995), 107–21.
31. A. Goldman, 'For Funerals, a Female Touch; More Women Undertakers', *New York Times*, 13 Feb. 1993; S. Murray, 'The Rise of Female Undertakers', *Guardian*, 23 June 2011.
32. Murray, 'The Rise of Female Undertakers'.
33. Pringle and Alley, 'Gender and the Funeral Industry'. See also White Lady Funerals <http://www.whiteladyfunerals.com.au> (accessed 17 Mar. 2011).
34. Ulrich, 'A Midwife's Tale', 117.
35. T. Walter, 'British Sociology and Death', in D. Clark (ed.), *The Sociology of Death* (Oxford: Blackwell, 1993), 264–95.
36. J. Scott, 'Family and Gender Roles: How Attitudes Are Changing', *GeNet Working Paper*, No. 21, Sept. 2006 <http://www.genet.ac.uk/workpapers/index.html#jscott> (accessed 4 Jan. 2011).
37. U. Björnberg, *European Parents in the 1990s: Contradictions and Comparisons* (New Brunswick, NJ: Transaction Publishers, 1992); J. R. Gillis, 'Marginalization of Fatherhood in Western Countries', *Childhood*, 7 (2000), 225–38.
38. Office for National Statistics, 'Work and Family 2008' <http://www.statistics.gov.uk/cci/nugget.asp?id=1655> (accessed 13 Jan. 2011).
39. L. McKie, S. Gregory, and S. Bowlby, 'Shadow Times: The Temporal and Spatial Frameworks and Experiences of Caring and Working', *Sociology*, 36 (2002), 897–924.
40. H. Graham, 'Caring: A Labour of Love', in J. Finch and D. Groves (eds), *A Labour of Love: Women, Work and Caring* (London: Routledge and Kegan Paul, 1983), 18.
41. Detailed statistics can be found in C. Brown, *The Death of Christian Britain* (London: Routledge, 2001).
42. The Bem Sex Role Inventory was devised in the 1970s by US psychologist Sandra Bem.
43. E. H. Thompson, 'Beneath the Status Characteristics: Gender Variations in Religiousness', *Journal for the Scientific Study of Religion*, 30 (1991), 381–94.
44. Thompson, 'Beneath the Status Characteristics', 389–90.
45. Richard Sipe is a former Catholic monk and priest who became a clinical psychologist and counsellor <http://www.richardsipe.com/Comments/2009-09-11-Are_American_Bishops_Gay.htm#_ftn17> (accessed 6 Apr. 2010).

46. Ruth Gledhill, 'Without Gay Priests Church would be Lost Claims Bishop Gene' <http://www.timesonline.co.uk/tol/comment/faith/article2155148. ece> (accessed 10 June 2011).

47. L. J. Podles, *The Church Impotent: The Feminization of Christianity* (Dallas: Spence and Company, 1999).

48. D. Shand-Tucci, *Ralph Adams Cram—Life and Architecture, i. Boston Bohemia 1881–1900: Queer Fishes and Queer Dishes* (Amherst: University of Massachusetts Press, 1996).

49. B. Bawer, 'The Gentlemen's Club', *Advocate*, 14 Dec. 1995, 120.

50. E. Waugh, *Brideshead Revisited* (Boston: Little Brown, 1978), 26.

51. Podles, *Church Impotent*, 6.

52. P. Jones, 'Journeys of Faith' <http://www.mccmanchester.co.uk/journey_philip.htm> (accessed 7 June 2011).

53. Brown, *Death of Christian Britain*, and Podles, *Church Impotent*.

54. D. E. Sherkat, 'Sexuality and Religious Commitment in the United States: An Empirical Investigation', *Journal for the Scientific Study of Religion*, 41 (2002), 313–23.

CHAPTER 7

1. Bureau of Justice Statistics, 'Homicide Trends in the US' <http://bjs.ojp. usdoj.gov/content/homicide/gender.cfm> (accessed 1 July 2011).

2. A. S. Miller and J. P. Hoffman, 'Risk and Religion: An Explanation of Gender Differences in Religiosity', *Journal for the Scientific Study of Religion*, 34 (1995), 63–75.

3. Miller and Hoffman, 'Risk and Religion', 69.

4. Miller and Hoffman, 'Risk and Religion', 73. This also points to the fact that it is femininity, rather than being a woman, that determines religiosity. Women who display a preference for risk-taking will fall into the masculine pattern of religiosity.

5. C. Glock and R. Stark, *American Piety: The Nature of Religious Commitment* (Berkeley and Los Angeles: University of California Press, 1968). The final chapter talks of the possibility of entering a post-Christian era.

6. R. Stark and W. S. Bainbridge, *The Future of Religion* (Berkeley and Los Angeles: University of California Press, 1985) and *A Theory of Religion* (New York: Peter Lang, 1987).

7. For a book-length exposition and critique of Stark's work, see S. Bruce, *Choice and Religion* (Oxford: Oxford University Press, 1999).

8. R. Stark, 'Physiology and Faith: Addressing the "Universal" Gender Difference in Religious Commitment', *Journal for the Scientific Study of Religion*, 41 (2002), 495–507.

9. A. S. Miller and R. Stark, 'Gender and Religiousness: Can Socialization Explanations Be Saved?', *American Journal of Sociology*, 107 (2002), 1406.

This paper also reports other tests of the importance of socialization that are less significant.

10. Miller and Stark, 'Gender and Religiousness', 1411.

11. Stark, 'Physiology and Faith', 496.

12. Stark, 'Physiology and Faith', 496.

13. E. Nissen, G. Lilja, A. M. Widström, and K. Uvnäs-Moberg, 'Elevation of Oxytocin Levels Early Postpartum in Women', *Acta Obstetricia et Gynecologica Scandinavica*, 74 (1995), 530–3.

14. J. Collett and O. Lizardo, 'A Power-Control Theory of Gender and Religiosity', *Journal for the Scientific Study of Religion*, 48 (2009), 213–31.

15. On Cameron, see BBC News, 'David Cameron: Life and Times of New UK Prime Minister', 11 May 2010 <http://news.bbc.co.uk/1/hi/8661964.stm>; on Clegg, see <http://en.wikipedia.org/wiki/Nick_Clegg>; on Miliband, see 'Ed Miliband: I don't believe in God', *Daily Telegraph*, 9 Mar. 2012 <http://www.telegraph.co.uk/news/politics/ed-miliband/8032163/Ed-Miliband-I-dont-believe-in-God.html> (all accessed 10 May 2011).

16. See M. L. Roth and J. C. Kroll, 'Risky Business: Assessing Risk Preference Explanations for Gender Differences in Religiosity', *American Sociological Review*, 72 (2007), 205–20.

17. Roth and Kroll, 'Risky Business', 217.

18. Miller and Hoffman, 'Risk and Religion', 72; B. Malinowski, *The Argonauts of the Western Pacific* (New York: E. P. Dutton, 1961).

CHAPTER 8

1. See the Wikipedia entry on <http://en.wikipedia.org/wiki/Mitzvah> (accessed 7 Aug. 2011).

2. S. Bruce, *Secularization* (Oxford: Oxford University Press, 2011).

3. K. M. Loewenthal, A. K. MacLeon, and M. Cinnirella, 'Are Women More Religious than Men? Gender Differences in Religious Activity among Different Religious Groups in the UK', *Personality and Individual Differences*, 32 (2001), 133–9.

4. K. Haw, 'Being, Becoming and Belonging: Young Muslim Women in Contemporary Britain', *Journal of Intercultural Studies*, 31 (2010), 345–61.

5. T. Benn and H. Jawad, *Muslim Women in the United Kingdom and Beyond: Experiences and Images* (Leiden and Boston: Brill, 2003).

6. A. Dale and S. Ahmed, 'Marriage and Employment Patterns amongst UK-Raised Indian, Pakistani, and Bangladeshi Women', *Ethnic and Racial Studies*, 34 (2011), 21.

7. F. Ahmad, 'Muslim Women's Experiences of Higher Education in Britain', *American Journal of Islamic Social Sciences*, 24 (2007), 46.

8. K. Bhopal, 'How Gender and Ethnicity Intersect: The Significance of Education, Employment and Marital Status', *Sociological Research Online*, 3 (1998), 1–16.

9. F. Ahmad, 'Modern Traditions? British Muslim Women and Academic Achievement', *Gender and Education*, 13 (2001), 137–52.

10. H. Jawad, 'Historical and Contemporary Perspectives on Muslim Women Living in the West', in T. Benn and H. Jawad (eds), *Muslim Women in the United Kingdom and Beyond: Experiences and Images* (Leiden and Boston: Brill, 2003), 9.

11. M. Wolhrab-Sahr, 'Conversion to Islam: Between Syncretism and Symbolic Battle', *Social Compass*, 46 (1999), 351–62; K. Brice, 'A Minority within a Minority: A Report on Converts to Islam in the United Kingdom', *Faith Matters* <http://faith-matters.org/resources/publicationsreports/218-report-on-converts-to-islam-in-the-uk-a-minority-within-a-minority, 2010> (accessed 5 May 2011).

12. H. A. Haleem, 'Experiences, Needs and Potentials of New Muslim Women in Britain', in Benn and Jawad (eds), *Muslim Women in the United Kingdom and Beyond*, 93.

13. C. Manning, *God Gave Us the Right: Conservative Catholic, Evangelical Protestant, and Orthodox Jewish Women Grapple with Feminism* (New Brunswick, NJ: Rutgers University Press, 1999).

14. Haleem, 'Experiences', 95.

15. Haleem, 'Experiences', 91. This difference between the USA and Britain is unsurprising, considering that Americans, on average, are more religious than the British and that conversion mostly occurs among individuals who have a positive disposition towards religion and/or spirituality.

16. Communities and Local Government, 'Empowering Muslim Women: Case Studies', <http://www.communities.gov.uk/publications/communities/empoweringmuslimwomen> (accessed 29 June 2011).

17. S. Gilliat-Ray, *Muslims in Britain* (Cambridge: Cambridge University Press, 2010), 212.

18. Gilliat-Ray, *Muslims in Britain*, 228.

19. Gilliat-Ray, *Muslims in Britain*, 202.

20. Gilliat-Ray, *Muslims in Britain*, 203.

21. *Good Practice Guide for Mosques and Imams* <http://www.muslimsinbritain.org> (accessed 7 Apr. 2011).

22. K. Brown, 'The Promise and Perils of Women's Participation in UK Mosques: The Impact of Securitisation Agendas on Identity, Gender and Community', *British Journal of Politics and International Relations*, 10 (2008), 480.

23. Brown, 'The Promise', 481.

24. Gilliat-Ray, *Muslims in Britain*, 213.

25. L. Nyhagen Predelli, 'Religion, Citizenship and Participation: A Case Study of Immigrant Muslim Women in Norwegian Mosques', *European Journal of Women's Studies*, 15 (2008), 241.

26. Nyhagen Predelli, 'Religion', 250.

27. Nyhagen Predelli, 'Religion', 254.

28. L. Deeb, *An Enchanted Modern: Gender and Public Piety in Shi'i Lebanon* (Princeton: Princeton University Press, 2008).
29. Deeb, *An Enchanted Modern*, 8.
30. Deeb, *An Enchanted Modern*, 36.
31. Deeb, *An Enchanted Modern*, 204.
32. Deeb, *An Enchanted Modern*, 206.
33. Deeb, *An Enchanted Modern*, 210.
34. Deeb, *An Enchanted Modern*, 211.
35. Deeb, *An Enchanted Modern*, 213.
36. Deeb, *An Enchanted Modern*, 218.
37. Deeb, *An Enchanted Modern*, 219.
38. F. Mernissi, *The Veil and the Male Elite: A Feminist Interpretation of Islam* (New York: Basic Books, 1991); L. Ahmed, *Women and Gender in Islam: Historical Roots of a Modern Debate.* (New Haven: Yale University Press, 1992); R. Hassan, 'Feminist Theology: The Challenges for Muslim Women', *Critique: The Journal of Critical Studies of the Middle East*, 9 (1996), 53–65.
39. R. Bokhari, 'Bihishti Zewar: A Text for Respectable Women?', in D. Llewellyn and D. Sawyer (eds), *Reading Spiritualities: Constructing and Representing the Sacred* (Aldershot: Ashgate, 2008), 135.
40. Bokhari, 'Bihishti Zewar', 140.
41. Bokhari, 'Bihishti Zewar', 141.
42. Bokhari, 'Bihishti Zewar', 142.
43. Bokhari, 'Bihishti Zewar', 145.
44. Bokhari, 'Bihishti Zewar', 147.
45. A. S. Kariapper, *Walking a Tightrope: Women and Veiling in the United Kingdom* (London: Women Living under Muslim Laws, 2009).
46. K. Brown, 'Realising Muslim Women's Rights: The Role of Islamic Identity among British Muslim Women', *Women's Studies International Forum*, 29 (2006), 425.
47. Brown, 'Realising Muslim Women's Rights', 428.
48. Haw, 'Being, Becoming and Belonging', 353.
49. C. Dwyer, 'Negotiating Diasporic Identities: Young British South Asian Muslim Women', *Women's Studies International Forum*, 23 (2000), 477.
50. J. Klausen, *The Islamic Challenge: Politics and Religion in Western Europe* (Oxford: Oxford University Press, 2005), 173.
51. Haw, 'Being, Becoming and Belonging', 353.
52. S. Rozario, 'On being Australian and Muslim: Muslim Women as Defenders of Islamic Heritage', *Women's Studies International Forum*, 21 (1999), 653.
53. D. E. Schultz, 'Competing Sartorial Assertions of Femininity and Muslim Identity in Mali', *Fashion Theory*, 11 (2007), 253–80.
54. M. Riesebrodt, *Pious Passion: The Emergence of Modern Fundamentalism in the United States and Iran* (Berkeley and Los Angeles: University of California Press, 1993).

55. Riesebrodt, *Pious Passion*, 64.

56. D. P. Sullins, 'Gender and Religion: Deconstructing Universality, Constructing Complexity', *American Journal of Sociology*, 112 (2006), 844.

57. J. Theophano, *Eat my Words: Reading Women's Lives through the Cookbooks they Wrote* (New York: Palgrave MacMillan, 2002), 70.

58. S. Sered, 'Food and Holiness: Cooking as a Sacred Act among Middle-Eastern Jewish Women', *Anthropological Quarterly*, 61 (1988), 131.

59. Sered, 'Food and Holiness', 131.

60. Sered, 'Food and Holiness', 134.

61. Sered, 'Food and Holiness', 135.

62. S. Sered, 'The Religion of Relating: Kinship and Spirituality among Middle-Eastern Jewish Women in Jerusalem', *Journal of Social and Personal Relationships*, 6 (1989), 309–25.

63. T. Hartman and N. Marmon, 'Lived Regulations, Systemic Attributions: Menstrual Separation and Ritual Immersion in the Experience of Orthodox Jewish Women', *Gender and Society*, 18 (2004), 389–408.

64. Hartman and Marmon, 'Lived Regulations', 398.

CHAPTER 9

1. Some feminists argue that the public/private division denigrates women. We take the view that it is a useful analytical device based on observable differences in law and social convention.

2. M. J. Neitz, 'Afterword', in K. Aune, S. Sharma, and G. Vincent (eds), *Women and Religion in the West: Challenging Secularization* (Aldershot: Ashgate, 2008), 222.

3. S. Bruce, *Secularization* (Oxford: Oxford University Press, 2011).

4. L. Woodhead, 'Gendering Secularization Theory', *Kvinder, Køn og Forskning*, 1 (2005), 1–25 (accessed 17 Nov. 2009). Woodhead's version of the secularization paradigm is misleadingly narrow. It rests on a psychologized version of Max Weber's pessimism about 'the iron cage of rationality' and ignores all the other causes of secularization.

5. P. L. Berger, G. Davie, and E. Fokkas, *Religious America, Secular Europe* (Aldershot: Ashgate, 2008), 13–14; R. Stark, 'Secularization RIP', *Sociology of Religion*, 60 (1999), 249–73.

6. T. Parsons, *Structure and Process in Modern Societies* (Glencoe, IL: Free Press, 1960), 304.

7. This is Karl Marx's theory of class formation.

8. D. Martin, *The Dilemmas of Contemporary Religion* (Oxford: Blackwell, 1978), 9.

9. E. Gellner, *Nations and Nationalism* (Oxford: Basil Blackwell, 1983); *Plough, Sword and Book: the Structure of Human History* (London: Collins Harvill, 1988).

10. This is the change that Durkheim captured in his distinction between societies based on mechanical and organic solidarity (E. Durkheim, *The Division of Labor in Society* (Glencoe, IL: Free Press, 1964)).

11. B. R. Wilson, *Religion in Sociological Perspective* (Oxford: Oxford University Press, 1982), 154.

12. F. Tönnies, *Community and Association* (London: Routledge and Kegan Paul, 1955).

13. We have no argument at all with the case made by social historians such as Callum Brown that many features of urban life permitted the better organization of religious association and hence, for a short time, produced a higher rate of church involvement for some people. See C. Brown, 'Did Urbanization Secularize Britain?', *Urban History*, 15 (1988), 1–14.

14. T. Asad, *Genealogies of Religion: Discipline and Reasons of Power in Christianity and Islam* (Baltimore: Johns Hopkins University Press, 1993).

15. P. L. Berger, *The Heretical Imperative* (London: Collins, 1980).

16. P. L. Berger and T. Luckmann, 'Secularization and Pluralism', *International Yearbook of the Sociology of Religion*, 2 (1966), 133.

17. T. Luckmann, *The Invisible Religion* (New York: Macmillan, 1970), 98–9.

18. R. Stark and R. Finke, *Acts of Faith: Explaining the Human Side of Religion* (Berkeley and Los Angeles: University of California Press, 2000), 61.

19. D. Martin, *The Religious and the Secular* (London: Routledge and Kegan Paul, 1969), 116.

20. The evidence is considered in detail in Bruce, *Secularization*.

21. R. Frankenberg, *Village on the Border* (London: Cohen and West, 1957).

22. S. Bruce, 'Religion in Four Welsh Parishes', *Contemporary Wales*, 23 (2010), 219–39.

23. D. De Vaus and I. McAllister, 'Gender Differences in Religion: A Test of Structural Location Theory', *American Sociological Review*, 52 (1987), 480.

24. A. Dubach, 'The Religiosity Profile of European Catholicism', in M. Rieger (ed.), *What the World Believes* (Gütersloh: Bertelsmann Stiftung, 2009), 509.

25. We are indebted to David Voas for this general point.

CHAPTER 10

1. To locate our position in the standard language of the philosophy of science, we are de facto positivists. We recognize all the criticisms that philosophers make of positivism but also acknowledge that there is no more plausible alternative. In distinguishing between proving and disproving we are endorsing Karl Popper's 'conjectures and refutations' view that science advances by the elimination of the least well-supported propositions. Again we are familiar with all the arguments against the Popperian view but find nothing preferable. See K. Popper, *Conjectures and Refutations* (London: Routledge, 1963).

2. R. Stark, 'German and German–American Religiosity', *Journal for the Scientific Study of Religion*, 36 (1997), 182–93. For a detailed critique, see S. Bruce, *Choice and Religion: A Critique of Rational Choice* (Oxford: Oxford University Press, 1999).

3. *Observer*, 24 Apr. 2010.

4. *Daily Telegraph*, 4 June 2011.

Index

Printed and bound by CPI Group (UK) Ltd, Croydon, CR0 4YY